CLARK

D0787363

SPY FLIGHTS OF THE COLD WAR

Spy Flights of the Cold War

Paul Lashmar

NAVAL INSTITUTE PRESS
ANNAPOLIS, MARYLAND

First published in 1996 by
Sutton Publishing Limited · Phoenix Mill
Thrupp · Stroud · Gloucestershire · GL5 2BU

Published and distributed in the United States of America and Canada by
the Naval Institute Press, 118 Maryland Avenue, Annapolis, MD 21402-
5035.

Library of Congress Catalog Card Number (Applied for)

ISBN 1-55750-837-2

This edition is authorized for sale only in the United States of America, its
territories and possessions, and Canada.

Printed in Great Britain on acid-free paper by
Butler & Tanner, Frome, Somerset

CONTENTS

Dedication

To Anna and Ben

ACKNOWLEDGEMENTS

I would like in particular to thank: Laurence Rees, the Editor of *Timewatch* and his team; Phillip Whitehead of Brook Associates, who fully understands the importance of history, and all at Brook – Jayne Rowe, Anne, Udi, Elaine; the team that made the 'Spies in the Sky' programme – Mark Anderson, Teresa Cherfas, Gary Bradley; and the British participants including Rex Sanders, Bob Anstee, Robbie Robinson, Monty Burton and Sir Neil Wheeler.

In 1993 I travelled across the sunbelt of America meeting pilots and I shall not forget the hospitality I received from Joe Gyulavics, Sam Myers, Fred Wack, Bruce Bailey, Richard Myers, Curly Behrmann and many others; I thank Hal Austin, Carl Holt, Richard McNab, John Lappo, Gen. Andrew Goodpaster, Don Welzenbach, Jeff Richelson, Peter Kornbluth, Dr Kathryn Weathersby and Sir Neil Wheeler. The team that made 'Russia's Secret War' – Nick Anning, Igor Morozov, Natasha Shallice, Chris Goddard, Franklyn Stevas and Alf Penn. James Oliver for his help. Maj. John Farquahar for sending me copies of his two excellent theses. Special thanks to Robert S. Hopkins III for a free and open flow of information and inspiration. Also Dr Paul Cole who has become a friend and colleague.

The individuals of the US-Russian Joint Commission investigating the fate of missing in actions who assisted me. All the families of MIAs who helped and welcomed me into their lives.

Teresa Cherfas, Nick and Igor for conducting the Russian-language interviews; Richard Riding and Lydia at *Aeroplane Monthly*; Roy Nesbit for advice and Paul Jackson for assistance; Andy Weir for his analysis of the bomber and missile gaps; and Jonathan Falconer at Sutton Publishing for his enthusiasm.

ABBREVIATIONS AND GLOSSARY

ACM Air Chief Marshal.

AFB Air force base.

AVM Air Vice Marshal.

Black Knight Air Force programme to procure RB–57D.

CINCSAC Commander-in-Chief Strategic Air Command.

COMINT Communications intelligence – technical and intelligence information derived from foreign communications by other than the intended recipients.

Crows Nickname given to US aircrew special operators who monitor electronic signals.

DCI Director of Central Intelligence.

ELINT Electronic intelligence – technical and intelligence information derived from foreign non-communications electromagnetic radiations emanating from other than nuclear detonations or radioactive sources.

EW Electronic warfare – military action involving the use of electromagnetic energy to determine, exploit, reduce or prevent hostile use of the electromagnetic spectrum and action which retains friendly use of electromagnetic spectrum. There are three divisions of electronic warfare:

Electronic countermeasures (ECM) – that division of electronic warfare involving actions taken to prevent or reduce an enemy's effective use of the electromagnetic spectrum. Electronic countermeasures include: electronic jamming – the deliberate radiation, reradiation, or reflection of electromagnetic energy for the purpose of disrupting enemy use of electronic devices, equipment, or systems; and electronic deception – the deliberate radiation, reradiation, alteration, suppression, absorption, denial, enhancement or reflection of electromagnetic information and to deny valid information to an enemy.

• Electronic counter-countermeasures – that division of electronic warfare involving actions taken to ensure friendly effective use of the electromagnetic spectrum despite the enemy's use of electronic warfare. Also called ECCM.

• Electronic warfare support measures – that division of electronic warfare involving actions taken under direct control of an operational commander to search for, intercept, identify, and locate sources of radiated electromagnetic energy for the purpose of immediate threat recognition. Thus, electronic warfare support measures provide a source of information required for immediate decisions involving ECM, ECCM, avoidance, targeting and other tactical employment of forces. Also called ESM. Electronic warfare support measures data can be used to produce SIGINT, both COMINT and ELINT.

Ferret An aircraft, ship, or vehicle especially equipped for the detection, location and analysing of electromagnetic radiation. (JCS Pub 1, page 143) In 1949, the term was defined as 'an aircraft specifically modified to perform electronic reconnaissance only.'

FEAF US Far East Air Force.

GCI Ground-controlled intercept – controller that guides interceptor aircraft to an air target using ground radar stations.

ICBM Intercontinental ballistic missile.

JCS Joint Chiefs of Staff.

LORAN Long range navigational aid – uses beacons to vector destination.

MiG Generic abbreviation for Eastern Bloc fighter aircraft. More accurately it refers to those designed by the Mikoyan-Gurevich team.

MINOS *Matériels d'Information Normalisées pour les Opérations Spéciales.*

MIT Massachusetts Institute of Technology, Cambridge, Mass.

NACA National Advisory Committee on Aeronautics (predecessor of NASA).

NAS US Naval air station.

NIE National Intelligence Estimate.

NRO National Reconnaissance Office.

NSA National Security Agency.

PAL Permissive action link.

PR Photo-reconnaissance.

PRF Pulse repetition frequencies.

PRU Photo-Reconnaissance Unit.

RAND Research think tank – from Research and Development – originally set up in 1946 to service the air force but gradually widened remit.

Redsox Codename for CIA operations infiltrating agents into the Soviet bloc.

RFC Royal Flying Corps – precursor of the RAF.

RS Reconnaissance squadron.

Ravens Nickname designating the pecking order of US aircrew special operators as Raven One, Raven Two and so on.

SAC Strategic Air Command.

SESP Special Electronic Airborne Search Program.

SHORAN Short range navigational air – uses beacons to vector destination.

SIGINT Signals intelligence – a category of intelligence information comprising all communications intelligence, electronics intelligence, and telemetry intelligence.

SIS Secret Intelligence Service (UK).

SRS Strategic reconnaissance squadron (US).

SRW Strategic reconnaissance wing – there are usually three squadrons in a USAF Wing.

SSBN Submarine-launched ballistic missiles.

TDY Temporary tour of duty abroad.

Ultra Codename for breaking of German radio codes during World War 2.

USAAF United States Army Air Force. The USAF initially came under army supervision – thus the name, which was used 1941–47. Post-1947 the word 'Army' was dropped from the title.

USN United States Navy.

A Guide to ELINT terms

The primary purpose of airborne electronic reconnaissance is locating enemy radar stations and analysing the performance characteristics of the equipment. The 'Ferret' uses radar intercept receivers to detect enemy radar transmissions and a pulse analyser to display the radio waves received upon an oscilloscope for analysis. The 'Ferret' operator (called radar observer, RCM officer, electronic warfare officer (EWO), 'Raven', or 'Crow' at various times) seeks the following performance characteristics:

Frequency – The usual way of recognising a radar is on the basis of the carrier frequency of the radio waves it sends out. This frequency is usually expressed in terms of megacycles, or millions of cycles per second. Thus, the radar frequency is like the radio channel of a conventional radio set.

Pulse repetition frequency – a measure of the rate at which radio pulses are transmitted. Radars do not transmit continuously. They must pause briefly in order to receive the returning echo. The rate of pulses, or PRF, produces an audible humming sound or whine. Proficient 'Ravens' recognise individual radar types by their sound.

Pulse length – the duration of the pulse of transmitted radio energy. The pulse lengths are usually so brief that they are expressed in millionths of a second or microseconds.

Beam width – a radar sends out a beam of radio-frequency energy much like a searchlight sends out a beam of light. The beam width is expressed in degrees. Less sharp than a beam of light, the radar beam usually measures 10 or 15 degrees wide. Although a sharper beam is more accurate, it is also more likely to miss an elusive target.

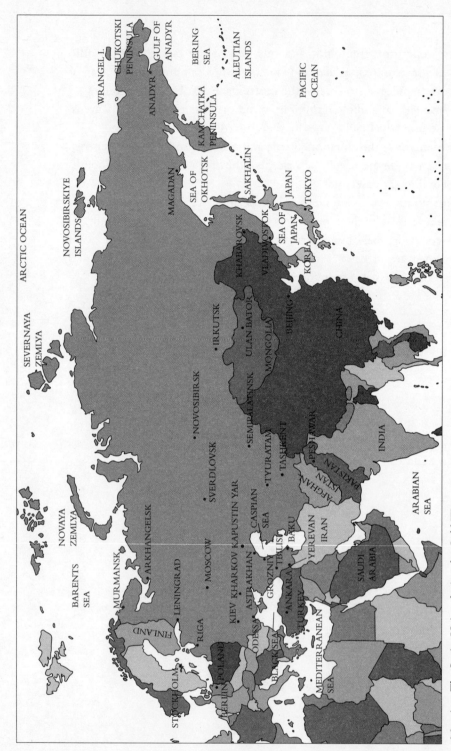

Map 1   The Soviet Union during the Cold War.

INTRODUCTION

History is a precious commodity. Cumulatively it provides the grey cells of the nation's collective memory. If the memory is fragmentary, partial or distorted it can warp today's perception and tomorrow's decision.

From an Institute of Contemporary British History editorial.

When General Curtis E. LeMay, head of Strategic Air Command, was briefing the crew of one of his aircraft that was about to undertake a dangerous and provocative overflight spy mission over the Soviet Union in May 1954, he made an astonishing remark. The plane's captain, Hal Austin, recalled the conversation in 1993: 'Well, I don't know whether it is appropriate to say or not. Of course, the old man's dead now, God rest his soul. But back at the briefing at SAC headquarters he said, "Well, maybe if we do this overflight right, we can get World War Three started". I think that was just a loose comment for his staff guys, because General (Thomas) Power was his hatchet man in those days, and he chuckled and General Power never laughed very much, so I always figured that was kind of a joke between them in some way or another. But we thought maybe that was serious.'

But if Austin thought at the time LeMay's comment might be just a dark joke, over thirty years later he discovered it was not. 'In the late 1980s I was involved with the Air Force Village West retirement community near Los Angeles. LeMay was the chairman of the board, and I was on the board for a while. He used to come in my office, sit down, and he'd been there a number of times before I brought up the subject of the mission we had flown. And he apparently remembered it like it was yesterday. We chatted about it a little bit. His comment there again was "Well, we'd have been a hell of a lot better off if we'd got World War Three started in those days". Of course he doesn't know that the Cold War is over now but he made that comment one day. "Maybe we'd all have been better off if we'd got it over with then." Well, who knows, we'll never know because history didn't go that way.'[1]

This exchange fascinated me and I resolved to understand what lay behind LeMay's remarks. The interview with Austin had been part of a BBC TV *Timewatch* documentary on Cold War spy flights that I was making in 1993. For three years I have undertaken further research to find out the basis of LeMay's remarkable comments.

When I first told friends and colleagues about the *Timewatch* programme they always assumed it was about the U-2 and Gary Powers. This was the most famous case where the Communists and West clashed over a spy flight but very few people were aware that the Powers case was only one example of many violent confrontations over spy flights during the Cold War. Few came to the world's attention. Fewer still remain in the collective consciousness. Most were not even admitted as spy flights. Throughout the Cold War there were stories of innocent Western aircraft being shot down by aggressive communists while on 'routine' weather, training or radio propagation flights. The public were never told that these aircraft were mainly spy planes operating close to Eastern Bloc borders.

The *Timewatch* documentary, called 'Spies in the Sky', was broadcast in the UK in February 1994 and in the United States on the Arts and Entertainment Channel in May 1994. Further material for this book was gathered while making two further *Timewatch* programmes on related topics over the next two years. They were 'Russia's Secret War', which revealed the Soviet involvement in the Korean War, transmitted in January 1996, and another on Strategic Air Command which was still being made at the time this book went to press.

In a recent essay, John Ferris laments the dearth of research and writing on American intelligence during the Cold War, 'We know less about American intelligence since 1945,' he writes, 'than we think we do, and this missing context ensures that much of what we do know does not mean what we think it does.' Of the Eisenhower years, Ferris notes that historians have been content to assume that US intelligence policy 'consisted essentially of coups and U-2s.'[1]

This book is an attempt to put together the fullest picture, as is currently possible, of the spy flights flown by the West against the Eastern Bloc in the first half of the Cold War. Much still remains secret. But I believe I have uncovered the major strands of these spy flight operations which were much more extensive than has been believed.

The gathering of intelligence is always a delicate affair in peacetime.

On the one hand a country must always be well informed of the capabilities and intentions of potentially hostile nations. Sometimes the gathering of intelligence in itself can endanger peace. This relentless and extremely dangerous secret war had taken place – high above national borders and civil airspace – between the Western powers and the Eastern Bloc. For over forty years the communist borders were under constant scrutiny by a range of Western aircraft. Some sources suggest there were as many as 3,000 missions a year.

The more eyewitnesses I found, the more flights came to light. From 1945 an undeclared war had been fought, the scope of which had only been hinted at, much less told. This war was not a 'hot war' like the Korean conflict but it took place nominally in peacetime albeit against the backdrop of the Cold War.

Decades of information blackout mean that the importance of aerial reconnaissance in the Cold War has been underestimated. Authors and historians have tended to concentrate on the big historical confrontations of the period or the more glamorous tales of spies and agents in popular fiction. But spy flights were important, if not crucial, to the direction of the Cold War. When Gen. Dwight D. Eisenhower took over the presidency of the United States in 1953 he was unhappy with the current state of US intelligence gathering and analytical capabilities. The president made reference to the postwar findings of the US Strategic Bombing Surveys which showed that the wartime analysis of aerial photography was extremely accurate. He pointed out that some 80-90 per cent of US military intelligence came from aerial reconnaissance. This book is intended to show how during Eisenhower's presidency, aerial reconnaissance was to take an even more global and political role than even he imagined. A number of the chapters in this book started life as articles in *Aeroplane Monthly*. They have been extended and amended to take note of the many useful comments from the magazine's readers.

In the course of the first chapter I have attempted to cover the rise of aerial intelligence prior to 1946. From there on I chart in much greater detail the rise of strategic aerial reconnaissance and the changes brought by the entirely new form of warfare of the nuclear age. This was primarily directed at the Soviet Union which, as the propagator of communist ideology, was seen as the most likely opponent. I try to concentrate on actual spy flights against the Soviet Union. British participation, in parallel to its involvement with the *realpolitik*, began as a major partner but gradually faded in importance as the United States grew as a superpower. By the time the British had reasserted their strength with their own thermonuclear capability after 1957, the US had little use for British reconnaissance capability.

As the research progressed I became aware this was more than just the story of daring intelligence missions. I discovered that aerial reconnaissance was much more central to Western military policy towards the Eastern Bloc than I had ever imagined. So the book, by the force of research, took on a wider brief than I had originally set for it.

The story of strategic reconnaissance is inseparably linked to the rise of one man, Gen. Curtis E. LeMay, the father of the strategic bombing. From early 1948 he was the head of Strategic Air Command, the world's first offensive nuclear strike force, during its formative years. As the prime user he set the tone for the collection of strategic intelligence for the era. LeMay is without doubt one of the great US military commanders, many historians rating him alongside Jackson, Pershing, Patton and MacArthur. His lack of recognition is probably accounted for by the fact he was an air force bomber general – not as glamorous as his equals – and possibly because his military brilliance was set against the bombing of civilians, not a practice with which the West likes to be associated too closely.

LeMay, as we will see, was the archetypal hawk and anti-communist and very much a man of his times. He did everything in his power to promote the growth of the USAF to confront the Soviet Union. During my research I uncovered a number of worrying pieces of evidence about his ultimate intentions. Aerial reconnaissance was to play a major part in these activities. Whether he ultimately overstepped his position is for the reader to judge. I have attempted to provide facts not opinions.

Above all, this book is the story of airmen who made these long flights, often in very uncomfortable conditions, over some of the most inhospitable terrain in the world. It was a war fought with enormous courage with many unsung heroes. Where possible I have used eyewitness accounts. I have found the pilots of all sides a delight to spend time with. There is a quality about men who have looked death closely in the eye and survived. I remain grateful.

This is also a book about secrecy. Many of those who took part were told never to divulge to anyone anything about their work. Forty years on some dutifully continue to obey this ordinance. Others, fortunately, realise that the need for secrecy has now gone. It was the Russians who were most forthcoming about their work. Although often motivated by patriotism, the totalitarian regime they once served has disintegrated and there is little to be loyal to any longer.

American participants displayed a common-sense attitude to secrecy but sometimes with reservations. I believe this sensible approach comes naturally to a nation that enshrines free speech in its written constitution. The American inclination is to talk to a journalist unless there is a good reason not to. Their British counterparts were the opposite and hardest by far to get to talk – something which I deduce to be partly about secrecy. The British pilots also come from a tradition of modest understatement and wish to play down any exceptional act they may have performed. The British Ministry of Defence was not helpful. In some cases fliers were told not to discuss flights that had taken place over forty years ago.

There is also a wider context to this book. The more I researched the more I realised that aerial intelligence had never been given its proper place or relevance in the history of the Cold War. The sheer extent of the West's air intelligence clearly affected the relationships between the Communist and Western world profoundly. I have tried to evaluate this impact impartially and not simply with knee-jerk pro-West concurrence.

This book has its limitations. It only covers part of the Cold War, up to 1962, when aerial reconnaissance was in its ascendancy before satellites became the mainstay of overhead reconnaissance. It does not try to deal with tactical reconnaissance. It concentrates on aerial reconnaissance and does not expand far into the wider intelligence context of signals intelligence and spies. It does not try to deal fully with Anglo-American spy flights against Mao's China, although along the way I try to give a sense of the breadth of these operations. Until the 1970s the United States War Plan intended the destruction of the major Chinese cities at the same time that Russia's cities would be attacked. (By 1961 the RAF's Bomber Command was integrated into this plan.) China was subject to a similar level of aerial surveillance. At this time only half the story can be told. China remains a closed society and access to participants and documents is very limited.

Neither does the book try to detail all the other reconnaissance missions that these aircraft undertook at targets other than the Eastern Bloc. Spy flights were flown against most politically significant countries in the world, especially if there was a crisis underway. Many of the U-2 missions were overflights of Israel and Egypt and other middle eastern countries.

I hope the what I have written does in some way add to our perception of the Cold War, so that we can learn and never have to repeat the experience of living for thirty years in fear of Armageddon.

1
SPIES IN THE SKY

On 29 October 1995 a USAF Lockheed U-2 spyplane crashed at RAF Fairford killing the pilot. This accident gave a rare public glimpse of a special intelligence operation that had been taking place every day for the previous three years over the skies of the strife-torn country that was once Yugoslavia. An American U-2 spyplane operating from a British base reflected the close co-operation with the United States in aerial espionage operations that has continued, often in conditions of the greatest secrecy, for over fifty years.

The U-2 was exactly forty years old in 1995. Built to fly high above the communist defences during the Cold War, it soared to notoriety when Gary Powers' plane was shot down in central Russia on May Day 1960. Its simple but efficient 'glider with a jet engine' design – a product of the famous Lockheed 'Skunk Works' – has survived into the satellite era, capable of obtaining intelligence better than virtually any other aircraft. But it is only one of the aircraft used in Anglo-American operations that have supported the UN and NATO operations in Bosnia.

In 1995 a journalist friend told me he had been staying at a hotel just outside Rome populated by a number of RAF crews. Friendly at the bar, all they would say about their work was that they were flying Nimrod aircraft and their posting was temporary and to do with the civil war in Yugoslavia. They were in fact crew of No 51 Squadron, the RAF's most secret unit, dedicated to gathering electronic intelligence. Closely allied to GCHQ (communications 'eavesdropping' agency, Britain's version of the NSA) these aircraft fly over the former Yugoslavia, listening in to radio, telephone and electronic signals from the fighting units and politicians. 'The former Yugoslavia is the most listened to, photographed, monitored, overheard and intercepted entity in the history of mankind,' said a former State Department official who handled the Bosnian conflict. Indeed, the world famous photographs showing the mass grave site near Srebrenica were taken by a USAF aircraft flown from Britain.[1]

A 1996 newspaper report also revealed that the US Intelligence community had played games with intelligence gathered from Bosnia. In 1992 the CIA had stated to the Senate's Foreign Relations Committee that air strikes against the Serbs would be 'impossible'. Yet several weeks before, U-2 photographs had showed that the Serbian artillery around Sarajevo was exposed in the hills. It was estimated that a single day of air strikes could have destroyed most of these weapons that day after day inflicted carnage on the civilians below. Deceit in the use of aerial intelligence, as we shall see, was nothing new.[2]

Their work is complemented by the men of the USAF's 55th Strategic Reconnaissance Wing (SRW). Flying missions under the codename 'Rivet Joint' their large Boeing RC-135 aircraft are also packed with sensitive electronic equipment for picking up electronic intelligence. (The RC-135 is a close relative of the Boeing 707 developed alongside the airliner.)

These sophisticated units are the result of development and refinement in the long history of aerial reconnaissance. Although the drama of the fighter and bomber has stolen the glamour, the history of aerial warfare is as much about reconnaissance as about its show-stealing counterparts. Reconnaissance was the original military motive and purpose of getting humans into the air. Its importance is continually underrated.

The first manned and free flight was made in a hot-air balloon in Paris on 21 November 1783, and the military possibilities were immediately apparent to observers. Two days after Joseph-Michel and Étienne-Jacques de Montgolfier succeeded in their flight, André-Giroud de Villette ascended in the balloon. He recognised the enormous military potential of aviation:

> From that moment I was convinced that this apparatus, at little cost, could be made very useful to an army for discovering the position of its enemy, its movement, its advances, its dispositions and that this information could be conveyed by a system of signals, to the troops looking after the apparatus.

In 1793 the first balloon corps was formed in France and was in due course used in military operations. The prime use was reconnaissance – a spotter in a balloon could observe enemy movements for miles around. The idea caught on. Captive observation balloons were used in the American Civil War of 1861-65, and free-flying balloons were used in the siege of Paris in 1870. A balloon section accompanied the British Army expeditions to Bechuanaland in 1884 and to the Sudan in 1885. A permanent balloon section was formed within the British Corps of Royal

Engineers in 1890. It carried out reconnaissance duties during the Boer War 10 years later, much to the annoyance of the Boers who considered such technology as unfair and not playing by the rules.

By the turn of the century events were taking place that would overshadow the balloon. On 17 December 1903 near Kitty Hawk beach in North Carolina, the brothers Wilbur and Orville Wright made a powered flight in their biplane. At first this extraordinary event met with indifference in America where the government dismissed them as charlatans. The British turned down the opportunity to use their aircraft. It was to be the French that would be at the forefront of aircraft technology and who bought the rights to fly the new aircraft. Even by 1912 the British only had a dozen aircraft in military use compared with France's two hundred.

In 1911, the Italians first used aircraft for military reconnaissance when they observed Turkish positions in Libya. In this short campaign, Italian aviators furthered the military potential of aviation by taking aerial photographs, experimenting with wireless communications and dropping bombs. Likewise, the French, Mexicans, Bulgarians and Turks used aircraft in various wars in 1912-13. The United States first flew visual reconnaissance missions in 1913 in the Philippines and along the Mexican border. Brig.-Gen. John J. Pershing's celebrated pursuit of Pancho Villa in the spring of 1916 introduced the potential of air observation to the American public.[3]

Seven days after the declaration of war on 4 August 1914, four squadrons of the Royal Flying Corps, with a collection of sixty-three aircraft, went to France. Aerial photography quickly assumed great importance and when the front lines stabilised, it became necessary to make longer flights over enemy territory to reconnoitre trench supply routes and ammunition dumps. These aircraft brought back reliable information about the attacking German forces in the retreat from the Mons and the Battle of the Marne. It was recognised that reconnaissance was a separate skill from dogfighting or bombing. Some aircraft were suited to it and some were not. By the Battle of Neuve Chapelle in March 1915, the Allies had photographed the German trench system and transformed the information into detailed maps. By 1918, reconnaissance aircraft and observer balloons provided commanders with vertical and oblique aerial photographs which enabled staff to map terrain, mark enemy troop positions, spot artillery and anticipate attack.

Strategic bombing began in a very unorganised form mainly aimed at terrorising and demoralising civilians on the home front rather than the destruction of military or industrial infrastructure. The Germans sent Zeppelin airships and, later, Gotha bombers to attack British cities. The British responded with a few attacks late on in the war. The reconnaissance work of the RFC[4] throughout the war was primarily to assist the army in its ground battles. The lack of range of aircraft and relatively embryonic abilities of the bomber force meant that bombing was primarily a tactical rather than strategic weapon.

According to Sir Walter Raleigh, the official British historian of the air war: 'Reconnaissance, or observation can never be superseded; knowledge comes before power; and the air is first of all a place to see from.'

In 1919 a British Member of Parliament said, 'We have beaten the Germans in nearly every invention or development of engines of war. But it is in the realm of aviation photography that our supremacy has been most conspicuous'.[5]

Following the 'war to end all wars' and particuarly as a result of a firm belief that such a war should never happen again, all nations reduced their air forces to the operational minimum. Little research and development was undertaken.

The difference between reconnaissance in peacetime and spying is a narrow one. But the use of disguised aircraft certainly pushes intelligence gathering deep into the realms of spying. With the rise of National Socialism, Germany – then bound by the Treaty of Versailles not to maintain arms – began a covert and aggressive strategy to expand its air force. It also effectively began proper strategic reconnaissance. In the mid-1930s Germany began the systematic, secret overflying of countries it considered to be potential opponents. Luftwaffe pilots posing, in a civilian aircraft, as a Lufthansa team exploring possible new airline routes took photographs over France and Britain. These missions were no longer tactical sorties to enable an army at war. They were missions designed to provide intelligence for full-scale bombing and invasion. They were looking for industrial and military targets that would be crucial in an all-out war.

While German spies overflew Britain and France, those two countries were teaming up to spy on the rising power of Germany. As early as 1929 the French had made some flights along the German border, taking photographs of German military activity. These missions resumed in 1936. Around the same time British intelligence realised that they needed better covert intelligence on what was happening in Germany and other potentially hostile European countries. This intelligence could not be gathered by official reconnaissance units and had to be secret. So Britain's Secret Intelligence Service (SIS) set up a special unit under the command of air intelligence specialist, Wg Cdr Fred Winterbotham.

Sir Neil Wheeler[6] says:

> . . . photographic reconnaissance was far removed from the concept of operations we knew from World War 1. The basic initiative for change came from one Wg Cdr Winterbotham, Chief of Air Intelligence in the Secret Intelligence Service. Winterbotham had been receiving the photographic results of some clandestine French flights in the late 1920s and early 1930s and it gave him ideas. He started looking around for someone to undertake such work in the late 1930s. He was steered towards a very remarkable man, Sidney Cotton, best described as a buccaneering entrepreneur.[7]

Winterbotham recruited an Australian pilot and adventurer called Sidney Cotton, a decision that was to pay dividends in the next months. SIS bought two Lockheed Electra aircraft which could take fourteen executive passengers and fitted them with hidden cameras so that exposures could be taken in flight of the ground they were overflying. Cotton and his team flew these aircraft all around Europe but especially over Germany and Italy on purported civil aviation flights. As the likelihood of war grew in 1939 so did Sidney Cotton's business trips to Germany. On these missions Cotton's cameras recorded the build-up of the Luftwaffe on airfields below his flight path.

In anticipation of war the Admiralty asked SIS and Fred Winterbotham to provide photographs of the warships and merchant ships in the port of Wilhelmshaven. They flew a small Beechcraft just inside the Dutch border and were able to get viable photographs. The German invasion of Poland and declaration of war put an end to Cotton's civil overflights.

Shortly after the outbreak of war Sidney Cotton's unit was absorbed into the RAF. Cotton was given a commission but the unit was taken over by regular commissioned officers. The new unit was called after its headquarters at the time – the Heston Flight. The RAF PR inventory consisted of the slow but stable overhead monoplane, the Westland Lysander and the Bristol Blenheim. Cotton had retained some influence and quickly recognised that neither aircraft was a suitable platform for reconnaissance over hostile territory. Both the Lysander and the Blenheim, a two-engined bomber, took terrible casualties in the first year of the war completely outclassed by German fighters.[8]

Cotton realised that you needed the fastest possible aircraft flying at high altitude to be successful reconnaissance aircraft. Cotton persuaded ACM Sir Hugh Dowding, then Commander-in-Chief of Fighter Command, to lend him two precious Spitfires. The Blenheim and the Lysander were, however, going to remain the RAF's main PR aircraft for some time.

The Spitfires went to join the British Expeditionary Force. Cotton's team was taken over to an airfield at Seclin near Lille where the unit operated under tight security, with its own private hangar and guards. On 18 November 1939 the converted Spitfire took-off on its first mission, with Squadron Leader Maurice Longbottom at the controls. It headed towards the German border and Aachen. While Longbottom did not reach his targets he was able to take several sequences of high quality photographs at 33,000ft over country next to the German-French border. Never before had such good quality photographs been taken at high altitude in wartime conditions.

Cotton's philosophy was to have a profound effect on photo-reconnaissance. He recognised that it was more important to be able to evade the enemy's defences rather than fight the enemy. It was better to remove the armament of a Spitfire to make it lighter and faster than to be able to combat German fighters. It was a philosophy that ran counter to the RAF's natural inclinations but eventually won the day.

After several name changes what had started as the Heston Flight became the Photographic Reconnaissance Unit (PRU) in July 1940. Each mission taken by the unit furthered not only Allied intelligence but the state of the PR art. In February 1940 the Admiralty asked for more photographs of Wilhelmshaven, to find out if the *Tirpitz* had left dry dock, as agents had reported. Blenheims had failed to crack the problem. The unit now had four Spitfire Type Bs (until the purpose-built PR Mk IV early PR Spitfires were designated Types A to G), and one was fitted with an additional tank to give it the necessary range. On 10 February both the ports of Wilhelmshaven and Emden were photographed at 30,000ft. In 48 hours plans of the port at Emden and the naval base at Wilhelmshaven had been drawn from the photographs, with all the ships in harbour identified. A Type C Spitfire became available with an even longer range and added the port of Kiel to the target list.

Following the retreat from Dunkirk in early June, aerial reconnaissance became vital to detect signs of the immediacy of the expected German invasion. The PRU looked for hard evidence. Initially the pilots were photographing the Dutch ports and the Channel coast and found little. There was no obvious build-up of invasion shipping. But a constant watch was needed and even when weather conditions prevented high altitude flights, low-level missions were flown.

By August these missions began to show signs that the plans for invasion of England were in gear. Landing craft were being built in the Low Countries' shipyards. Photo-interpreter Michael Spender discovered five 130ft barges with modified bows at Rotterdam. By mid-August they could report that the invasion fleet was being assembled at Antwerp, Rotterdam and Amsterdam. The climax came on 17 September. There were more than 1,700 self-propelled barges and 200 seagoing ships gathered in various ports.

The whole matter hinged on the Battle of Britain. Hitler knew he had to have air superiority. He came very close. The RAF was under enormous pressure taking greater losses than it could recoup without a respite. But Hitler's decision to move bombing from military targets including airfields to urban targets lifted the pressure just enough. On 12 October the Luftwaffe's failure to destroy the RAF led to the cancellation of the invasion of Britain – Operation 'Seelöwe' (Sealion) – until the next spring. Photographs brought back from the coastal ports were the hard evidence of this decision as the invasion fleet was stood down.

Sir Neil Wheeler described the difficulties the new team faced:

Most of our early problems came from the altitude we were flying. It has to be remembered that there was not much flying before the war above 20,000ft. My log book shows thirty times over 10,000ft in five years before 1939. Most of our Spitfire PR sorties took place between 25,000ft and 35,000ft where temperatures were around -50°C. In the early days we had problems with, for example, the vent of the oil tank and some form of heating was required. The same was true of the cameras.

Frankly I found the extreme cold most uncomfortable. On my feet I wore a pair of ladies' silk stockings, a pair of football stockings, a pair of oiled Scandinavian ski socks and RAF fur-lined boots. On my hands I wore two pairs of RAF silk gloves and some special fur-backed and lined gauntlets which I had to buy for myself.

As the RAF slowly began to go on the offensive, PR was vital for

Bomber Command who needed detailed targeting intelligence. Photographs were needed of all the enemy's main industrial-military targets for accurate bombing. PR was also providing feedback showing the ineffectiveness of the Bomber Command's attacks on Germany. The British had switched to night bombing because the German air defences were too effective during the day. In June 1941 Bomber Command was ordered to concentrate on rail and transport centres when the moon was up. The majority of the time it was to attack major cities with the joint objectives of causing economic damage and demoralising the civilian morale.

Initially PR of these targets was limited. The city of Mannheim was hit twice. Crews reported that most bombs had hit the target with the centre of the city being left in flames. On the second raid, in daylight, photographs taken from Spitfires showed that there had been significant damage but over a very wide area and a lot of it was outside the target area. In April 1941 a detailed study of wide-area daylight photographs of later raids established that the estimate of accuracy of 300yd in good conditions for night bombing was wildly optimistic, usually it was at best upwards of 1,000yd.

As well as assessing actual damage, post-strike PR became essential in producing independent evidence so that reliable techniques of bomb aiming could be devised. New navigation equipment was developed like 'Gee', 'Oboe' and 'H2S' which permitted far more accurate night bombing.

The importance of aerial reconnaissance would be paramount during the Battle of Ruhr bombing offensive, which began with a raid on Essen on 5 March 1943 and was the first to use 'Oboe' extensively. It helped guide the 442 aircraft to their targets. The campaign continued for over three months with over 15,504 sorties dropping 42,349 tonnes of bombs. Supporting day and night aerial reconnaissance showed a marked improvement in accuracy.

Perhaps the best known story of RAF photo-reconnaissance is the identification of the sites of manufacture of Hitler's V-weapons, the V-1 and V-2 rockets. The V-weapon campaign seriously damaged British civilian morale and was a very cost effective means of attacking Britain. The famous story concerns the recognition of an unusual new construction by the WRAF photo interpreter Constance Babbington-Smith. This intelligence work was crucial to the systematic bombing of launch sites by the RAF before they could make a significant difference to the war.[9]

Aerial reconnaissance was key to the successful launching of the invasion of Europe in 1944. From 1942 Spitfires and an increasing number of American aircraft constantly photographed a 30-mile wide strip of the European coast from Holland to Spain. As D-Day neared, low level photographs shot at an angle to allow shadows to reveal the depth of ground objects became vital. From these photographs the planners could estimate the best landing places and the type of equipment that would be needed to get the invasion force ashore. Once the battle had been joined, PR units provided vital tactical intelligence of the enemy's military dispositions. Of course this kind of operation was taking place in every sector of the war by both sides. The Germans had the highly capable Theodore Rowehl who had been their equivalent of Sidney Cotton, secretly photographing Britain, France and the Low Countries before the outbreak of war posing as 'civil flights'. But it was the British and Americans who refined aerial reconnaissance to a higher form of military science.

When the US air forces began to arrive to assist the British they were relative novices. The United States Army Air Corps capability was mainly the product of the work of Gen. George W. Goddard, 'the father of US aerial reconnaissance'. Born in Tunbridge Wells, England, in 1889, Goddard had left for America at the age of fourteen. At first a successful cartoonist, he became fascinated by aircraft while watching the intrepid woman aviator Ruth Law conduct aerobatics over Keuka Lake, Chicago in the summer of 1916. Goddard went to Cornell University training school but while he was there he was told the military did not want any more pilots but instead they wanted men trained in aerial photography. Goddard took the course and began a life-long career.

He never made it to the war in Europe but shortly after World War 1 ended he was sent to Carlstrom Field in Arcadia, Florida to learn to fly. There he started experimenting with cameras attached under the aircraft and as a result came to the attention of the pioneer military aviator Gen. Billy Mitchell. In 1924 Goddard became Director of Research and Development at the Photographic Laboratory in Dayton and spent many years innovating new methods of aerial photography.

On 12 May 1938, three of the new B-17 Flying Fortress bombers took off from Mitchell Field, New York to demonstrate a potential new role for the air force. They intercepted the Italian liner *Rex* some 725 miles out of New York. This extraordinary piece of navigation was conducted by 1/Lt Curtis E. LeMay. Col. George Goddard was in one of the B-17s to record the success for posterity. His photographs of the ship, with two B-17s just behind at mast height appeared in over 1,800 newspapers and magazines.

When World War 2 began in Europe the supply of superior German optics ceased. Realising that good optics would be vital in war, Goddard organised an optical centre at Harvard University. With the help of the young optical genius Dr Jim Baker, they gathered the best people in the field. As a result the United States was not caught totally unprepared for the forthcoming air war.

The British, though had already been getting war experience of PR. As Sir Alfred Ball said:

> I formed and took No 4 PRU to North Africa for the 'Torch' landings in October 1942. We found that our Benson experience was invaluable and thoroughly applicable throughout the Mediterranean theatre and we advised the American 7th Photo Group, straight over from the States and with whom we formed a joint PR Wing, accordingly. These practices were adjusted and developed with local experience as the Wing advanced from Algiers through Tunis to San Severo in Italy.[10]

As Gen. Goddard has said, they were quickly taught by the British. Goddard especially praised the capabilities of Sidney Cotton. Once the huge American industrial complex had begun to support the war effort huge leaps were made in the technology. A three-way partnership was formed between the military, universities and industrial companies. One of the great examples was the relationship between the military, MIT in Boston and companies like Polaroid. Run by Edwin 'Din' Land, Polaroid was involved in a number of key breakthroughs as diverse as the synthesising of quinine, rangefinders for gunners, polarised goggles for troops and pilots. Other men came to the fore, like Jim Baker who began the first in a series of camera and lens development that would break technological boundaries. Over at MIT, Baker, an English major and editor of MIT's *Technological Review*, found himself placed in charge of the administration of the first federally-funded research project.

If the Americans learnt the modern arts of photo-reconnaissance in North Africa and Europe, their own proving and developing ground was to be in the Pacific theatre. There US forces could not use the results of British reconnaissance – because there was none. To develop target folders, the USAAF relied on strategic photographic reconnaissance to identify military and industrial targets.

Goddard himself devised a strip cameras that was revolutionary, eliminating the need for shutters on cameras by using the principle of image-motion compensation. This annoyed many of the big companies as they already had $40 million of contracts to build aerial cameras and optics. Now Goddard's invention was threatening this arrangement. He proved its unique worth and showed in a test off Palm Beach that it could be used to determine the depth of water and height of water. This was crucially important to the United States Navy who used it to chart the reefs around Okinawa and not one life was lost in the landings during the invasion.

The British welcomed Goddard's invention. The RAF Reconnaissance 'went wild about the strip camera', he said. They modified the camera to take night photographs at 20,000ft. Goddard pointed out the importance of strip cameras for today, saying at the end of his 36-year career:

> The pictures of the moon and Mars were made with what we now call the panoramic camera: we took the strip camera at 32,000ft and put a crank on it across the line of flight from horizon to horizon. The strip camera changed cameras. There are no pictures taken in space with a shutter camera.

World War 2 was to take the basic tasks of aerial reconnaissance and make them into a sophisticated discipline each with its own specialists: pre-strike, post-strike, mapping, intelligence, photo-interpretation, daylight, night reconnaissance, tactical battlefield and strategic intelligence.

But the rapid pace of technological development was to lead aerial reconnaissance into whole new areas. Signals intelligence (SIGINT) had begun with the first interception of an enemy message. Listening to the enemy's radio messages had begun in the war and had become increasingly sophisticated as both sides started coding their messages. The art of cryptology came into its own. The British and American success at decrypting German and Japanese signals was a deciding factor in World War 2.

World War 2 was to be the first electronic battlefield. Before the war both the British and the Germans were secretly pioneering the use of radio waves to spot approaching objects, often many miles away. The British had developed the cavity magnetron amplifier and realised its potential application as the 'radio-detection and ranging device', known for short as radar. The British grasped the significance of radar technology by developing early warning and ground-controlled intercept (GCI) stations which alerted defences to the approach of enemy aircraft and directed fighters to intercept even at night. The Germans also later devised their own radar systems.

Again the Cambridge, New England campus of MIT became the site of the US Government-sponsored radiation laboratory, which rapidly caught up and improved on the British version. This in turn led to the development of a family of radars including 10cm waveband radar for use in submarine hunting aircraft, several precision gun-laying radars, and a long range navigational system known as LORAN. As each new technique appeared on the electronic battlefield then so did the opposition devise methods to counter it, beginning a long running cat and mouse game. This was known as electronic countermeasures (ECM).

Another aspect of the electronic battlefield was its use in navigation. In the summer of 1940 the Germans introduced a radio-aided navigational device, known as *Knickebein* (knock-knees), to improve night bombing accuracy. The British strategy to counter it started the 'Battle of the Beams'. The British developed their own navigational aids including 'Gee' and 'Oboe', 'H2S' airborne radar and radar countermeasures. 'Window', for instance, was thousands of thin strips of aluminium dropped from aircraft in the bomber stream. These produced multiple echoes on the German radar screens and misled and confused the radar operators as to the true route and target of the attacking force. They misdirected the night-fighters who in turn, failing to find their targets, ran low on fuel and had to refuel and get airborne again, by which time the bombers had long since gone out of range. The Germans replied with night-fighters equipped with SN-2 airborne radar.[11]

The allies began to identify the characteristics of the different types of German radar: the *Freya* early warning radar, the *Wurzburg* ground-controlled intercept radar and the *Gema* coastal surveillance radar.

In 1942 a special top secret RAF unit, No 1474 Flight, was set up and dedicated to investigating German radar patterns and wavelengths. The RAF designed the first electronic intelligence (ELINT) aircraft by placing special receivers in converted Wellington bombers. No 1474 Flight was redesignated No 192 Squadron on 4 January 1943. It absorbed No 1483 Flight, a unit with a similar role, on 27 January 1944.

These pioneering days were a hit and miss affair. In 1944 experts were convinced that radio signals were directing V-2 rockets. No 192 spent fruitless hours on 'Big Ben' patrols in an attempt to discover the correct frequency. Sqn Ldr Bob Anstee, the veteran of more than fifty bomber missions over Germany, was transferred to No 1474: 'I joined RAF Bomber Command and was with No 214 Squadron 1943-45. I did missions in Short Stirlings and B-17s. I was taken off for electronic warfare missions.' He joined No 1474 Flight using converted Lancaster bombers flying up and down the English Channel monitoring for radio signals. 'Finally they discovered that the signals did not exist,' he said. The V-2s were guided by an inertial system.

The Americans realised the significance of ELINT very early in their war effort. The Office of Scientific Research and Development headhunted Dr Frederick E. Terman from Stanford University. He was to head that Radio Research Laboratory responsible for radar and radio countermeasures. They quickly began work on electronic reconnaissance and radar jamming. In early 1942 Terman directed the adaptation of SCR587 radar intercept receivers for use on board aircraft. This equipment was a rudimentary effort to identify enemy radar sites and the signals they sent out.

At the Radar School at Boca Raton, USA, they set up a radio countermeasures course to train aircrew specialists on radar detection. These operators were nicknamed 'ravens', or the later derivative 'crows', names which stuck. The first American ELINT mission was flown by a modified B-24D on 6 March 1943 to collect data on Japanese radar on Kiska Island in the Aleutians. The flight was codenamed 'Ferret 1', another term that has stuck as the generic name for all subsequent ELINT flights. The 'ravens' were 2/Lts Bill Praun and Ed Tietz and they observed signals in the 100-megacycle range. Following the 'Torch' landings in North Africa and the beginnings of the massive influx of American forces into the European and North African theatres came more 'ferrets' and 'ravens'. In May 1943, 'Ferret 111' entered service with the 16th Reconnaissance Squadron. Between May and September 1943 'ferrets' in the Mediterranean sector flew 184 sorties and discovered 450 enemy radar sites. This unit tested the new RC-156 jammer that worked against gun-laying radar.[12]

By the end of the war aerial reconnaissance had become vital for strategic warfare and had become a highly technical profession. Members of the reconnaissance squadrons tended to stay in the discipline much more so than fighter or bomber pilots. By 1945 a huge reservoir of experienced aerial reconnaissance crews had been built up with huge accumulated expertise. But with the end of the war many of the lessons would be forgotten and later, would have to be relearnt the hard way.

2
THE SECRET EXPLORERS

In the relief and optimism following World War 2, both the USAF and RAF were radically reduced in size. The United States Army Air Forces personnel was reduced from a peak of 2.4 million to around 400,000. The RAF budget was reduced to only £173 million for the year 1948/9. But quite quickly there was a realisation that there was going to be little opportunity for a peace dividend. The uneasy alliance with the Soviet Union was already under strain and no longer was 'my enemy's enemy, my friend,' now the Axis was defeated. The communist remit was spreading and within two years it would encompass East Germany, Czechoslovakia, Poland, Hungary, Romania, Yugoslavia, Albania, Bulgaria, North Korea and China.

Lessons had been learnt from World War 2 and the success of the air force had finally won it equal status with the other military services. The German Luftwaffe had failed in its effort to mount a strategic bombing campaign against England largely because of the Luftwaffe's prewar concentration on tactical operations. It did not have the capability to carry out a devastating bombing campaign. The German attack on Russia prevented further resources being diverted into strategic bombing. Only the United States and Great Britain had shown they had the organisational and technical means to carry out sustained long-range bombing attacks. The Germans had, however, made the first effective use of rocket technology. The British had no way to defend against the V-2 once it was launched.

The aftermath of war saw a number of major reorganisations of the US air forces. In March 1946 the surviving US strategic bomber units were combined in the new Strategic Air Command (SAC) within the US Army Air Force. SAC's formal missions were: to conduct long-range offensive operations independently or in co-operation with land and naval forces; to conduct maximum range reconnaissance operations; and to provide units capable of operations employing the latest and most advanced (i.e. atomic) weapons.

On 18 September 1947, the United States' air forces became fully independent of the army. Gen. Carl Spaatz, an outstanding wartime leader, became the first chief of the United States Air Force. Although the US Navy continued to maintain its own air arm, the USAF quickly assumed responsibility for strategic bombing, national air defence as well as tactical and logistical support of the ground forces.

At SAC's formation the new command possessed a front-line strength of 148 B-29 Superfortress bombers, 85 P-51 Mustang escort fighters and a reconnaissance squadron. As part of the reorganisation, the 46th Squadron (Very Long Range) had been formed in early 1946. As the only effective unit with a strategic capability it was assigned to the newly formed SAC. Until recently the missions of the 46th have been shrouded in secrecy and mystery for 40 years. It has now become clear that they successfully completed more dangerous operations, under the most hazardous and difficult conditions, than probably any other American air unit in peacetime. In 1946 it was to be at the forefront of the radical new strategies designed to meet not only a new enemy but an entirely new form of war.

The first stage in this new form of war involved looking for land the US could lay claim to in the Arctic. On 14 June 1946 the squadron was mobilised to participate in Operation 'Nanook' at Ladd AFB in Alaska. The *Washington Post* of 9 June 1946 printed an innocuous report of what was, in reality, a highly classified operation:

> The Air Force disclosed earlier that a squadron of converted B-29 long range bombers has been assigned to Alaska to make frequent weather flights over the Arctic, termed by ranking military men the world's most strategic stretch of geography in an age of atom bombs and 10,000 mile planes.

The real purpose of 'Nanook' was to search for undiscovered land masses in the Arctic regions. This was considered to be important, for both offensive and defensive military installations could be built on land but not on ice. To make a land claim in the Arctic, land needed to be found and as far as was known the Arctic was mainly solid ice. Some early explorers thought they had seen land in the polar region. The US explorer Robert E. Peary, in 1909 the first man to reach the North Pole, reported land 120 miles north-west of Axel Heiburg Island. But these reports were vague.

The matter was getting urgent. The United Nations was preparing an international agreement for the ownership of any lands found in the North Arctic areas, that would be determined by the converging lines of longitude to the North Pole. This would give the United States jurisdiction over only about 8 per cent of any land found near the pole, but would give the Soviets 47 per cent of the area, Europe about 29 per cent and Canada about 16 per cent. Therefore it was in the best interests of the United States to immediately lay claim to all lands that might be found in the Arctic areas. The original mission, Project 'Nanook', was ordered for 180 days. It was to last three years.

A senior air force officer, Gen. Curtis E. LeMay, was later to say of Nanook:

> It was known that the Soviets were active in air exploration of the Arctic as early as 1937 and had operated temporary testing stations on ice floes off their coasts. But the polar ice cap had never been explored by air and there was concern that the Soviet Union might find and operate forward aggressive military stations that could be a threat to the United States.

Fred Wack and his brother Joe were officers with the 46th. Fred had enlisted in the Army Air Corps Aviation Cadet Program in 1942 aged seventeen. He stayed on after the war and was transferred to the unit as a lieutenant.[1] In retirement Fred wrote a history of the unit.[2]

> At first, our job was to look for land, number one. If we found land and could claim it on behalf of the United States, we could get forward bases closer to the Soviet Union, instead of way back in Alaska and into Canada.
>
> There's a general feeling that if there was going to be a war with the Soviet Union, they were going to come over the polar area. So according to General LeMay and many of the other authorities of the day, if there's going to be a third world war, it will start over the pole.
>
> When we went to Alaska, we were told that we have to look at the world completely different now. The North Pole is going to be the centre of the world, because that's where the war is going to start, and so you have to get used to looking at the world from the top of the globe. And we looked at it with Canada and the United States, Alaska, on one side of the North Pole, and the Soviet Union, a very broad country, on the other side.[3]

Working from Ladd AFB was tough. The first winter the 46th arrived was the worst for 30 years.

> We were in a special area on the other side of the runway, about four miles from the base proper. It was very rugged and men were living in Quonsets[4] and modified

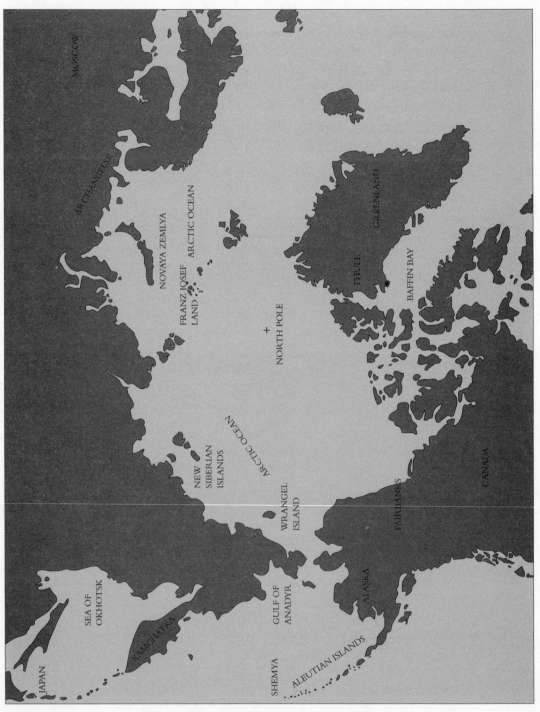

Map 2   'A different view of the world' with the North Pole at the centre.

maintenance buildings. Many of the men built their own homes, as rugged as they could be. It was an experience, a great experience, actually.

The 46th had to pioneer flying in the appalling Arctic conditions. They sometimes flew in ground temperatures of -50°F, so cold that the fuel would freeze. Their aircraft underwent many modifications to enable them to fly in such cold temperatures. In the learning process they lost a number of aircraft and crews.

> We were flying B-29s and when we first took them up there, they were not very reliable to fly in that kind of polar regions because at 40 and 50 degrees below zero carburettor cooling would happen on take-off. We lost several of our aircraft. But we had B-29s, 10 of them, and some of them were F-13s [photo-reconnaissance variant of the B-29], which were modified for cold weather flying. It was very difficult for the maintenance people to get the aircraft in condition, to get it off the ground. Especially we're talking about in the fall, winter and the spring, when the temperatures were very low.[5]

Ice often formed on the propellers which upon take-off would be thrown off against the side of aircraft inflicting damage to the skin. Cameras installed in the unpressurised area of the F-13 would not work properly in the freezing temperatures – they had to be moved to pressurised sections. Only one in ten of the cameras was winterised.

In the rundown postwar air force, obtaining spares was a major headache. In October 1946 Gen. LeMay visited the squadron. The squadron navigation officer explained they lacked reliable minimum precision gyros that could be trusted in Grid Navigation. LeMay quickly diverted over $500,000 in budget money for a gyro testing unit at Ladd's Cold Weather Testing Branch.

With this kind of backing the 46th could get on with its job. While flying an early 'Nanook' mission, an Arctic ice island, 'T1', measuring 17 miles long by 8 miles wide was spotted on a ground mapping radar. But although the 46th were to fly hundreds of hours over the Arctic they never found any land. However, they were to find more ice islands and they were named unsurprisingly, 'T2' and 'T3'. They were later used as spy bases against the Soviet Union. Fred Wack:

> Another job for the 72nd was to get up there and lay the ground work for those defences such as the early warning network, that came about in the 1950s. The

maps and the information that we gathered up there, helped to create that early warning network, even to the creation of installations on ice islands, as listening posts.

As SAC gradually realised the complexities of their future role, more and more tasks were assigned to the 46th in Alaska. Fred Wack again:

Another job was photographing the land for mapping. Most of the maps of those days were blank spaces, even the Canadian archipelago, and we had no maps of the Soviet Union, the coastal regions and the northern areas. The 46th was assigned to photograph, literally photograph, five and a half million square miles of area. That includes the ice pack, the northern polar areas, the Canadian archipelago, much of Alaska, much that had never been photographed, and the northern areas of the Soviet Union, coastal areas.

Another breakthrough for the 46th was to devise an accurate method of navigating the polar wastes. The difficulties of Arctic navigation are shown by an error made by one experienced crew. On 20 February 1947 one of the 46th's B-29 Superfortress aircraft *Kee Bird* returning from the pole became lost and went 1,500 miles in the wrong direction landing in a remote part of Greenland. This was not the stupid mistake it sounds but an all too easy error to make in those latitudes. The rescue operation is an extraordinary tale, only made possible by a stroke of genius by one of the rescuing navigators. He realised that when the *Kee Bird* crew had reported their estimated position by radio they had seen the sun setting. He calculated that to have seen the sun setting they must have been at several hundred miles further away. The search aircraft homed in on the position he had calculated. They then started to pick up weak radio signals and eventually found the aircraft.

Today Jumbo jets routinely fly over the North Pole but in the late 1940s it was the 46th that trailblazed these transpolar routes and navigating techniques. Their pioneering missions would enable the bombers of Strategic Air Command to fly over the Arctic to deliver their bombs to the Soviet Union by the shortest route. Fred Wack said:

We had to devise a new system of navigation, so that was also one of our primary reasons for being there. Now, the British and the Canadians had already devised a thing called grid navigation, but it had not been perfected. So during the next three years, from 1946 to 1949, we perfected grid navigation, to make polar flights feasible and possible.

Another 46th discovery was that there were three North Poles, not one. From October 1946, Lt Frank Otto Klein undertook a study of all known magnetic bearings. To this was added bearing reports from missions of the 46th. All the textbooks stated that a magnetic compass was useless in the Arctic. Klein said in the unit's history, 'To our surprise, early flights in the fall of 1946 suggested that the fluxgate compass was not entirely useless.' He requested readings so that magnetic bearings could be turned into a reliable compass chart. 'Such a chart would provide polar navigators with back-up means of navigation, particularly in an emergency.'

His report indicated a main North Pole on the Prince of Wales Island and two lesser, local magnetic poles, one on Bathurst Island and the second on Boothia Peninsula. When news of this was released in October 1947 it made headlines in all the major US papers. Members of crews of the 46th who flew over the North Pole were presented with 'Pole Vaulters Certificates'.

In October 1947 the unit's name was changed to the 72nd Strategic Reconnaissance Squadron. It was part of a SAC decision to give several squadrons long and meritorious history to boost unit loyalty. The 72nd had been a bomber unit during World War 2 with a distinguished history going back to 1918. As the months went by the new 72nd Reconnaissance Squadron (Very Long Range) acquired a wide range of secret projects. It began to have less contact with the other units at Ladd AFB and stuck to its remote corner of the airfield.

The Soviet Union was posing a tough intelligence and reconnaissance problem for the Pentagon. Within its sealed borders was a vast, virtually unknown landmass, a closed society with a totalitarian government and effective internal repression. The only maps of the USSR were captured Luftwaffe World War 2 aerial photographs which only covered the Western side of the vast country. Otherwise there were only pre-World War 1 Tsarist maps.

The air force wanted to know the state of the Soviet defences – what airfields and military installations existed or were in construction. At first the Americans were concerned with defences that might oppose the SAC bomber force. Then the West was startled to discover that the Soviets had started to manufacture their first intercontinental bomber, the Tupolev Tu-4 (NATO reporting name 'Bull').[6] In August 1947, as a climax to the Soviet Aviation Day at Tushino airfield near

Moscow, three of these bombers made their public debut. For the Western observers it was the first hard evidence that the USSR was building a strategic bombing capability. For the first time, a potentially hostile bomber was capable of taking a bomb load to any number of mainland American cities.

America's immediate concern was to find the airfields for the new generation of Soviet bombers that for the first time brought the US mainland into range. The main area of interest was the Kamchatka Peninsula because it was the closest and therefore the most threatening location for the US Pacific defences, Korea and Japan.

On 5 April 1948, Stuart Symington, Secretary of the Air Force, sent a short note to Gen. Carl Spaatz, Air Force Chief of Staff:

> A pretty queer looking map was sent to me along with a memorandum I was sending to Secretary Marshall on what we know is across from the Bering Straits. I asked that the map be looked into, found it was wrong in some places, and attach it. In addition, however, I also found that there are no pictures of any kind of these airfields. Isn't there some way we could take pictures?[7]

SAC also needed to know in what state of Soviet defences were on the most likely bombing routes into the Soviet heartland. Discussions were held between the USAF, State Department and JCS over the minimum distance outside Soviet borders the planes would be required to stay within the confines of international law. This concluded in August 1948. As a result the 72nd began flying missions, apparently codenamed 'Leopard' against a variety of locations on the Chukotski peninsula. Photo-reconnaissance aircraft would fly along the Soviet borders with special oblique cameras capable of photographing targets dozens of miles inside the Soviet Union. The oblique photography of the Uelen, Lavrentiya, Mys Chaplino, and Provideniya areas of the peninsula revealed 'very little activity in those areas at the time of the missions, and no visible bases at these particular sites from which any long range bombing attack could be launched.'[8]

By October 1949, in addition to the 'Leopard' missions, other sets of missions with codenames such as 'Rickrack', 'Stonework' and 'Overcalls' had been flown and had produced over 1,800 photographs. The 'Overcalls' missions began on 30 October 1948 and continued through to 27 July 1949, focusing on twenty-eight targets ranging along the Far Eastern seaboard of the USSR. They revealed no signs of reported airfields in the Provideniya Bukhta area but revealed the existence of airfields at Velkel, Anadyr and Lavrentiya as well as storage and barracks areas. There was a clear increase in military activities in these areas.[9]

The 72nd was the first unit to be ordered to conduct spy flights over the northern Soviet Union, initially photo-reconnaissance missions, looking for military bases. Fred Wack was sent as part of a team to Wright AFB at Dayton, Ohio to bring back the first B-29 to be converted with an oblique camera. Fred Wack recalled it could photograph sites 100 miles away. This aircraft, number 871, was known as the 'Dreamboat'. All the gun turrets and armaments were removed. This increased its aerodynamic profile, and its top airspeed rose to 357mph at 25,000ft. He continued:

> The aircraft were stripped down in order to reach a higher altitude. To reach a longer range and fly in from Fairbanks over to the island of Novaya Zemlya, you're talking about 5,000-mile missions 24 to 30 hours of flying time, and to fly in over areas like Kamchatka Peninsula and the coastal areas and the Northern Siberia areas in order to avoid possible interceptions by hostile aircraft, we wanted to get up to 35,000ft. And no fighters in those days could get up to 35,000. They were building airfields in the northern areas of Russia, and along the coastal areas, they were building submarine bases and airfields, that we suspected were for offensive purposes.

Initially this job fell to the 72nd. It was a tough and dangerous job. Fred Wack said:

> Some of the missions were over 24 hours. Those missions you would get very tired, after about 6 or 7 or 8 hours. In my case I'm looking at a radar scope almost all of the time. After about 13 or 14 hours you think that you can't go any further but you continue to work at it. We even took something to keep us awake. Now today that's not, you know, you're not supposed to take those kind of things today, but we were taking Benzedrine to keep us awake. Anyway, after about 17 hours, you reached a point where it really didn't matter any more, I think you could just continue to work for a long time and 17 to 30 hours or 28 hours did not seem that bad.

All these missions were flown in radio silence throughout and they were not without incident. Several aircraft reported interceptors including identified MiG fighters but they were unable to reach the Dreamboats. As important, difficult and hazardous as these flights were, no recognition was afforded those participating crew members nor were any medals awarded until one crew in late 1949 was assigned a special project with a side-installed 100in camera, flew several missions in the vicinity of Kamchatka Peninsula and were awarded DFCs and Air Medals.

The fledgling Central Intelligence Agency tried to establish spy networks behind the Iron Curtain, but it was a military programme – Project 'Wringer' – which provided the bulk of intelligence for strategic planning. 'Wringer' employed 1,300 specially trained military and civilian personnel in Germany, Austria and Japan to question thousands of repatriated prisoners from the Soviet Union. Begun by the joint service Far East Command in December 1946, it had so expanded its scope by 1951 that the US gleaned most of its strategic intelligence from it.

To supplement this information was a growing number of reconnaissance units following in the footsteps of the 72nd RS. A number of well informed sources say that in 1950 the USAF used the giant mixed-powerplant Convair RB-36 'Peacemaker' carrying fourteen cameras in two of its four bomb-bays, to conduct intrusion flights inside the borders of the USSR. One writer, Vic Flintham, in *Air Pictorial* (June 1971) said, 'although it is unlikely that long overflights took place during the period.'

Little remained of the electronic warfare teams that had been built up during the war, just a few specialists assigned to headquarters staffs. From 1946 on, the British, Americans and other western countries began to rebuild their ELINT operations and monitor the development of communist defences. These first missions were piecemeal. A B-17 Flying Fortress with special equipment was sent up to Greenland after reports of suspected Soviet radar units. Nothing was found.

When a C-47 transport in Europe had strayed over Soviet-occupied territory and had come under quite accurate anti-aircraft fire despite low cloud, two wartime electronic warfare officers were sent to check out if the Soviets had fire control radar. They were in luck. On their first mission they picked up 'familiar signals' of a German *Wurzburg* radar at 570MHz. It turned out the signals emanated from a German radar school captured by the Soviets.[10]

Initially, in the first years of the Cold War, the Russians had few radars and were poor at disguising their radio signals. Most Russian electronic equipment had been supplied by the West during World War 2 or were direct copies. Early warning radars RUS-2 operating at 75MHz and P-3 ('Dumbo') were copies of World War 2 Allied equipment. The Russians' main gun-aiming radar was the SON-2, a straight copy of the British Mk 2 gun-laying radar designed in 1940.

But work was underway in haste in the Soviet research institutes. One of the most important projects was to copy the American SCR-584 E-band fire control radar and in 1947 the first Soviet-built set, designated the SON-4 ('Whiff') had passed its acceptance tests. The most ambitious Soviet radar development project of this period was the P-20 ('Token') early warning and ground-controlled intercept radar, which had obviously had been based on the American CPS-6. The first Soviet airborne microwave frequency radar was the *Kobalt* ('Mushroom') I band ground mapping radar, copied from the APS-15 carried by the B-29.

The Soviets were increasingly conscious of the potential of nuclear attack by Strategic Air Command. In response they set up a specific national air defence system, the PVO. Initially these Soviet air defences were poor. Most of the Soviet electronic defence equipment was sent to the priority area of Western Europe or to help the Chinese in Korea. There were great holes in the Soviet radar net on the northern side, which allowed the 72nd to intrude with impunity. When looking for these defences the ELINT operators would have receivers capable of picking up the frequency range used by radars.

Col. John 'Curly' Behrmann described the process:

> The main thing that you hear is pulse rate, a radar sits on the ground and that big antenna sweeps around in a search radar, or it's a gun layer he points at you, and sends pulses. And let's say he's sending a thousand pulses per second, well, that's like a tone of a thousand rpm, like music, you know. It's a note of a certain vibration, OK? A thousand vibrations per second, and that has a tone. It's like, beeeep. And if it is a high frequency pulse, this particular radar you run across, puts out 2,500 a second, well that's considerably higher, beeeeeeeep. And then you begin to hear radars that put out diffuse PRFs [Pulse Repetition Frequencies]. They're running at one and they may throw in extra pulses once in a while, and you can hear this. You know, it's going along at a steady tone, oooooo-bup-oooooo-bup if there's an increase or something like that. So all of these things are what you listen for. When you find the ones you want, you record them, and you photograph the cathode ray tubes of what the pulse shapes look like and things like that.[11]

An operator could establish what kind of radar was tracking the aircraft and also its exact position. In early 1947 B-29 s/n 45-21812 was sent to Wright Field, Dayton, Ohio to enable it to gather ELINT. It had all its gun turrets removed and a pressured cabin with room for six countermeasures operators was fitted in the rear.[12] When the 'Ferret' was ready, its crew was summonsed to the Pentagon for a briefing by Maj. Guiton, the staff officer. Fred Wack's brother Joe recalled later:

> Guiton told us that there was growing concern over what the Soviets were doing and the Army Air Forces needed to know what they were using in the way of electronic systems in case these might later have to be countered. Our mission would be to fly long range Ferret missions off the north of Siberia to gather information on Soviet radars operating in that area. The secrecy of the project was impressed upon all of us.[13]

On 21 May the aircraft arrived at Ladd AFB where the crew named their aircraft *Sitting Duck*. On 13 June they set out on the first of their missions, a 13-hour flight along the coast of Siberia. No radar signals were picked up at all. This was the first in a series of flights. Little radar information was found except around the port of Petropavlovsk or Kamchatka where some radars were picked up. By the third week of August the crew had flown eight operational missions and spent more than 100 hours airborne. On 25 August the B-29 returned to Andrews AFB. Following a debriefing at the Pentagon the crew were awarded the DFC or Air Medals.[14]

The *Sitting Duck* team was next sent to Germany where the crew decided it was best to patrol the Berlin corridor. The mission was to be flown at 10,000ft because the Soviet authorities would not clear aircraft to fly higher. On a mission on 12 September they were intercepted by two Yak fighters. Shortly afterwards the crew was ordered to return to the USA.[15]

After the success of the *Sitting Duck* missions the ELINT role for the northern perimeter was passed over to the 72nd. Their aircraft had ELINT operators added to the crews and flew missions often combining photo-reconnaissance and ELINT operations.

For three years from 1946 the 72nd RS was Strategic Air Command's main operational reconnaissance unit. Other units were now being formed to assist in the gathering of aerial reconnaissance for a strategic bomber fleet. The 72nd was transferred to Europe in 1950.

Members of the unit remained proud of their years in Alaska. Fred Wack remembers:

> We knew we were doing something that was very important, and something that was needed, especially this top secret reconnaissance was very beneficial to the country and to the world, we felt. And so although it was very difficult it was very, very satisfying.

Following the visit of the *Sitting Duck* the 7499th Squadron, a B-17 unit, took over the ELINT role in Germany. It was to take part in the Berlin Airlift, when in June 1948 the Soviets halted all road and rail communications into the isolated city of Berlin. The RAF and the USAF (under Gen. LeMay) ferried enormous quantities of basic supplies into the city. This meant there was a constant stream of transport aircraft flying along the Berlin air corridors. Aircraft from the 7499th would join in the flow to monitor communist defences covertly but they could not land or the aircraft – bristling with antennae – would give the game away. One crew member, Inky Haugen, recalled:

> When we got to Berlin we could not land. Our B-17s bristled with antennae and looked quite distinctive and, by agreement, Soviet officers had to be allowed to watch movements from the control towers. When we reached the city we had to call up and say we had landing gear trouble. Although these flights detected a few new radar sites, we found no new radar types.[16]

The importance of ELINT in any forthcoming confrontation was beginning to be recognised and full units were set up to deal with ELINT and ECM duties. In 1949 the 324th Reconnaissance Squadron based at MaGuire AFB, New Jersey, was the first training unit with B-29s fitted with receivers. In that year they assigned a section of their aircraft up to Ladd AFB to operate in the area. With the advent of the Korean War the 324th transferred most of its operational flights to Yokota AFB in Japan. As well as monitoring North Korean defences they still continued to target the Soviet Union. They found more Russian activity along the Gulf of Anadyr and the Kamchatka Peninsula. They picked up standard Soviet radars, the RUS-2 and the 'Dumbo'. They also recorded intercepts from Soviet ships.[17]

In July 1950 343rd SRS conducted reconnaissance missions against the Soviet Far East. Flying from Ladd AFB, Alaska, RB-29 'Ferret' aircraft probed Soviet air defences from Wrangel Island to the Kamchatka Peninsula.

There was an early recognition that such flights had a political overtone. By July 1949, the USAF agreed to co-ordinate the pattern and frequency of flights with the State Department. By 1949 the air force supported by the navy extended the informal programme of electronic-collection flights. These aircraft, converted USAF B-29 bombers and USN P-2V patrol planes, tended to concentrate on communist ships and naval bases. In the new decade aerial reconnaissance was to expand out of all recognition, as the Cold War tensions grew.

3
ATOMIC WAR

At the end of the 1940s one question began to dominate strategic thinking: what would be the role of atomic bombs in the new world order? In 1946 Bernard Brodie, the pioneering nuclear strategist, observed: 'Thus far the chief purpose of our military establishment has to been to win wars. From now its chief purpose must be to avert them.'

One air force general would play a greater part in defining the strategic role of nuclear weapons than any other individual over the next decade and a half – Gen. Curtis E. LeMay. Aerial reconnaissance was to become a vital tool in his strategy.

In October 1948 Gen. LeMay was appointed to take over Strategic Air Command by Gen. Carl Spaatz, the USAF's first Chief of Staff. SAC was suffering from the dramatic post-World War 2 cutbacks; it was disorganised and morale was at rock bottom. LeMay was later to say, 'I should go on record and say this flatly: we didn't have one crew, not one crew in the entire command, who could do a professional job. Not one of the outfits was up to strength – neither in airplanes nor in people nor anything else.'[1]

A career officer who had joined the air force in 1928, the cigar-chomping, brusque LeMay was an early advocate of strategic bombing. 'Fighters are fun but bombers win wars,' he later remarked. Rising rapidly in rank after the USA's entry in to the war, he had helped mould the philosophy of the massive daylight bombing of Germany by the 'Mighty Eighth', the US Eighth Air Force. LeMay was no armchair warrior, he flew on the earlier missions himself.

After a brief stint as a commander in the India–China theatre, in early 1945 LeMay was transferred to take command of the XXIst Bomber Command which had been fighting a patchy air war against Japan. He realised that the once mighty Japanese air force was so depleted it had few aircraft for home defence. On 10 March LeMay broke with previous precision bombing tactics and sent 325 B-29 Superfortress heavy bombers loaded with incendiary and napalm bombs over Tokyo. He briefed his crews, 'You're going to deliver the biggest firecracker the

Japanese have ever seen.' The in-flight commander of this operation was Thomas Power, who circled the city for two hours taking notes and photographs of the destruction. Power was to be LeMay's deputy for a good part of the next twenty years.

The subsequent United States Strategic Bombing Survey stated that more civilians lost their lives by fire at Tokyo than at any other one act in the history of war. Over 16 square miles of Tokyo were razed to the ground. More than 80,000 people were killed and tens of thousands injured. LeMay was so pleased with the results that he began a systematic campaign against Japanese cities, devastating one at a time.

In late April, LeMay sent a message to his immediate commander Gen. Lauris Norstad:

> I am influenced by the conviction that the present stage of development of the air war against Japan presents the AAF for the first time with the opportunity of proving the power of the strategic air arm. I consider for the first time strategic air bombardment faces a situation in which its strength is proportionate to the magnitude of its task. I feel the destruction of Japan's ability to wage war lie within the capability of this command, provided its maximum capacity is exerted unstintingly during the next six months, which is considered to be the critical period. Though naturally reluctant to drive my force at an exorbitant rate, I believe that the opportunity now at hand warrants extraordinary measures on the part of all sharing it.[2]

By the end of the war in August 1945, sixty-three cities had been devastated and more than a million Japanese civilians killed. LeMay precisely estimated the day the war would end – the day when they had destroyed every Japanese city – 1 September 1945. Only the dropping of the A-bombs on Hiroshima and Nagasaki in early August forced the Japanese to surrender before LeMay could finish the job.

Initially LeMay was hesitant about the use of atomic weapons. He took the view that the Japanese would have surrendered when the bombing had obliterated most of urban Japan. He felt that the devastating power of atomic bombs had allowed the Japanese High Command to justify surrender. In a November 1945 speech to the Ohio Society of New York City he added it was 'obvious that the atomic bomb did not end the war against Japan. Japan was finished long before either one of the two atomic bombs were dropped. They gave the Japanese an opportunity to surrender without losing too much face.'[3]

The next war, he warned, would be fought with fantastic new

weapons – a war of 'rockets, radar, jet propulsion, television guided missiles, speeds faster than sound and atomic power.' Before the next war, he insisted, 'the air force must be allowed to develop unhindered and unchained. There must be no ceiling, no boundaries, no limitations to our air power development.'

LeMay, the consummate commander, was the obvious choice to invigorate Strategic Air Command. He brought in his tried and trusted subordinates from the Pacific War: Thomas Power as his deputy, with Gens. 'Rosie' O'Donnel and J.B. Montgomery in senior positions. LeMay rapidly turned SAC into a highly disciplined military force and quickly became highly regarded, if somewhat feared, by his men. Fred Wack said, 'He was the air force officer to many of us. He presented the epitome of discipline and professionalism.'[4] Col. Hal Austin, an ex-SAC pilot, said:

> General LeMay was a real task master. I don't know of anyone that I served with, in my 34 years in the air force, that didn't have a great amount of respect for LeMay. You knew he was tough. I tried to pattern my military life after the guy.
>
> He had a reputation that preceded him of course; gee whiz, I don't know how long he'd been Commander in Chief of SAC before I ever saw him the first time. He ruled with an iron hand, that was the iron fist of SAC. But by golly, he built one of the greatest military forces the world has ever known.[5]

For fifteen years LeMay was able to make SAC the first violin of the USAF, always with the highest priority in budget, men, equipment and in forging strategy.

Initially the strategic mission was to contain the burgeoning Eastern Bloc with the threat of strategic attack.[6] This was at first to be by conventional bombing but as the nuclear arsenal grew it was to become the dominant strategic weapon. The growth was, in fact, initially quite slow and it was not until the new decade that the USAF had a substantial nuclear arsenal.

At first nuclear bombing appeared to be a one-way traffic. In the case of war only the Americans were in a position to launch a nuclear attack against the Soviet Union. This had been spelt out in a magazine article by Gen. Spaatz, published the week he retired as chief of the USAF in mid-1948. He wrote of obliterating 'A few hundred square miles of industrial area in a score of Russian cities'. He also stressed acquiring forward bases for US bombers, from which the United States could mount an air offensive against Russia's industrial heartland until the introduction of intercontinental supersonic bombers and missiles carrying nuclear warheads made the bases unnecessary.[7]

This article and other public statements over US policy had caused alarm within Stalin's government and increased pressure to formulate a response. The Soviets had no tradition of strategic bombing but a new factor was about to enter the equation and the arms race was to begin proper.

In his last years in the USAF, Gen. Spaatz conducted high levels inquiry boards to establish the lessons of the last war. According to John Farquahar:

> The Spaatz Board's criticism of US intelligence systems reflected American experience with British intelligence during World War 2. Despite occasional lapses, the British intelligence system represented a successful fusion of data collection, collation, analysis and dissemination of intelligence information. Unfortunately, except for a few Americans involved in 'Ultra' and Y-service communications intelligence, the British controlled the Allied intelligence organisation. Because of their close association with the British, Spaatz, [Gen. Hoyt S.] Vanderberg and [Gen. Lauris] Norstad appreciated their counterparts' attributes. Nevertheless, they believed that although the United Kingdom remained a close ally, the United States could not afford to be dependent on British intelligence. As a result the Spaatz Board recommended an intelligence organisation capable of knowing the strategic vulnerability, capabilities and intentions of any potential enemy.[8]

With the appointment of LeMay a series of new initiatives were undertaken. A series of discussions between SAC headquarters, USAF intelligence and the 311th Air Division identified six essential aerial reconnaissance tasks:

1. Radar scope photography.
2. Bomb damage assessment photography.
3. Target verification photography.
4. 'Pioneer' or target development photography.
5. Procurement of weather intelligence under combat conditions.
6. Procurement by 'Ferret' methods of intelligence concerning enemy electronic emissions.[9]

Separate but even more importantly, the West lacked any real intelligence on Soviet atomic research. In 1947, the US Atomic Energy Commissioner, Lewis L. Strauss, suggested an airborne atomic detection programme. Aircraft would be used to see if they could detect traces of radiation from Soviet tests. The principle was tested during the US's own 'Sandstone' atomic tests the next year. The project was nicknamed 'Snifden' and regular runs were initiated to use the upper air currents from parts of the Soviet Union likely to be used by the Soviets for nuclear tests. Each aircraft carried a filter unit that would collect any post-test radioactive dust. This would enable the size and location of a nuclear explosion to be determined. The island of Novaya Zemlya, north of European Russia, was the atomic and nuclear testing area for the Soviets. Aircraft from the 72nd RS not only photographed the island but were among those fitted with these 'scoops'. Within a year a Boeing WB-29 conducting a 'weather' flight near Alaska returned with intelligence that was to shock the West profoundly.

The WB-29 had picked up radioactive samples that revealed the testing of the first Soviet atomic bomb on 29 August 1949. Both this and the 'loss' of China to communism shocked the West and accelerated growing tensions with the communists. The Soviet bomb derailed Truman's defence policy of containment of the Soviet threat. Truman ordered a review of US national security policy. The resulting document, *NSC-68*, of April 1950 outlined a single comprehensive statement of the Soviet threat, US strategic aims and foreign policy assumptions. Retaining the term 'containment', *NSC-68* revised Keenan's concept defining as an effort:

> By all means short of war to (1) block further expansion of Soviet Power, (2) expose the falsities of Soviet pretensions, (3) induce retraction of the Kremlin's control and influence and (4) in general, to foster seeds of destruction within the Soviet system that the Kremlin is brought at least to the point of modifying its behaviour to conform to generally accepted international standards.[10]

In conjunction with *NSC-68*'s reassessment of national security, the prospect of Soviet nuclear weapons forced changes in the military strategy. SAC now argued that, at its current strength, it was incapable of destroying simultaneously Soviet atomic delivery capability, Soviet ground and tactical air forces and Eastern Bloc war industries.

With such a policy in force, LeMay received the political support to turn SAC into a formidable unit especially from Air Force Secretary, Stuart Symington, a fellow hawk who was to support LeMay politically over the next decade. In 1949, the Symington said: 'The existence of this strategic atomic bomber force is the greatest deterrent in the world today to the start of another global war.'

LeMay's SAC began to receive the major bite of the cherry of the defence budget much to the annoyance of the other services. The levels of disagreement can be seen by the statement to a Congressional committee by Rear-Adm. Ralph A. Ostie, USN: 'We consider that strategic air warfare, as practised in the past and as proposed for the future, is militarily unsound and of limited effect, is morally wrong, and is decidedly harmful to the stability of a postwar world.'[11]

Before LeMay took it over SAC had 49,589 personnel with 713 World War 2-vintage aircraft. By 1955 this was to grow to 200,000 personnel and 3,068 aircraft, mostly jet bombers. SAC had forward bases around the world forming an 'iron ring' around the Soviet Union. Britain, 'the unsinkable aircraft carrier', provided one of SAC's forward key bases.

Nuclear war plans evolved accordingly. The December 1948 Joint War Plan 'Trojan' called for attacks on 70 Soviet cities with 133 atomic bombs: the October 1949 Joint outline Emergency War Plan 'Offtackle' listed 104 urban targets to be destroyed by 220 atomic weapons, plus a re-attack of 72 weapons. Additionally, aircraft capable of delivering this equipment increased proportionally. In 1947 SAC possessed just thirty B-29s modified to carry nuclear weapons, known as 'silver-plated'; by June 1950 the number of nuclear-capable aircraft had reached 250. This assisted a huge turnaround in SAC organisation and morale.

Col. Fred Wack recalled training flights for such missions in B-29s at the end of the 1940s. He described going to the bomb bay to arm the weapon:

> We crawled down a tunnel in the aircraft and put uranium in the bomb and then it was a nuclear weapon. These were one-way missions, you understand. If we did go on one of these, we would never be able to return. Not in the 1940s. So you had a weapon on board, the bombers would be prepared to fly over there, drop the weapon, and then bale out somewhere over enemy territory.

Every SAC crew was given a nuclear target in the Soviet Union in case of war. Col. Sam Myers was a jet bomber pilot in the 1950s. He revealed this for the first time in 1993: 'OK, my target for my crew was Gorky and we did have full weaponry aboard. And I think that it's been pretty well understood in all these years, forty-two years after that period, that we did have nuclear weapons.'[12]

By the early 1950s LeMay had become legendary for keeping his men on a constant war footing. SAC regularly ordered wing commanders to fly their war missions only recalling them when the unit had gone a long way towards their target. There are many stories of wing commanders being routed out of bed in the early morning by a flashlight-holding LeMay, cigar clamped in mouth, ordering such a 'no-notice' mission.

The rapid pace of change placed huge pressure on SAC's reconnaissance capability. This was accurately predicted by the World War 2 PR expert Richard Leghorn in a lecture he gave in December 1946:

> . . . it will be profitable to consider the probable effects of the birth of atomic warfare on military aerial reconnaissance.
>
> There will be two principle effects. In the first place, strategic operations will dominate the military scene and will assume the position of prime importance. The situation means greater centralisation of facilities and will permit the use of the most highly technical type of equipment. Long-range reconnaissance of any place on earth from established bases will be a necessity.
>
> The second effect will be a greater demand for aerial reconnaissance prior to the outbreak of hostilities. At the present time, we are seeking national security through the building of an adequate international political structure, and it is generally agreed by military men that political security is probably the only effective means of protecting the nation against atomic bombs. However, should an adequate political structure not be established, or if a suitable one is formed which should break down at any time in the future, then military intelligence becomes the most important guardian of our national security. The nature of atomic warfare is such that once attacks are launched against us, it will be extremely difficult, if not impossible, to recover from them and counter-attack successfully. Therefore it obviously becomes essential that we have prior knowledge . . .
>
> . . . Aerial reconnaissance, as one of the principal information collecting agencies of military intelligence, can play an exceedingly important role in this period prior to the outbreak of hostilities.[13]

In 1949 Gen. LeMay wrote to the Chief of the Air Force, observing that they must prevent a surprise attack on the US. He proposed that he instigate a pre-hostilities strategic overflight reconnaissance programme to warn against attack, and then a pre-emptive strike should follow. The proposal was not approved.[14]

However, LeMay's recon units still had their work cut out. Not only did SAC's reconnaissance units have to photograph and ferret out Soviet defences but they now had to find ways of watching for the emergence of an offensive Soviet bomber force. But the Soviet Union was taking a new aggressive stance and this was going to make the task much more difficult.

In the late 1940s the Americans and British had been able to fly around the periphery of the Soviet Union with some impunity. At first the Soviets did little to tackle the activities of 'ferret' aircraft around their borders; their defences were still rudimentary. Occasionally they sent up fighters to warn off the ELINT aircraft. As early as 1946 the Soviets were making diplomatic complaints about missions.[15]

One of the earliest protests was communicated by the Soviets to the US Embassy in Moscow. Dated 15 April 1946 it charged that on 5 April two US aircraft had crossed the Soviet-Iranian border in the vicinity of Astara and had penetrated 6km into Soviet territory. The US Ambassador, Bedell Smith, promised an immediate investigation. Neither the Soviet Union nor the United States made a public disclosure.

A Soviet note to the United States on 25 February 1947 complained of various violations of Big Diomede Island. The United States indicated that no conscious violations had occurred and those that had, had happened because of bad weather. Another complaint was lodged by the Soviet Embassy in Washington on 5 January 1948. It stated:

> On 23 December 1947 at 14.15 an American airplane violated the Soviet frontier in the region of Cape Chukotsk, flying for about seven miles along the coast of the Chukotski Peninsula at a distance of two miles from shore.
>
> In communicating the foregoing, the Embassy upon instructions of the Soviet Government, requests that the case of violation of the Soviet frontier by an American airplane be investigated and that measures be taken not to permit such violations in the future.

Air crews were instructed in the autumn of 1949 to claim they were on a long-range navigation training mission if they fell into communist hands.[16]

There seems to have been a difference between the State Department and the Pentagon. Declassified documents from the late 1940s show the State Department discussing the borders of the Soviet Union and whether air force flights should stay 3, 12, 20 or 50 miles off the coast of the Eastern Bloc. The State Department made it clear that it thought boundaries should be respected. The USAF sought to evade the regulations.

The rising tension also created problems in the corridors to Berlin.

The Western allies were forced to fly down narrow air corridors when flying into Berlin, now isolated in Soviet territory since the Soviets had cut off the land routes. The Soviets policed the corridors tightly. But there were numerous examples of the Soviets harassing and attacking aircraft actually in the corridors. A number of American military flights in and out of Vienna were also attacked but these were primarily by aircraft of Tito's Yugoslavia.

The Soviets concentrated their most sophisticated defence equipment including radars along the European borders. Improving defences along other borders meant that the Soviet air defence became more aggressive coming out to meet the probing 'ferret' aircraft. During 1949 and the early part of 1950 Soviet interceptions increased. Most were non-hostile but the level of aggression was increasing. For example on 22 October 1949 two Soviet Lavochkin La-7 fighters intercepted a US Boeing RB-29 over the Sea of Japan in daylight. The Soviet fighters made four passes and the lead aircraft fired a short burst of three to seven rounds past the B-29's nose.[17]

But then came the first spy plane casualty. On 8 April 1950 a Consolidated PB4Y-2 Privateer of the US Navy's VP-26 Squadron on patrol over the Baltic, along the Latvian coast, was shot down by Soviet Lavochkin La-11 fighters. Lt Jack Fette's crew had taken off from Wiesbaden AFB in West Germany. Their job was to eavesdrop on Soviet Navy and harbour communications. In their protest note, the Soviets claimed that the aircraft was a B-29 and that it had flown 10 miles inland of the port of Libau in Latvia when it was intercepted and refused to land. The US always maintained that the aircraft was intercepted and without warning shot down over international waters. Ten men were lost, only two bodies found.

The event was to show the potential of aggressive aerial reconnaissance to heighten international tensions. Three days after the incident Soviet Foreign Minister Andrei Y. Vishininsky summoned the US Ambassador Alan G. Kirk and delivered a official diplomatic protest, in which he wrongly described the aircraft type:

> According to verified data, on 8 April this year at 17.39 hours, there was observed south of Libua a four-motored military airplane B-29 (Flying Fortress) with American identification signs which went into the territory of the Soviet Union for 21 kilometres. As the American aircraft continued going deeper into Soviet territory, a flight of Soviet fighters arose from a nearby airdrome, demanding that

the American airplane follow them for landing at the airdrome. The American airplane not only did not submit to this demand but opened fire on the Soviet airplanes. In view of this the leading Soviet fighter was compelled to return fire after which the American airplane turned toward the sea and disappeared.[18]

In his 1955 RAND secret report on overflights, analyst Alexander L. George[19] noted the shootdown:

> . . . marked a major turning point in Soviet policy toward air encroachment around the Soviet perimeter. For the first time in the postwar period the Soviets asserted the right to force foreign planes suspected of violating their territory to land upon Soviet territory, and to shoot them down if they refused.[20]

He stated that the Soviet action appeared to be deliberate. 'The best evidence of this comes from highly classified Swedish intelligence sources. Swedish intelligence intercepted radio communications to Soviet fighter aircraft ordering them to pursue the plane and to shoot it down.' He got this information from a Department of State memorandum of a conversation between U. Alexis Johnson and Ambassador Boheman of the Swedish Embassy. Boheman added that, for security reasons, such information could not be used publicly against the Soviets, since to do so would give away the fact that Swedish intelligence was intercepting Soviet military communications.

The shootdown created an outcry in sections of the American media and among some politicians. The *New York Herald Tribune* reported a 'proposal by the House Democratic leader, Representative John W. McCormick of Massachusetts, that the United States should sever diplomatic relations with the Soviet Union or, perhaps, recall Ambassador Kirk.' Representative Carl Vinson compared the incident to the Japanese attack on the USS *Panay* in 1937:

> Here in the same pattern, the same manner for the same purpose, with the same ruthlessness, with the same contempt for life, for democratic institutions, for international law, for decency – a barbaric attack is made on an unarmed, defenceless American aircraft.

Reminding Americans of their unpreparedness for the last war, Vinson called for increased spending for military aircraft to 'maintain sufficient force to ensure Russian respect.'

Over the next few weeks American reporters uncovered the aircraft's secret mission. Marquis Childs in the *Washington Post* disclosed that:

> The Russians believed that the American plane was carrying a recently developed type of reconnaissance equipment. This electronic equipment makes it possible to conduct reconnaissance at much greater distances than has ever before been possible.

Columnist Drew Pearson claimed the Navy's posted list of crew members showed the presence of electronics experts, and broadcast the aircraft's mission to the Russians even before take-off: 'They knew the plane was equipped with high-powered radar and electronics equipment that could watch amphibious manoeuvres and the flight of rockets over the Russian's most secret testing ground – the Baltic.'

In his *Washington Post* column, Walter Lippman speculated that the Soviets destroyed the USN Privateer as a deliberate act of policy. He believed the Soviets set a trap for the aircraft:

> The known facts indicate that the Soviet intelligence had advance notice that the plane would fly a course over the Baltic Sea, that though it was known to be unarmed, the Soviet intelligence believed it carried important electronic equipment, and that orders were given to the Soviet fighter command to intercept it, to capture it if possible and failing that to shoot it down.[21]

No wreckage was produced on Soviet territory implying the Soviet version, that the aircraft had been over land, was not true. Lippman questioned the motives of the Soviets decorating the fighter pilots credited for the kills:

> The ostentatious award of the 'The Order of the Red Banner' to four Soviet flying officers was plainly intended to advertise the exploit. The award was particularly significant, it seem to me because the officers did not in fact succeed in doing what, according to M. Vishininsky, they tried to do.

Answering his question, Lippman postulated that the incident served a twofold purpose, 'One, which probably failed, was to capture a plane with valuable military secrets; the other was to demonstrate to the world that the Soviet air defence are able to repel American Strategic air power.' Obviously, the second objective proved more important.[22]

The shootdown created great tension between the US and USSR. President Truman was worried that it might provide an excuse for Soviet military action. During the Berlin Airlift the Eastern Bloc air forces had been very aggressive, occasionally firing at Western aircraft in the air corridors on their way to the beleaguered city. Truman ordered a 30-day suspension of flights until the situation could be assessed. The political volatility of the missions had to be weighed against the need for intelligence, especially as concern over the prospect of Soviet surprise attacks increased. As Omar Bradley stated in a memorandum to the Secretary of Defense,

> It is recognised that there is a risk of repetition of such incidents upon resumption of these flights, but it is felt that there would be more serious disadvantages occurring to the United States if the cessation of these operations were to be extended over an excessively long period.

On 5 May 1950 the Joint Chiefs of Staff formalised the goals and operating procedures of the 'ferret' missions, now called the Special Electronic Airborne Search Project (SESP).[23] In a memorandum to the Secretary of Defense, later briefed to President Truman, Gen. Bradley outlined the programme. The aim of the SESP was to obtain 'the maximum amount of intelligence concerning foreign electronic developments as a safeguard to national defense.' The JCS scheduled the missions to be flown along the borders of the Soviet Union to locate and analyse enemy air defences. The new operating procedures set down:

• Flights will not be made closer than 20 miles to the USSR or satellite controlled territory.
• Flights will not deviate from or alter planned courses for other than reasons of safety.
• Aircraft engaged in these operations over routes normally flown by unarmed transport-type aircraft, in other words the land masses of Allied occupied zones and the Berlin and Vienna corridors, will continue to operate with or without armament. (The president scribbled 'which?' on the copy forwarded to him. A later memo explained that statement meant to 'permit operation of either armed or unarmed aircraft dependent upon whether the armed or unarmed type is available at the time.')

President Truman's approval of the SESP was a watershed in the history of aerial reconnaissance. No longer would 'ferret' operations be conducted informally by the military service; from 1950 onward, reconnaissance operations played a significant role in US foreign policy. The programme was divided between the two armed services: the navy was to be mainly responsible for Southern Europe, while the air force was to cover the Baltic and Murmansk.

According to a number of sources Truman gave strict orders: no overflights without his specific permission. Former CIA historian, Don Welzenbach said :

> Truman had the Korean War on his hands, and he found that any attempts at overflight got in his way, bothered him, disturbed him. He had too many other things going on, and he didn't appreciate overflights.[24]

The explosion of the Soviet's first nuclear bomb created a new series of intelligence problems. The banning of overflights was to prevent the obvious way to gain much strategic intelligence about Soviet capabilities. On the other hand the increased anxieties of war with the Soviet Union galvanised policy makers into an expanded strategic aerial reconnaissance programme. On 6 June 1950, the president gave permission for the air force to resume ELINT missions in the Baltic. The flights twice a week kept a close watch on Soviet radar developments in Europe.

In July 1950 there were urgent US-UK strategic talks in late July 1950. The two allies sought to outline agreed strategies in the light of the plummeting temperature of the Cold War. Present were Gen. Omar N. Bradley, Chairman of the Joint Chiefs of Staff, and Ambassador Phillips C. Jessup on the American side and on the British Lord Tedder, Marshal of the RAF and Chief of the Air Staff, and Sir Oliver Franks, Ambassador to Washington. They sought to limit the involvement of troops on the Asian landmass in light of the potential threat to Europe. Consequently, the American and British leaders decided to increase military strength, to establish joint planning staffs and to study further options in the event of Communist Chinese intervention. However, in one key area the two sides disagreed. The Americans rejected a British intelligence study of Soviet military capability. The British believed the Soviets would not be prepared to engage in general war before 1955. The Americans emphasised their estimate that the Russians would be prepared by 1952, or earlier, and before that time the Russians would attempt to 'cause maximum difficulties short of general war'.

These discussions were to made all the more urgent by the outbreak of war on the other side of the world.

4
THE FORGOTTEN WAR

On 25 June 1950 the army of communist North Korea crossed the 38th Parallel and swept deep into the south, the start of a brutal three-year conflict. At the time the West suspected Stalin's hand behind the attack. The Soviets continued to deny involvement until after the end of the Cold War forty years later. Many in the West then believed, particularly in the US government and military, that this was Stalin's first move in his plan for a communist-dominated world and that an attack in Europe would be next.

New evidence from former communist eyewitnesses and the Soviet and Chinese archives shows this was not the case.[1] It now transpires that Stalin was reluctant to approve the attack on the south. It took over a year for the North Korean leader, Kim Il Sung, to persuade him that North Korea could overwhelm South Korea in a matter of days and that the Americans would not intervene. Certainly leading American politicians, including Secretary of State Dean Acheson, had given this impression by making statements that Korea was outside the American defence perimeter.

Since 1993, American academic Dr Kathryn Weathersby has been given unique access to the archives of the former Soviet Union. She said,

> Stalin considered this request from Kim Il Sung for, oh, nearly a year from March 1949 to January 1950, before he finally approved it. He, a number of times, said no over the course of 1949. It was not 'advisable' was the word that was always used. It was not 'advisable' or not 'expedient' for North Korea to engage in offensive action against South Korea.[2]

Stalin only cautiously agreed in principle in January 1950. The telex said:

> I understand the dissatisfaction of Comrade Kim Il Sung. But he should realise that such an immense operation of the sort he wants to undertake in relation to South Korea, requires much preparation. The operation should be organised in such a way that risk is minimised.

Before any attack was launched Stalin made sure that the north had Russian arms, munitions and advisers to give them the edge over the south. Ultimately Stalin was seduced by the idea that, for relatively little effort, his allies would remove all American influence from mainland Asia.

Stalin did not want confrontation with the Americans. There is a great deal of evidence that he did not believe that the USSR would be capable of taking on the Americans for some years to come. Gen. Sir Anthony Farrar-Hockley fought in and is the official British historian of the Korean War:

> Stalin would not have allowed the war to be started at all if he had thought that the Americans were going to intervene. The initial involvement was undoubtedly on the understanding that Kim Il Sung was going to pull off a quick victory against the weak South Korean forces and present the world with a fait accompli.[3]

The north very nearly succeeded – but against all communist expectations the Americans intervened extremely quickly. The West was alarmed by seeing a tank-led blitzkrieg attack – based on a war plan drawn up by Russian advisers with World War 2 experience. Within hours the United Nations had condemned the invasion in a resolution drawn up by Secretary-General Trygvy Lee. Russia was unable to exercise its veto. The Russian representatives were absent, boycotting the UN Security Council over the refusal to recognise the newly communist China. Troops from the United States and twenty-one other countries were sent to South Korea.

After a difficult period compressed into the south-east corner of Korea, the 'Pusan perimeter', UN troops began to push back the North Korean army. In September a task force under Gen. Douglas MacArthur staged a daring amphibious landing at Inchon, cutting the North Korean army in two. MacArthur then swept north toward the Chinese border. Mao Tse Tung was alarmed by this rapid turn of events. Seeing the UN army heading toward China, Mao hesitated but then decided he had to act.

On 19 October 1950 hundreds of thousands of Chinese troops began attacks that drove the UN forces back past the 38th Parallel in disarray. But despite their success, the Chinese peasant army urgently needed sophisticated military support from their Soviet comrades. The UN had total air superiority and it was making life very tough for the Chinese. Stalin promised Mao air support but then procrastinated for over two weeks before sending MiG-15 units to Chinese air bases on the Korean border.

According to Gen. Anthony Farrar-Hockley,

> Mao turned to Stalin (we know the wording of his telegrams now and the actions of his intermediaries) saying, look, we need your help. Stalin made various promises, some of which he ratted on. The most prominent of those was withholding air support when the Chinese came into Korea. A defection on his part, which caused Mao to have a nervous breakdown for 24 or 36 hours.[4]

When the Soviet aircraft were finally sent, Stalin was anxious that the Soviet presence should be covert. This had some bizarre aspects. Soviet pilots were dressed in simple Chinese uniforms. Capt Boris Abakumov was a MiG-15 pilot with the Soviet display team:

> An instruction came from above to send a group of pilots to China. They dressed us in Chinese uniforms so that our Soviet uniforms wouldn't attract prying eyes. We wore reddish brown boots, cotton trousers, like workers used to wear, tucked into the boots, and green dress-jackets.[5]

They were told to speak in Chinese on the radio and when flying would have a clipboard on their knee with a list of commands in Chinese. As one Soviet veteran said, 'This would be fine as we are sitting here today but in the middle of an air battle it was ludicrous. As you can imagine it soon broke down.'[6]

Stalin prohibited his pilots from flying out of communist airspace so that none would be captured. The increasing involvement of the Soviets was dramatically changing the effectiveness of the communist air defences. MiG-15s made daylight operations very difficult for the B-29 bombers and other propeller-driven planes. The UN pilots knew that some of the MiG-15 pilots they were up against were Russians. There were tales of Caucasians with red beards seen dangling from parachutes after dogfights. Few UN pilots know, even now, that the *majority* of combat missions were flown by Soviet pilots.

The involvement of the superpowers – it was the only time they were all to meet in a 'hot war' during the Cold War – in Korea quickly turned what had started as a civil war into a dress rehearsal for World War 3.

US reconnaissance aircraft were to play a vital role in the war. They had been on the scene from the beginning, part of the United States Far East Air Force based in Japan. The FEAF reconnaissance aircraft provided vital information during the critical first few months of the conflict. Although undermanned and intended for strategic reconnaissance, crews of the 31st SRS engaged in tactical reconnaissance, providing photo-mapping, photo-reconnaissance and bomb damage assessment. Their work was augmented by the Lockheed RF-80A Shooting Stars of the 8th Tactical Reconnaissance Squadron.

On 16 November 1950, the 31st SRS was replaced by the 91st SRS. Based in Yokota, Japan, it flew the improved version of the Boeing RB-29 Superfortress, redesignated the RB-50B. This had a substantially improved range, helped by a new aluminium wing which was over 25 per cent more efficient for a reduced weight. It could also carry up to nine cameras and had improved radar equipment. It fell to the 91st SRS to monitor the new Soviet-enhanced air defences to help devise countermeasures. Covertly the Russians began to supply radar fire control for anti-aircraft defences. At first these were radars originally supplied by the Americans to the Russians during World War 2 but then Soviet uprated copies began to arrive. In early 1951 the 91st SRS's ELINT operators began picking up signals from the first early warning radars (RUS-2s) deployed in North Korea. Shortly afterwards they identified the first fire-control SON-2 radars to be deployed, in the Pyongyang area.

The missions flown by the 91st SRS in March 1951 provided an example of the ELINT effort during the Korean conflict. Missions 178 and 179 showed FEAF interest in the air defences of north-west Korea. The mission identified the probable locations of enemy radars, which proved useful in the planning of FEAF B-29 bomb strikes.[7]

These discoveries also enabled the UN forces to fit electronic countermeasures equipment to confuse the communist radar operators. This was effective, as a pilot of the 19th Bomber Wing after a mission on 29 November 1951 described:

> One aircraft attacked Namsi and encountered intense flak. When the flak was first sighted it was aft and low. In approximately 30 seconds the flak walked up to the aircraft and began tracking with good accuracy. Although the ECM operator on board intercepted no signals he jammed the radar frequency. The flak became inaccurate.[8]

The cat and mouse game of electronic measures and countermeasures was to last the length of the war. From spring 1952, darkness alone gradually ceased to afford protection to B-29 bombers attacking targets in North Korea. During April and May crews reported occasional sightings of enemy fighters at night but the aircraft – mostly MiG-15s – lacked airborne radar and failed to press their attacks.

On the night of 10 June the defenders adopted a new tactic. As four B-29s of the 19th Bomber Wing carried out bombing runs of the rail bridge of Kwaksan using SHORAN radio navigation techniques, they found themselves caught in up to 20 searchlights and pounced on by a dozen MiGs. Two bombers were shot down and one suffered serious damage. Only one of the B-29s attempted electronic jamming and it emerged unscathed. The communist defences had learnt to intercept the American navigation beams.[9]

Over the next year the electronic war became more and more sophisticated with both sides developing techniques to counter the other. For the final seven months of the war, up to the end of July 1953, UN bombers conducting night attacks received protection from electronic jamming, chaff and friendly night-fighters. They were forced to fly at 18,000ft and above. The US estimated that three times as many B-29s would have been shot down if electronic countermeasures had not been employed.

The 91st SRS was to be the core reconnaissance unit for the rest of the war. A collection of smaller specialist units were attached to the 91st which by the end of the war was to grow to the largest unit in the theatre with over 400 aircraft. Amongst the first attachments were three North American RB-45C Tornado aircraft detached in November 1950 from the completely separate 91st Strategic Reconnaissance Wing then based at Barksdale AFB in Louisiana.

The B-45 Tornado was the first American medium multi-jet aircraft with any range to be ordered into production and could be refuelled in flight.[10] It could fly high and fast for the time – at a maximum of Mach 0.72 up to 37-38,000ft. The reconnaissance variant carried a substantial array of cameras of different types and configurations and it also carried the state of the art ground radar and a camera capable of taking pictures of the radar screen.[11] Its capability for high resolution imagery of the ground terrain made it ideally suited for radar reconnaissance.

The RB-45C was immediately put into a top secret role. It was used for reconnaissance against the Chinese border. Said Capt. Louis Carrington, RB-45C pilot:

> We had our wings sticking over in China, because we were photographing the Yalu River every day. Particularly that time of year, after the Chinese invaded, we photographed the river every day so they could count the footprints in the snow to see how many came over.[12]

These missions were soon to become reconnaissance for potential nuclear attacks. Early on, LeMay's SAC had sent ten nuclear-capable B-29 Superfortresses to Johnson field in the Philippines to be available for atomic strike. Only nine actually arrived as one crashed and killed the unit commander Gen. Travis. They had bombs but not the nuclear components. The nuclear weapon remained a possibility for the US during the entire war.[13]

In a few months the Korean War had grow from a civil war into a potential full-scale confrontation between the superpowers. Behind the scenes, the hot war of Korea was to be a proving ground for Cold War intelligence in all its forms for both sides. Much of this activity has remained secret until very recently.

Early on the Soviets lost a major intelligence opportunity. On 12 December 1950, a RB-45C flying over the Yalu was intercepted by newly arrived Russian MiG-15s and shot down. I discovered the full story of this flight while making the BBC TV *Timewatch* programme on the Korean War. In addition to the three-man crew on board for the mission was a passenger (unusual because the aircraft was a tight squeeze anyhow). The passenger was a senior USAF intelligence officer, 46-year-old Col. John R. Lovell, who worked for the USAF Director of Intelligence Maj.-Gen. Pearre Cabell at the Pentagon. Lovell had left his family hurriedly on Thanksgiving Day for a secret mission.[14] The American government always believed the entire crew died in the crash. In fact the pilot of the aircraft, Capt. McDonough, was badly burnt but survived some days. Lovell, unhurt, survived the crash to become the most senior intelligence officer captured during the war. I discovered that not only had he survived, but was captured and interrogated.

A Soviet officer, Pavel Fironov, said he was asked by a North Korean air force general called LaFark [phonetic spelling] to attend Lovell's interrogation:

> When we got in, the North Korean general was particularly incensed that the prisoner didn't get to his feet, that he didn't stand. After all, this was a general, the man was on his territory, he was undoubtedly a prisoner – this behaviour angered him.[15]

Col. Lovell was carrying a classified manual on the Soviet order of battle: Fironov said, 'In this manual were a lot of photographs of the commanding officers of our Air Force, plus short biographical details. Vasily Stalin was there, so too was Krasovsky, Marshal of Aviation.' Col. Lovell's importance was becoming clear. But before Fironov could organise another interrogation, disaster struck. The North Korean general, angered by Lovell's belligerence, had the colonel marched to the local town with a placard round his neck proclaiming him a 'war criminal' where he was beaten to death by the local people.

The record of the North Koreans for brutality against PoWs was unsurpassed. Gen. Sir Anthony Farrar-Hockley was himself a prisoner:

> In 1950 the North Korean treatment of prisoners was appalling. With rare exceptions prisoners were denied treatment for wounds or sickness, they were shot arbitrarily on the line of march. They were denied food and water, people drank water out of the paddy fields and thus got dysentery and all sorts of diseases and so on. And a great number of prisoners died early on and more continued to die through the winter.

The Soviets could not allow acts like the death of Col. Lovell to continue. Such a wasted intelligence opportunity must not be repeated. The whole POW policy was changed and the job of looking after prisoners was taken over by the Chinese. They co-operated with the covert Soviet systematic interrogation of prisoners.

If Stalin's direct involvement in the war was reluctant, he decided to make the best possible use of a bad situation. The USAF was in the process of dropping 600,000 tonnes of bombs on the north, devastating the cities and decimating the civilian population. Stalin was convinced that it was only a matter of months before the Soviet Union faced such destruction. The Soviets had never been systematically bombed but the Nazis had overrun a considerable part of the USSR and had reduced it to a smoking ruin with a scorched earth policy during their retreat. Stalin knew that the Soviet military urgently needed to catch up with the West's technical superiority. He ordered a full-scale intelligence operation in Korea.

As Gen. Anthony Farrar-Hockley said,

> We've seen why Stalin came into the war, but he was an opportunist. And once the battle was joined with the United Nations forces, clearly there were going to be opportunities to discover a good deal about equipment, weaponry, aircraft and so on.[16]

The Soviets were particularly interested in the latest American equipment – especially that which might be used in the expected World War 3. By Christmas 1950 the United States had begun to send its new North American F-86 Sabre to Korea. This was the only western aircraft capable of equalling the MiG. The MiG-15 had a greater ceiling and firepower but the F-86 was more manoeuvrable. The MiG's advantages were gained by keeping the aircraft as simple as possible. It was essentially a World War 2 fighter with a jet engine. By contrast the Americans had used new technology to make the F-86 highly sophisticated. The metal technology was cutting edge. It had many fail-safe systems, air conditioning and a radar gunsight all of which made it heavier. Ironically, the swept wing technology of both the MiG and the F-86 had been developed from the scientists of Nazi Germany that had been scooped up after the war by both sides.[17] The Soviets were particularly interested in the secrets of Western aircraft and tactics and made special efforts to interrogate UN pilots.

Only now are the Russians reluctantly admitting that they were involved in the interrogations, often disguising their nationality when sitting in with the Chinese interrogators. Col. Viktor Bushuyev was a Soviet air force intelligence officer in Korea:

> One of our translators was a man called Nikolay Munkuyev. He was a Buryat, with Mongolian features and therefore he was allowed to be seen there in person. As far as I recall he dealt essentially with prisoner interrogations and actually took part in interrogations. Essentially the questions were about tactics. The questions were tailored to each prisoner.[18]

According to Soviet documents they interrogated 262 USAF pilots and crew. Some fifty-seven preliminary interrogation reports have been declassified by the Russians. They show how successful the Chinese were at breaking some prisoners.[19] In one report a pilot describes US tactics in detail. Another interrogation includes a diagram of the F-86 radar gunsight, a piece of technology in which the Soviets were particularly interested. In another a pilot had drawn an exact map of one of the major US air bases. Another, a map of the UN flight routes.[20]

These dossiers were considered so important that they were sent directly to the top Soviet leaders. The interrogation of the first F-86 pilot to be captured in December 1950 was sent to Stalin, Molotov and Beria.

But the Soviets also needed captured equipment – especially state of the art technology. Most of all they wanted an F-86. Col.-Gen. Nikolai Petukhov, Soviet Air Force Intelligence said:

> In one dogfight our pilot Pepelyayev damaged an American Sabre and it landed out in the estuary, on the sand, and the aircraft wasn't destroyed. The Americans came in, in force, and managed to rescue the pilot, but they left the aircraft behind. Well the Koreans and Chinese quickly camouflaged it there and, to cut a long story short, this aircraft ended up with us at the Andung airbase. I saw it there with my own eyes. Later that Sabre was sent to Moscow.[21]

I have been able to obtain a photograph of that aircraft taken at the crash landing site. It was serial number 1319, shot down on 6 November 1951.[22]

In May 1952 an even better opportunity arose with the capture of both a new F-86E model and its pilot, 34-year-old Col. Bud Mahurin. He was commander of one of the two American F-86 wings in South Korea. He describes his shootdown:

> . . . as I circled the target I saw a truck going down the highway and – and I thought well, I'll just go down and shoot that truck up and then go home and I'll have a big-time story to tell the people at the bar. And unfortunately I got slowed down, and just as I started to fire at the truck it turned off the road and I got hit with what I assumed to be 40 millimetre cannon fire.[23]

Four days later Gen. Lobov, commander of the Russian 64th Fighter Air Corps, sent an urgent telegram to Moscow stating that the F-86 was to be transported to the Soviet capital. It said, 'Colonel Mahurin was captured and taken prisoner. The F-86 plane is almost completely intact.'[24] Mahurin's downed F-86 was shipped to the Soviet air force's secret research institute outside Moscow.

The Soviets also obtained at least one helicopter, lured in behind the lines by a deception. The Soviet helicopters of the time were very primitive and none were used in Korea. The US was making great use of the helicopter in many new roles, including search and rescue and casualty transfer as immortalised by the TV show MASH.

A special intelligence team lured a US search and rescue helicopter by persuading a captured US pilot to send a distress signal. Col. Valentin Sozinov was an adviser to the North Korea leader Kim Il Sung:

> The captured pilot gave another signal to the helicopter. There was a little clearing and the helicopter started to land. Right then something happened. It looked as if

the pilot had only just landed and started to climb very fast. At that point we opened fire. The fire was hot. The rotors were damaged, and the helicopter fell from about 50 or 70m. It fell on its side when it hit the ground, but it wasn't badly damaged, and when it crashed the crew survived and the helicopter was then dragged away into some bushes.[25]

Valentin Pak was an aide and translator to Kim Il Sung. He said:

There was a command from Moscow, instantly, to take the helicopter apart and send it back to Moscow. The helicopter was the newest kind. Of course they sent it back. I heard personally how they took it apart and packed it into crates and everything literally down to the last screw was sent immediately back to Moscow. For this operation, Namsir, Simon Timofeevich, who was colonel in the KGB, was rewarded with the Order of the Red Banner.[26]

These aircraft were taken back to the Soviet Union and taken apart rivet by rivet. They enabled the Soviets to catch up on vital areas of western technology.

Through captured aircrew and wreckage of reconnaissance aircraft the Korean War enabled the Soviets to learn about the USAF's strategic reconnaissance capabilities. On the plus side, the war was providing cover for Strategic Air Command to conduct extensive strategic nuclear reconnaissance. But all air force units in the theatre fell under the control of FEAF, a situation that was increasingly frustrating for LeMay and SAC as FEAF gave the immediate tactical needs of the war a higher priority than SAC's strategic needs.

The 91st SRS conducted special photographic sorties over 'sensitive' areas. Often located on the borders of the Soviet Union or the People's Republic of China. For these missions, RB-29s specially equipped with the K-30, 100in focal plane camera, attempted to take long-range, oblique photographs of communist military sites. Examples of this were two special photo missions flown on 8 and 11 August 1951, concentrating on the Soviet-controlled Kurile Island, adjacent to Japan. In addition an RB-29 penetrated Chinese airspace to photograph the city of Shanghai on 25 August 1951. Severe technical problems marred the missions, but these added to American knowledge of enemy capabilities.

ELINT flights flown in March and August 1951 revealed a shift in emphasis from north-west Korea to the Soviet coast. Missions 199, 200 and 204 probed Soviet air defences over the Sea of Japan and near Vladivostok. Other missions, numbers 201 and 202KZ, continued surveillance of China.[27]

Correspondence at the highest levels of the USAF reveals that SAC was having difficulty in getting its agenda through. SAC urgently wanted radar and photo-reconnaissance of key Soviet and China nuclear targets to be conducted by the RB-45Cs. These were in line with the 'Sarsfield list' of key communist targets which was the basis of the SAC operational plan. The correspondence shows that at first it was thought that such missions could be flown under the authority of the theatre commander. However, it transpired that he could only give permission for flights over the war zone and a limited part of China. Other flights over China had to get higher authority.[28]

Eventually, a number of missions over China were approved. In addition flights were allowed over portions of Soviet-controlled islands. On 9 October 1951, an RB-45C took-off from Yokota AFB at 10.30a.m. on Designated Project 51. The aircraft's mission was to conduct reconnaissance over the southern end of Sakhalin Island. At an altitude of 18,000ft, employing both regular and radar cameras, all the targets were photographed. The plane landed back at base at 2.40p.m.

Documents in the Library of Congress reveal that the commander of FEAF had authority to authorise missions over some parts of China and Manchuria – all other areas requiring JCS authority – but Russia was off the menu. A telegram from LeMay said that in the case of nuclear war with Russia the 91st SRS would have to do the all the Far East pre-strike missions on the day.

However it was a risky business. In October 1952 a B-29 of the 91st SRS had been shot down carrying a crew of eight; it disappeared after 'radar equipment had picked up an unidentified plane approaching it from the direction of the Russian held Kurile Island.' The radar site located the scene of the attack eight miles north-west of Nemuro, a city on the Japanese island of Hokkaido. The FEAF spokesman concluded his statement by reporting that radio operators monitored a distress call and voice shouting: 'Let's get the hell out of here!' According to a note from the Soviets on 12 October 1952, the incident occurred near the Soviet-occupied Yuri Island in the Kurile chain.

Reconnaissance aircraft continued to take casualties. On 18 January 1953, the day before Eisenhower's inauguration, Chinese anti-aircraft guns brought down a US Navy Lockheed P-2V Neptune near the port of Swatow in southern China. Compounding the disaster, a USN Martin PBM Mariner rescue seaplane crashed on take-off after picking up ten of the Neptune's survivors. Only ten of the twenty-one men on the two planes survived.

In March 1953 Stalin died. He had been ill for some time and remained an obstacle to peace. While having a veto on the peace negotiation he had no great interest in ending the war. It was Chinese, North Korean and UN blood that was being spilt and for relatively little Soviet investment he was keeping his enemies busy and getting important intelligence back. As Kathryn Weathersby said:

> We know also from the documents that the armistice could not have been concluded without Stalin's approval. And consequently, because Stalin did not think that it was necessary to reach an armistice settlement, at least not necessary to make any significant concessions to do so, an armistice was never reached. It was only after his death that the Soviets, the Chinese and the North Koreans, were able to move toward reaching an armistice.

Perhaps the most remarkable feature of the Korean War is that it did not escalate either into a one-sided nuclear war or trigger another world war. Ultimately there was a great deal of restraint by the leaders of both sides. If Stalin ordered his pilots to pretend they were Chinese, then Truman ordered his not to attack enemy aircraft in Chinese airspace. (Although there were exceptions to this rule and it was frequently broken by gung-ho F-86 pilots.) Truman fired the UN commander and World War 2 hero, Gen. Douglas MacArthur, in 1951; MacArthur had been itching to extend the war into a greater confrontation. In the archives are MacArthur's plans to create a 10-mile wide radiation cordon across the top of Korea.

If the Western public did not know the extent of Soviet involvement then, certainly the leadership and intelligence chiefs did. Col. Phillip Corso was a senior US military intelligence officer involved in the Korean War:

> I personally sent a report to Washington that I compiled which was made official by Washington, that there were actually 22,000 Soviet combat troops involved in Korea. Actually involved in the fighting. These were advisers, tanks and so forth. Their tanks were run by Soviets, their aircraft: the MiGs across the border were all Soviet controlled – not Chinese – because we picked up the voices during combat. They had 200 MiGs right over the border and our policy makers won't let us bomb them.[29]

In Washington, President Truman kept quiet about the Soviet presence in Korea. He feared a public clamour for war with the Soviet Union. In a newsreel address at the time he said:

I believe we must try to limit the war to Korea for these vital reasons: to make sure that the precious lives of our fighting men are not wasted: to see that the security of our country and the free world is not needlessly jeopardised and to prevent a third world war.

Immediately after the signing of the armistice it was Cold War business as usual. On 29 July 1953, two days after the ending of hostilities in Korea, Russian fighters downed an RB-50 of the 343rd SRS over the Sea of Japan, about 90 miles south-east of Vladivostok. Attached to the 91st SRS at Yokota AFB, Japan, the RB-50 conducted a 'routine' electronic reconnaissance mission along the Soviet coast continuing the practice established during the Korean War. According to Capt. John E. Roche, the co-pilot and lone survivor of the crew of sixteen, the Soviets attacked the aircraft without warning from the rear. Although the RB-50's gunner fired a few bursts in self-defence, the MiGs raked the slower reconnaissance aircraft with cannon fire causing it to burst into flames.

The Soviet government announced that 'a four-motored bomber of the type B-50' violated the Soviet coast twice, at Camp Gamova and then at Askold Island, near Vladivostok. When challenged by two Soviet fighters on defensive patrol, the American intruder opened fire, seriously damaging one of the planes. As a result, the remaining Russian interceptors counter-attacked and the American bomber 'disappeared in the direction of the sea.'

Rejecting Ambassador Charles E. Bohlen's note of protest the Soviets diverted attention from the RB-50 incident. They claimed American fighters 'invaded' the airspace of Soviet China in the last hours of the Korean conflict and shot down a Soviet passenger plane, killing the six crew members and fifteen passengers. Immediately, US analysts linked the two incidents, speculating that the Soviets downed the RB-50 in revenge or simply manufactured the story as a ploy to shift public attention from their act.

Despite the Soviet charge, American newsmen pressed their attack on Communist brutality. A *New York Times* editorial condemned the Russian protest as a mere propaganda move:

All Soviet history shows Moscow's belief that a good attack is the best defence – in the diplomatic as well as the military arena. That this maxim is again being applied seems the most likely explanation for the Soviet charge . . . that American planes shot down a Russian transport flying over Chinese territory. One can hardly blame Moscow for preferring to press this charge rather than defend the cold-blooded murder committed last week by the Soviet pilots who shot down an American B-50 plane over the Pacific Ocean 40 miles from Soviet soil . . .

Any study of the chronology involved in Moscow's latest complaint shows how flimsy the charge is. The United States Air Force reported last Monday that one of our pilots had shot down a Soviet-built transport flying about 10 miles south of the Yalu River over North Korea. But it was not until four days later, last Friday, that Moscow suddenly charged that this plane was a Soviet plane shot down over Chinese territory. In between . . . occurred the shooting down of the American B-50, and the international commotion thereover. If the facts had been as Moscow claims, the world would have heard the Soviet complaint last Tuesday or Wednesday, not last Friday.

The *New York Times* journalist had only half the picture, he knew nothing about certain events in England the previous year. They were, after all, top secret.

5
SCULTHORPE SKULDUGGERY

At the beginning of the 1950s the United States was trying to decide what would be the most effective use of its growing stockpile of A-bombs in an attack against the communist nations. At that time the list of targets was drawn up under the guidance of the Joint Chiefs of Staff. In December 1950, Gen. Hoyt S. Vanderberg, who had replaced Gen. Spaatz as USAF Chief of Staff, asked Dr Bernard Brodie, noted expert and author on atomic strategy, to inspect and comment on the current JCS target list. This list represented the work of the Air Intelligence Production Division (later the Air Targets Division) of the Air Force Directorate of Intelligence and formed the basis of SAC's operational plans.

Dr Brodie strongly criticised the air planners' failure to calculate the overall impact of the strategic air offensive. His review also showed significant intelligence gaps. For instance, air force intelligence did not know where all the major Soviet power plants were located. Without this knowledge, Brodie pointed out, the total damage to Soviet industry could not be accurately calculated. It became apparent that air force planners had expected the Soviet Union to collapse following nuclear attack.

SAC commander, Gen. LeMay, attacked the target list from another position. At a high level meeting on 22 January 1951, LeMay said that many of the targets on the current war list placed unrealistic demands on the navigation abilities of his crews. Too many relied on visual, pre-strike reconnaissance and isolated, unfamiliar target complexes would be difficult to locate by radar especially in periods of bad weather.[1] LeMay argued, 'We should concentrate on industry itself which is located in urban areas': so that even if the bomb missed, 'a bonus will be derived from the use of the bomb.'[2]

On arrival at SAC, one of LeMay's greatest concerns had been bomb accuracy (even with the nuclear bomb!). Initial SAC bombing rehearsals had produced appalling results. Vigorous retraining was improving competence but one major problem remained. To bomb the Soviet Union successfully SAC aircraft would have to fly at high altitude and possibly in bad weather or at night making it difficult to identify targets visually. Navigation beacons could not go far into the USSR either, so the navigators had to be able to recognise their targets from radar images of the ground.

Radar portrayed large towns and geographical features quite clearly. But it was difficult to predict a radar picture of features like factories and missile sites. For accuracy it was important that bombardiers should be provided with photographs of the radar images of their targets. LeMay wanted to send SAC reconnaissance aircraft over the Soviet Union to obtain radar photographs but was prevented by President Truman. As John Farquahar said:

> A closer look at American war plans revealed a lack of intelligence data that jeopardised US strategic air war doctrine. Without target information, air planners could not determine the enemy's vital centres . . . American experience in the Korean War revealed the limits of American reconnaissance capabilities and demonstrated the impact of intelligence flaws upon war planning.[3]

But how to find out?

Like their USAF counterparts the RAF had been allowed to run down after World War 2. Although it tried to disguise the fact, Britain was having severe difficulties maintaining its status as one of the major powers. The war had eaten up one third of the British national reserves. The empire was rapidly disintegrating and the job of policing what was left was expensive. The descent of the Iron Curtain and all that it implied caused problems for the British government. It was committed to being a nuclear power but did not really have the resources to effect it.

Britain was trying to maintain its role as equal partner with the Americans. By contrast the Americans had come out of the war, almost unexpectedly, a global power and the first nuclear power. America, out of range of the German and Japanese bombers, had suffered relatively little damage to its infrastructure. Its industry was thriving.

The only way for the British to maintain status was to rely on American goodwill. With the increasing tensions of the Berlin Airlift, the British government agreed to provide air bases for American aircraft. By 1949 B-29 Superfortress bombers were based in the UK but under the ultimate command of the US president.[4] This was the beginning of a long role as one of the key forward bases for Strategic Air Command, a role that gave Britain the sobriquet, the 'Unsinkable Aircraft Carrier'.

Britain's role as the main forward US air base in Europe made it a primary target for any Soviet attack in the region. To keep its end up the RAF had to provide both an effective force to defend the UK and develop an independent nuclear-capable offensive bomber force. The approach to aircraft procurement during this period was more appropriate for the low-cost 1930s with several different types of the same aircraft ordered. But aircraft were becoming increasingly specialised and expensive and fewer put into service. The Korean War showed the British primary jets, particularly the Meteor, as outmatched by the MiG-15. As a result the British had to buy over 400 American F-86 aircraft. In a remarkable decision the British government ordered three different types of nuclear bomber: the V-bombers – Vickers Valiant, Handley Page Victor and Avro Vulcan – which were scheduled to come into service during the 1950s.

These new aircraft were expensive and costs had to be cut elsewhere. One of the main places to suffer was reconnaissance. At the time the photo-reconnaissance section of the RAF held an annual conference. In 1950 it was held at RAF Benson – the last year before the PR units moved en masse to RAF Wyton. Invited to the meeting were a number of SAC reconnaissance officers. The notes of the meeting and their papers show the Americans in confident mood, in the process of obtaining a new generation of jet aircraft for their broadening remit.[5]

By comparison the British cupboard was rather bare. The RAF was still relying on World War 2 propeller-driven aircraft like the Spitfire and Mosquito, which even if uprated were no match for the MiG. No 541 Squadron was equipped with the PR version of the first operational British jet, the Meteor, but it had limited capability and range. The great hope was the PR version of the new Canberra medium jet bomber. But that was not due in service until 1953. However, the RAF did have one major contribution to make. Its senior officers were anxious to show that they had something to contribute to the special relationship.

As early as 1951 the Truman ban on overflights was proving a real problem for Strategic Air Command. It needed to know how targets looked on a bomber's radar to achieve any level of accuracy, even when using atomic bombs. The best and ideal method was to fly a reconnaissance mission over the target and get photographs of the radar screen. These pictures could be given to SAC navigators and bombardiers so they would recognise their target should they be required to deliver their nuclear bombs. Targets were scattered across the Soviet Union but the main concentration was in the most populous and industrial regions to the West.

As we have seen, SAC's boss Gen. LeMay was able to get some radar reconnaissance photographs of targets in the eastern islands of the Soviet Union and China under the cover of Korean War operations. This delicately avoided Truman's ban. However, this ruse was not possible for the far more important targets in the European half of the Soviet Union.

In the absence of the real thing a special department was set up in SAC to predict and reproduce radar images of targets that could be supplied to SAC navigators. But this only worked when you knew what the topology of the target actually looked like and of what materials the different buildings and natural obstructions were made. There were a number of key targets on the European side where they did not have such knowledge. But the USAF believed that there was no way Truman was going to give permission for these flights.

LeMay discussed the problem with his boss, deputy head of the USAF, Gen. Nathan L. Twining, and the other Joint Chiefs of Staff. They decided to ask the British, who were more gung-ho and anxious to prove their worth in the special relationship. The US Joint Chiefs of Staff made overtures to the British Joint Chiefs of Staff for a set of special missions but the RAF did not have aircraft capable of penetration missions. The British radar reconnaissance effort relied entirely on World War 2 style bomber aircraft, the Avro Lancaster and Lincoln. They were equipped with the British air-to-ground radar which had a small screen and poor resolution. So a deal was hatched that the US would provide the aircraft and the RAF would fly the missions. The USAF would then share radar target plots with the British bomber force.

The project is still kept secret in Britain. In 1993 I wrote to the Cabinet Office and was told that the material had been reviewed and it would not be released – so often the case in such matters because of the British obsession with secrecy. I had to cross the Atlantic and utilise the more enlightened attitude to openness in the archives. I discovered some declassified correspondence about the flights in the papers of Gen. Twining, now in the Library of Congress. (Twining was first deputy to and then successor of Gen. Hoyt S. Vandenberg after the latter's premature death as Chief of Staff in 1953.)

A top secret letter from ACM Sir Ralph Cochrane reveals that in July 1951 the RAF was worried that Prime Minister Clement Atlee would not give approval and was hedging its bets – 'We have not yet obtained the political agreement which will be necessary if the full project is to be undertaken.'

The RAF had been flying penetration flights for some time. Grp Capt. Vic Cramer, who is now retired and living in Australia, told me that he flew some 'interesting' missions in late 1948. He had been assigned to No 13 PR Squadron in July 1948. The squadron was based at Fayid airfield in the Canal Zone, equipped with Mosquito PR34s – very long-range versions of the earlier PR16. He was 'detached to Habbaniya, Iraq, for special intelligence operations during October, November and December 1948.' The group captain will not give further explanation of these operations but it seems that they were penetration flights over the Soviet Bloc.[6]

The Americans found out that the British had been photographing the southern shoreline of the Caspian Sea in missions flown from Crete. Documents declassified from the US National Archives show that in December 1948 the Directorate of Intelligence wrote to the Air Attaché in London telling him to get hold of copies. 'It is requested that we be furnished at the earliest, practicable data film positives or duplicate negatives and overtraces of such photography as they may have obtained in the area.'

British Public Records show that the British were flying reconnaissance missions out of Hong Kong over islands held by the communist Chinese. On a number of occasions the communists had opened fire on the British aircraft. One set of documents show a deputy to the British air minister gave permission for flights while his boss was away. When the Chinese filed diplomatic protests the British air minister wrote a furious rebuke for not being informed beforehand. The full details of these British missions over China are still withheld.

The military on both sides were proving enthusiastic about overflights even if their political masters were not. They entered into discussions about a spectacular set of overflights. On 15 August 1951, ACM Sir William Elliot, head of the British Joint Services Mission in Washington, wrote to ACM Cochrane. 'This afternoon Vandenberg asked me to come and see him. He told me that, on the American side, the true purpose of the project had been kept extremely secret and was only known to himself, Twining, LeMay and White.' It does not say whether President Truman was informed.

ACM Cochrane, the RAF's Vice Chief of Air Staff, was placed in operational charge. He asked Sqn Ldr Micky H.B. Martin, DSO, DFC, AFC, a former World War 2 member of No 617 Squadron of 'Dambusters' fame, to set up a special top secret unit. Cochrane had been his boss during the war.

Flt Lt Rex Sanders, a veteran navigator of thirty-three bombing missions over Europe in World War 2, was in a desk job at the time:

> In 1951 I was a flight lieutenant in the Air Ministry responsible for navigator training. And one June morning Sqn Ldr Martin came into the office. He said he'd just been to see the Vice Chief and been told that he was going to be put in charge of a small band of people to do some special flying. For security reasons he wasn't able to tell me what this flying was about. He said, 'I've come to you. I'd like you to nominate or find me a good navigator.' Well, Micky was well known for his exploits in the war. So I realised this was going to be an interesting project. So I said to Micky, 'I nominate myself.' I'd be silly if I didn't. And happily he accepted.[7]

The aircraft that had been chosen were the USAF's North American RB-45C Tornados, which had in-flight refuelling capacity enabling them to extend their range greatly. On 12 July 1951 Martin and Sanders went to look at the RB-45Cs of a detachment of the 91st Strategic Reconnaissance Wing at the USAF base at Sculthorpe, near Fakenham in Norfolk. This was the same unit that was flying daring missions in the Korean conflict. Only thirty-three RB-45Cs were built and the 91st SRW was the main operating unit with three squadrons. One squadron was on temporary duty in England, another in Yokota in Japan and one at the unit's HQ in the United States.

Hal Austin was an RB-45C pilot with the 91st who did several tours of duty at Sculthorpe. He describes their UK workload:

> We had a daily mission, we had two airplanes launched every morning at eight o'clock. We went over to Europe. Our mission called for uncontrolled mosaic photography of the Rhine River, all the way from the English Channel to Switzerland. So they were tying together the maps they had for that area which had been very poor in World War 2. We typically flew 10-hour missions with the RB-45. We'd take-off, go over and do some photo work over Europe. And then a KB-29 tanker would meet us, we'd take on 6,000 gallons of gas and go at it again and so when we got back, we'd typically run 10, 10½, 11 hours . . . The rules were to stay a minimum of 50 miles and our commander added another 50 miles, so our rules were to stay 100 miles away from eastern Europe.[8]

As we have seen in the last chapter the RB-45C had proved vulnerable in Korea to the MiG-15 in daylight. However, the new secret missions were planned as night flights because radar reconnaissance, unlike photographic reconnaissance, was not reliant on light. All the same the Americans sent the British a report by an RB-45C crew describing a MiG attack in Korea.

The RB-45C required a crew of three – pilot, co-pilot and navigator. So nine RAF men and a doctor were posted to the secret unit. They were not all volunteers and most had no idea what they were to do. The initial group included Flt Sgt Joe Acklam and Flt Sgt Bob Anstee who were normally crew members on Washingtons – what the RAF called the B-29 Superfortress – operating with the RAF's No 115 Squadron. Flt Lt Bill Lindsay and Flt Sgt John Hill were on No 35 Squadron. The selected few were given medicals for high altitude pressurised flying and it was discovered that Sqn Ldr Martin's lungs could not take it. Another unit leader had to be found. John Crampton was the squadron leader of No 101 Squadron at Binbrook, one of the first RAF squadrons to fly Canberra jet bombers. Another World War 2 veteran who had flown Handley Page Halifax bombers over Germany, well over 6ft tall, he was known as 'Big John'. He was a noted figure for his upright manner, capacity to drink and the alarming way he drove his Maserati sports car.

The secrecy surrounding the project had caused problems as the USAF Director of Operations, Gen. Roger Ramey, not knowing of the true purpose, objected to the loan of three much sought-after RB-45s to the British. This presented a tricky diplomatic problem that had to be delicately handled by Twining.

In September 1951 the secret RAF unit was sent for training first to Barksdale AFB, Louisiana and then Langley AFB near Colombus, Ohio. Only Crampton and Sanders knew what the real reason for the training was. Bob Anstee thought they were assessing the RB-45C for possible RAF use:

> The idea we went there with, which was wilfully given to us, was that we were doing an assessment, probably with the idea of obtaining them on the same system as the B-29s were obtained and to be used as photo-reconnaissance here.[9]

He points out that the Americans were baffled by the RAF's class system. USAF crews were all officers and therefore all belong to the same mess. When the RAF unit arrived half would go to the officers' mess and the other crew, being NCOs like Bob Anstee, went to the NCOs' Mess for meals and relaxation. Now retired in East Anglia, Anstee's photo album is full of pictures taken at the time with his new American friends who showed the RAF boys around.

Early in December the unit returned to Sculthorpe for further training with mixed USAF and RAF crews. A couple of the original team had not been deemed suitable for jet flying and replacements had to be found. 'We flew missions over the UK and over Europe, day and night missions. Live camera and radar, so at that stage we were still assuming that we were doing the straight assessments,' said Anstee. He was very impressed by the RB-45C radar and did not yet know its significance as far as the mission was concerned. 'Most radars in the RAF were small but in RB-45s they were 18-19in in diameter.'

The American crews from the resident squadron from the 91st SRW also did not know the real purpose of the RAF unit. Capt Sam Myers was one of the USAF pilots. 'I recall that the RAF also flew some RB-45s on penetration missions, and we trained those crews in the RB-45s.' He said, 'I was not privy to the details of those penetration missions that they made, even though I was aware that they had been made.'[10]

The Sculthorpe operations were happening at a key moment in East–West relations. In the meantime the British voters had elected a Conservative government. According to a conversation recorded by Churchill's private secretary, John Colville:

> The Prime Minister said that he did not believe that total war was likely. If it came, it would be on one of two accounts. Either the Americans, unable or unwilling any longer to pay for the maintenance of Europe, would say to the Russians you must by certain dates withdraw from certain points and meet us on certain requirements: otherwise we will attack you. Or, the Russians, realizing that safety did not come from being strong, but only from being the strongest, might for carefully calculated and not for emotional reasons, decide that they must attack before it is too late. If they did so their first target would be the British Isles, which is the aircraft carrier. It was for that reason Mr Churchill was anxious to convert this country from its present status of a rabbit into that of a hedgehog.[11]

In January 1952 Churchill went to Washington in the hope of restarting the talks that had been broken off the previous September. This time Churchill was given access to the inner thinking of the Truman administration, including a briefing on US War Plans and a promise from

Truman that Britain would be consulted about the use of nuclear weapons.

The RAF apparently found the great wartime leader Winston Churchill much more approachable than Atlee. He gave permission for the flights to take place. On 21 March 1952 the first special mission was flown by one RB-45C with Crampton, Sanders and their co-pilot, Sgt Joe Acklam. They went up and down the Berlin corridor, fast and at maximum height. It wasn't for radar reconnaissance, but to see how the Soviets responded to a medium jet aircraft flying through particularly sensitive airspace.[12]

'Bomber Command planned that we should fly down the Berlin corridor to Berlin and back out again at high altitude and fast just to see what the reaction would be. At this time the Berlin air space of course was extremely sensitive as the airlift hadn't long finished,' said Sanders. At the time, Soviet defences used radios rather than telephone lines and the border region was dotted with secret British units listening in to the way the Soviet forces reacted to any perceived threat. 'The Y-service of GCHQ was listening in. We were not told whether the Y-service picked anything up,' said Sanders.

Then, on 16 April 1952 Crampton and Sanders were called to Bomber Command headquarters at High Wycombe some miles to the north-west of London. Sanders said:

> A few weeks later we were called down to Bomber Command again, just John and I, and there in the command operations centre we saw the Commander-in-Chief of the RAF and he said, 'This is the real thing this time.' And on the wall map they had marked out the routes and there were three routes. One was from Sculthorpe through Germany to the Baltic states, the second was south of that, through Germany towards Moscow. And the third was south of that, going down through the centre of Russia and then arcing down south on the way out taking in some of the industrial complexes in the south of the Ukraine. So we went back and briefed the other two crews.

Very few of the C.-in-C.'s staff knew about the operation. In the Command Operations Room the big wall operations map, normally covered by curtains, had three routes marked on it. Up to this point the other RAF crew members did not know the real purpose of the unit. Bob Anstee, the co-pilot, was a flight sergeant who had flown more than fifty bombing missions over Germany during World War 2. Most crew members did not survive more than twenty missions. He was already a statistical aberration and did not fancy chancing his luck another time. He remembers:

We arrived to do another flight and the navigator and the captain arrived back at the aircraft and I saw the flight plans for the first time and I was told what was going to happen. I thought at that time 'Oh my god, what have they let us in for? Why? Why us? Why did we get lumbered with it?' I was only shown the flight plans and shown the targets we had to do which was a patchwork of targets. It's too long ago to remember but they were basically south of Moscow. Most of us knew nothing of what really was happening until that stage.

In case they were captured by the Soviets, the crews were given cover stories that they had got lost. They carried a bag of false navigation plots and maps. Anstee said:

We did carry a complete set of false flight plans and a complete set of false tales that we got ourselves beautifully lost but how much that would have worn with all the equipment on the aircraft I don't know. And if that couldn't have been destroyed we wouldn't have stood much of an argument with them at all.

The three aircraft were wheeled out of the hangars. All the USAF markings had been taken off them and they were resplendent with RAF roundels, much to the surprise of most of the station personnel. They took off, rendezvousing over Denmark in the dusk to be refuelled in-flight by USAF KB-29 tankers also from Sculthorpe.

Once we left Copenhagen on our way in there were quite a few lights and ground features you can see from the air. Lights on the ground always give you some reference but once you get into Russia itself, Russia is one large black hole with lights, odd lights here and there. Nothing like flying over a densely populated country or flying over any big areas, like France and Germany.

I asked Bob Anstee what he thought when he saw Moscow out of the window. 'I thought I'd be very happy when I didn't see it any longer and was going the other way again,' he said.

Crampton and Sanders took the most southern route and the longest:

The flight I was involved in was rather a long one, we had to refuel over Germany before we went in, and we flew about a thousand miles into Russia and then arced our way southwards to come back. And on the way out we had to refuel again to get back to base. Our total flying time for that mission was about ten and a half hours.

The other crews also returned safely. Bob Anstee said:

I think the only thing we thought about when we came back was thank Christ nobody found out about it. At least we presumed we got away with it. What would have happened I don't know. Thinking back afterwards what happened to Powers I hate to think what would have happened if we had three aircraft over there doing the same sort of job. I don't think there'd be very many friendly people around for a while.

A Canberra came in from RAF Wyton to take the film to the Central Reconnaissance Establishment. All aircrew involved were given an Air Force Cross or Air Force Medal for the missions. In 'peacetime' these medals were given for missions that in wartime would have probably earned the Distinguished Flying Cross. The AFC required no citation and during the Cold War they were awarded to crew that flew intelligence missions.

The Soviets had detected the flights and were furious. It may have been the catalyst for a special commission that was set up to examine the ineffectiveness of the air defence system against Western intrusion flights. The commission included L.P. Beria, N.A. Bulganin and A.M. Vasilevski. Over the next six months, a commission official, K.A. Vershinin examined every unauthorised flight near or into the borders of the Soviet Union. His conclusions were a wholesale criticism of the air defences. As a result of the commission, air defences were given a revamp and new equipment. On 9 May 1952 Crampton and Sanders flew their aircraft back to Lockbourne AFB via Goose Bay. Gen. LeMay wanted to congratulate the British crew at Lockbourne. Sanders said:

> We were invited to General LeMay's office and he was very polite to us and very nice to us and congratulated us and then said, 'Where would you like to go? We'll lay an aircraft on for you to wherever you like.' Which was rather nice. In fact we went to Washington for a couple of weeks.
> We were flown back to Sculthorpe and then we all dispersed back to our units. I went back as Squadron Leader of Operations at Marham and John Crampton went back to command his squadron of Canberras.

Another document in the Twining archive is a letter dated 12 September 1952 from Sir John Slessor to Gen. Vandenberg. Another similar operation under the codename 'Ju Jitsu' was being proposed. Slessor's letter is full of bullish enthusiasm and he suggested a joint mission.

> I gathered from Nate [Twining] that the President's reactions were 'Why don't you do more of it?' On that, I suggested to Nate that we might each find three crews and do six sorties simultaneously in November.

I think it would be a great help in getting the Old Man's [Churchill] approval to do another 'Ju Jitsu' if we could say that the US as well as British crews would take part.

However the Americans did not use their crews. SAC's London HQ sent a cryptic telex to Twining, informing him of the problems of failing to participate:

Firstly one of the races scheduled will be over a course in which we have a primary interest and second, it is entirely possible that without our participation the Betting Commissioner [code for Churchill] here may reject Sir John's application.

In retrospect, it has to be asked if Twining had not exaggerated, to Slessor, President Truman's enthusiasm for the missions and whether the Americans were playing a canny game encouraging the gung-ho Brits to go ahead while knowing full well they would not be able to participate. On 18 September 1952 Vandenberg wrote to Slessor about making RB-45s available:

I agree with you it would be desirable for participation by aircrews of the USAF in the operation for the reasons you have stated. However, I regret to say that it will not be feasible to do so because of political considerations.

In October Sqn Ldr Crampton was asked to prepare the unit for the mission. The unit did a lot of training including a lot of night refuelling. There needed to be some crew changes. Bill Lindsay had been badly injured in a B-29 crash. Two new recruits, Flt Lt H. Currell and Flt Lt McAlaistair Furze, joined the unit. The Americans were not all delighted to see the RAF crews again. Sanders said:

When they found out after the first mission what we were doing some of them reacted a bit annoyed that they weren't able to do it themselves. They felt this was a thing the USAF should have done for themselves. They were a bit sorry about the political inhibitions on the American Air Force. But other than that they supported us well.

The exercise carried on for about five weeks: 'And then all of a sudden the whole exercise was called off. I presume that security had been compromised. We were dispersed back to our units again. And once again I thought that was that,' said Sanders. Then the mission was cancelled, apparently because the element of surprise had been lost. 'We were not told why we didn't do it but I think someone had opened their mouth,' said Anstee. (It is possible that the mission was leaked by Kim Philby or one of the other Cambridge Soviet agents.) The crews were grilled as to whether they had breached security. Sanders again:

> Nothing happened then for a year and two months, when once again John came onto the telephone and said, 'Rex, it's on again.' So we formed up again at Sculthorpe and we did about a month's intensive training. This time we were developing the radar side. We were improving the radar, we were improving the camera facilities. So we had quite a lot of work to do. And we were flying with the Americans. Once again appearing as ordinary exchange crews.

More crew changes needed to be made, Flt Lt Bill Blair, an RAF exchange pilot with the 91st, was recruited. Weeks of intensive training followed and again the call to High Wycombe.

'Then we were called up again to headquarters Bomber Command for a briefing. And once again there were three routes, roughly the same as last time. One north, one for the centre and one for the south. Just a lot longer,' said Sanders.

They were told that the Y-service was going to monitor the operation. They were told that the mission was as important for the Y-service test of Soviet Defences as the actual mission. A senior RAF officer said that even if they failed to achieve their primary mission, from the RAF point of view, the Y-service element was sufficient to justify the mission. The RAF was very interested in the organisation of the Soviet Air Force.

'We also were told that aircraft would be flying from the American side listening in to the Russian reaction,' said Sanders.

GCHQ's Y-service geared up for the missions weeks in advance. The unit was given a date and was told it couldn't be changed.

'Everything was extremely secret, very few people in the Air Force knew about this. Very few people in Bomber Command knew about it. And in my case, I never even told my wife about it,' said Sanders.

The aircraft had RAF roundels but no serial numbers. All American insignia had been blacked out. The routes were similar but a lot longer than the first mission and Crampton again chose the longest, the southern route that penetrated Soviet airspace by about 1,000 miles and covered some thirty targets. 'These targets were fairly scattered over the southern part of Russia. We were zigzagging from one target to another, in quite a piece of evasive routing, I suppose, which might have added to our safety. I don't know. It certainly prolonged our time over Russia,' said Sanders.

The British crews had little idea of the commotion they had caused in Russia. The whole Soviet Air Defence network was alerted. Gen. Vladimir Abramov was the commander for the Kiev region. In 1993, he described how he ordered his pilots to try to ram Crampton and Sanders' plane.

'Since it was the dead of night and our MiGs had no radar then, we tried to direct pilot Batyshev and the second pilot into a head-on collision,' he said.[13]

One of the Soviet pilots was Lt Nikolai Sysoev. He now said: 'Ideally, we weren't meant to ram head-on, but to ram the most vulnerable parts of the plane.'[14] Despite guidance from Soviet ground control radar, the MiG pilots could not find the intruder in the dark. So the British crews knew nothing of the Soviets' intended kamikaze tactics. But they had other problems. 'On the way back we experienced quite a bit of heavy flak, which was a surprise. We didn't expect anything in that particular part of the world. But it didn't do us any harm. My only reaction was that it was going to spoil my radar reconnaissance work and I tried to let it not do so,' Sanders told me with his deadpan manner, barely betraying his ironic stiff upper lip humour. He continued:

> As we came out of the Iron Curtain countries across into Germany, we tried to pick up the tanker aircraft, but unfortunately it was unable to give us fuel, and we were getting pretty low. So we had to land at the American air base Furstenfeldbruck, which caused some consternation. Here was an aircraft coming from the east landing about three in the morning that shouldn't be there. So we were very quickly refuelled and sent on our way back to Sculthorpe.

The only public reference ever made was a paragraph in the *Daily Telegraph* the next morning referring to unidentified aircraft refuelling over Copenhagen.

These flights were a terrific gamble. Although the MoD still refuses to release the files there can be little doubt that Churchill personally approved the flights. That is what the crews were told. What did Rex Sanders think of Churchill's gamble?

'I think it was an amazing decision and very much reflects the character of Churchill. It was a great risk. Had we gone down there would have been quite a furore.'

But was there a risk of the Soviets mistaking the missions for nuclear attacks? Sanders said:

> It did cross our minds that they might be thinking that we were doing something more serious than just taking reconnaissance photographs. We had no real way of knowing what they would make of it. It did cross our minds that they might think this was an actual attack by three aircraft.

Did Rex Sanders think the flights had caused tensions? 'I'm sure they did. But I think, from the Russian air force point of view, they probably recognised them for what they were.' In 1992 the Russian military writer, Lt-Col. Anatoli Dokuhaev, referred to the last flight in an article in the armed forces magazine *Red Star*. He said that although it had been thought by the defence units that they were reconnaissance flights, 'Specialists of the day could not rule out that there were not nuclear weapons on board.' The Russians had identified the aircraft as B-47s and thought they were USAF flights.

This was to be the last British radar recce mission. 'Why?' I asked. 'The Russian defences were improving all the time. They were getting new fighters, improved fighters, and the speed and height of the RB-45 was becoming a bit obsolete. I think the risks would have been too great, with that aircraft,' said Sanders.

6
'NEVER AGAIN . . .'

In 1953 Western intelligence began to get reports of a new Soviet missile testing site at Kapustin Yar, a remote site near the Volga River. Former CIA officer Dino Brugioni said, 'We found out about the missile tests at Kapustin Yar from the German scientific returnees.'[1] The German V-weapon campaign against Britain had already shown the missile's capability for terrifying populations. The V-2 had proved almost impossible to stop once it had been launched. It was now possible to envisage adding a nuclear warhead to a rocket. This would be the perfect weapon of terror. The West desperately needed to know how far the Soviets had got with their missile programme.

At the end of World War 2 the Soviets, like the Western allies, captured a large number of Nazi scientists, and set them to work often with fat salaries and privileged conditions.[2] Especially sought after were those who had devised the V-1 and V-2 rockets. Some of these German scientists had been involved with the use of slave labour and were suspected of war crimes but this was overlooked as the new tensions of the Cold War provided overwhelming pressures for the former allies to steal the technological march. Unlike the Americans, who allowed Werner Von Braun and others to naturalise and remain part of the space effort, the Soviets debriefed the Germans for every bit of useful information and gradually replaced them with their own scientists. Surprisingly some of these Germans were allowed to return to West Germany.

These returnees were scooped up by Project 'Wringer', the vast intelligence operations targeted at the Soviets. Both the American and British intelligence services debriefed every returnee whether POW or refugee. Hundreds of thousands were subjected to detailed and broad-ranging interrogations. One of the highest priorities was new evidence of Soviet military building. Many of the returnees had been used as slave labour for the Soviets and could describe extensive new military building works in the Eastern Bloc countries. This enabled many airfields, barracks, manufacturing or testing sites to be located. Even a main power line spotted running across a remote area might point to a new secret military installation.

Given the difficulties of overflying or infiltrating agents behind the Iron Curtain, this operation became the main method of obtaining intelligence on Soviet activities for some years. The returning German scientists knew more than generalities. They knew that the new Kapustin Yar site was one of the most important military testing grounds in the USSR. The Soviets had realised the potential of missiles as a delivery method for nuclear weapons.

As CIA historian Don Welzenbach said:

> Kapustin Yar marked the beginning of the real Soviet rocket programme, where they began launching Soviet designed rockets. It was the period in which they divorced themselves from the Germans. When Kapustin Yar was up and running, the Germans were sent off to an island in the middle of a lake somewhere for a couple of years, that was the end of the German involvement. The Soviets were very good at missile technology, and had made great strides. It was important for the western world to know what Kapustin Yar was like.[3]

According to American sources the secrets of Kapustin Yar were revealed by overflights – not an American overflight because they were still banned in the Western European sector – but an RAF flight. The official record of this mission is still secret and putting the story together was a slow and difficult process. The first tantalising clue came from Bob Amory, the Deputy Director of Intelligence at the CIA during the 1950s in an oral history interview he gave to an American university in 1964:

> When we first heard of the Russian missile centre in 1952, or about then, at Kapustin Yar on the Volga, we demanded that we get photographs of it. 'We just can't ignore it. This is going to be a major new thing, this whole missile development, and we've got to get on top of it in the beginning and judge it.' And Nathan Twining [Chief of Staff of the USAF] said it couldn't be done. The RAF actually did it for us with the Canberra all the way from Germany to the Volga and down into Persia, a risky thing but they got some fair pictures. And then we said, 'Well this is fine.' But the British said: 'God, never again,' so to speak. The whole of Russia had been alerted to the thing, and it damn near created a major international incident. But it never made the papers.[4]

This first account appeared publicly in a book, *The Centre*, by Stewart

Alsop,[5] published in the USA in 1968 with the additional assertion that the aircraft had sustained some kind of damage during the flying as a result of the Soviet air defences. Alsop was a intelligence writer who knew Amory well. The second source was the 'father of US Aerial Reconnaissance', Gen. George Goddard of the USAF, in his ghost-written autobiography.[6] Goddard refers to the RAF director of intelligence but confuses his name.

During early 1993 I spent time in the Public Record Office looking through the records of the RAF's photo-reconnaissance squadrons of the time and asking around RAF contacts of that period. I could see nothing that would shed light on the flight. The mission would have taken place in conditions of greatest secrecy and on a 'need to know' basis. Probably only some top brass, the station commander and the actual crew would have known. The mission would also have had to be approved by the then Prime Minister, Winston Churchill.

The idea of the RAF flying such a mission made perfect sense. First, the presidential ban on the USAF from overflying the Soviet Union. Second, the Canberra was the only aircraft capable of taking photographs during the day, as was necessary. It was the only aircraft with sufficient range and altitude to be able to carry out the mission and fly too high for the Soviet air defences. On 4 May 1953 Canberra B2 WD952, testbed for the Bristol B1.99 engine, established a new world altitude record of 63,668ft flown by W.F. Gibb from Filton.[7]

The next piece in the puzzle came when I was put in touch with a retired CIA historian Don Welzenbach, who had spent his last few years at the agency putting together a history of the U-2 project. He too had seen the Amory interview and was curious because it was the prehistory of the U-2. At the time, in the mid-1980s, Bob Amory was very elderly but still alive. They had spent a very pleasant evening on the balcony of Amory's house discussing the matter. It turned out that the former DDI had little to add to his interview. He had not been directly involved in the project and could give no details. 'And sometime, in the time frame 1953, 1954, a flight was made from Giebelstadt in West Germany, over Kapustin Yar in the Soviet Union, and the plane landed in Iran. Now my knowledge of this is very indirect, I've put it together from many sources,' Welzenbach told me. Giebelstadt was the base that the very earliest operational U-2 flights were to be flown from.

Don also had clearance to look at CIA documents and was only excluded from the highest category of secrecy. He told me that it was unlikely, given that the Americans do not have the same obsession with long-term secrecy as the British, that this project would still be top secret. But he had not found any mention of the overflight.

Welzenbach went to see Jim Baker, the camera designer and brilliant interpreter of photographs. Baker said that in late January or early February 1954 he and Amron Katz, another key photo expert, had visited England. Baker had gone to see the RAF's Director of Intelligence, AVM Fressanges, on his own as Katz did not have a sufficiently high level security clearance. According to Baker, Fressanges bragged of the RAF flight over Kapustin Yar. Baker had the impression that the flight had taken place in the summer of 1953.

Helping to confirm the story I found in Bomber Command's *Operational Record Book* an entry that Cdr A.H. Katz and Cdr J.G. Baker (SAC USAF) along with Grp Capt. D. Wilson had visited the commanding officer at headquarters on 11 February 1954. Don Welzenbach had finally had to give up on the exact details of the flight: 'And it was a fairly good mission. Obviously, they've kept it secret, for all these years. Even today, we don't know who flew it, even which airplane was used.'

Welzenbach believed the codename for the operation was Project 'Robin' and that it involved a modified Canberra with 'wet wings' and extended range. This sounded like the PR7 which was the first Canberra with fuel tanks in the wings. My inquiries showed that No 540 Squadron, a PR squadron, appeared to be the only unit capable of the mission. The first PR3, the photo-reconnaissance version of the Canberra, came into service in late 1952 with No 540. By May 1953 there were only four PR3s in the squadron, the rest of its strength being made up of converted Canberra B2s. Two of the squadron officers pioneering the PR3 were 'Monty' Burton and Bob Reeve. In April 1953 No 540 Squadron was given the high profile task of delivering the films of the coronation to Canada, called Operation 'Pony Express'. The Canberra aircraft involved were WD987, WE136 and WE142. No 540 Squadron was based at RAF Wyton in Cambridgeshire which had become the home of the British strategic reconnaissance force.[8] At the time that meant Nos 540, 82, 58 and 541 Squadrons. But 540 was the first to convert to the Canberra.

About the same time the RAF decided to compete in the London to

New Zealand air race in October 1953, an event that was going to need an great deal of preparation. In the original plan the RAF race team was going to fly three PR7s – improved versions of the PR3 – in the race. The Public Record Office file on the race shows that because of production problems they had trouble getting enough PR3s let alone PR7s to rehearse. The RAF only had one PR7 ready for the race and it was a No 540 Squadron PR3 – WE139 flown by Monty Burton and his navigator Don Gannon that won. The PR7 developed a couple of faults which slowed it down.[9]

It crossed my mind that maybe the race team sneaked in the Kapustin Yar flight not least because Monty Burton and Don Gannon had picked up two AFCs each that year (the AFC was often awarded to aircrew that had undertaken risky peacetime intelligence flights).

I tracked down Monty Burton to France[10] and Don Gannon to the West Midlands.[11] They were most helpful, but Monty said that he had certainly not done the flight although he felt it would have been a No 540 Squadron operation. Don Gannon remarked that he had only once been over communist territory and that was during the race:

> Our 'accidental' incursion over communist territory on 8 October during the race itself which cut a slight corner off the track from London to Basra, and may have secured our first speed record – together with some other unconventional actions.

Over the next months I tracked down as many surviving members of No 540 Squadron as I could find. John Unwin had left the unit by late 1953 to go to an operations conversion unit. He said he knew the flight had taken place but could not remember any details. He thought the aircraft used was PR3 WE142.[12]

Looking up No 540 Squadron records, I found another tantalising reference. On 27 and 28 August 1953, 'long range operations sorties' were carried out by Wg Cdr Freddie Ball, Sqn Ldr Don Kenyon and Flt Sgt Jim Brown in WH726 and Flt Lt Gartside and Flt Sgt Wigglesworth in WH574. Similar missions were flown by different crews using WH726 and WH800 on 23 and 26 August 1954: the reference shows 'Went on Operation Robin. 240 exposures obtained.'

Jim Brown explained that Operation 'Robin' was a series of flights involving WH726 which had been specially converted:

> The Americans gave us a 100in focal length camera and said, 'Do what you want

with it. Don't tell us but give us copies of the pictures.' The camera stretched right along the fuselage and pointed out to port and could be used obliquely.[13]

According to Brown the plane was used for 'over the border' photographs looking over the border into communist territory. Apparently the camera was so good that during a test it was able to get clear shots of St Paul's Cathedral while flying off the coast of Dover.

Brown said that he did not fly the Kapustin Yar flight. He did admit that they had penetrated East German airspace. 'The purpose of the second aircraft was to follow WH726 and make sure that it was not contrailing and giving its position away.'

Another No 540 Squadron veteran, Norman Metcalfe, recalled picking up an experimental side-facing camera from Warton, Lancs and this was later fitted to Canberra WJ573:

> I flew several local camera trials in September/October in WJ573, including one with Don Kenyon (CO at the time) when we 'squinted' across the West German border in to East Germany. The camera could have been a prototype for the one fitted to WH726. I left the squadron in November 1953.[14]

When I told Don Welzenbach about this he explained that this type of 100in camera had been designed by Jim Baker and only six had been made. He had also found that the Kapustin Yar operation had not been commissioned by the CIA, despite the impression given by Bob Amory, but was a USAF operation under General Lewis. I tracked down other surviving crew that had flown WH726. It seemed that it was more a special Wyton aircraft than a squadron aircraft. Sir John Gingell, then a flight lieutenant on No 58 Squadron, later Black Rod at the Houses of Parliament, first flew it in October 1953. But he was not a regular user until after April 1954 when he took it the United States for a week: 'My recollection of WH726 is that it was a very useful addition to the Canberra fleet operated by numbers 58 and 540 Squadrons at a time when the full complement of PR3s had not been delivered.'[15]

Entries in the Wyton *Operational Record Book* showed that on 1 March 1954 Gingell and Downs were detached to the USA for the purpose of carrying out joint RAF/USAF trials. The aircraft concerned was a 'modified B2 Canberra WH726' and the trial given the name Project 'Robin'. Originally planned for two weeks, the detachment was extended to six weeks and the crew successfully completed the trials, returning to the squadron on 10 April 1954. In all I was able to piece together a long series of 'Robin' flights right up to late 1955. None of the former crew members I spoke to could recall 'going over the fence' into communist airspace. One remembered a friend telling him about such an operation flown in WH726 out of Malta. E.C. Waterer was a flight lieutenant with No 540 Squadron. He said:

> I did not come onto Operation 'Robin' until late April 1954, flying escort sorties on 23 April, 8 and 11 August 1954. An abortive sortie was flown in WH726 on 15 June, camera testing on 19 and 21 July and another camera testing with Frank Slaymaker on 23 August followed by a 'Robin' sortie on 26 August and another camera test on 30 August 1954.[16]

So did WH726 fly the Kapustin Yar flight? The mystery is not yet resolved. Unfortunately many of the members of Nos 540 and 58 Squadron are now dead. No 540 lost several crews in the period in accidents. If the flight was made on a need to know basis then the secret might be lost. No 540's commanding officer at the time is dead. Several other officers involved with No 540 Squadron, including Gordon Cremer, Don Greenslade and Harry Currell, were part of a separate top secret unit which flew the Sculthorpe missions. Certainly the flight and others were made. In 1993, Col. Aleksandr Orlov, a Russian military intelligence expert in this area, confirmed spy flights over Kapustin Yar. He said:

> The site was set up in 1951, and in 1952, the Americans and the English knew that missiles were being successfully produced there. 'But what kind?' They must have asked themselves. 'Inter-continental, medium-range, anti-aircraft missiles?' They didn't know. And that's why they carried out reconnaissance all the time, moreover, by aeroplanes, and especially the English Canberra.[17]

Russian air force lieutenant Mikhail Shulga recalls trying to intercept a Canberra in his MiG fighter in the Kapustin Yar region. He was guided by Soviet ground control:

> I began to climb to 48,000ft, to 48,500ft, and they said, 'Look around you. Look to the right and look to the left.' I looked. They said, 'Look higher and look a bit to the right.' I looked up and there a few thousand feet above me I saw the plane. They asked me, 'Can you see it?'
> I said, 'Yes, I can, shimmering beautifully in the sunshine.' They said, 'Prepare your guns.' So I accelerated and climbed up towards the plane – 4,500ft, 5,000ft, 5,500ft higher – and my plane was stalling. Nothing came of it. The plane was flying higher than me. They said, 'Do it again.' I tried again. 'Can't you reach it?' 'No, I can't.'[18]

So it would seem that the RAF did undertake a daring mission over Kapustin Yar. Which aircraft and crew flew still remains a mystery. Was it WH726? There are other possibilities. It could have been a PR3 using a F52 camera. The PR3 had greater range and altitude than the B2. But with a 100in camera WH726 would not have needed to get so close to the missile site, so it still looks like the best contender.

The former Soviets report other intrusion flights by Canberras including a flight from Iran over Grozny in summer 1954. Recently an overhead photograph of the city of Baku in the Soviet Crimea was found in a British PRO's file that contained photos taken just before World War 2 by two RAF pilots using Sidney Cotton's Lockheed 14. But this picture, dated 1956 and misfiled in the file, said 'Baku Nov 56 1:34000'. The picture size is about 8in x 7in which corresponds to the F52 camera used by the RAF at the time. It was taken from 13,000ft.

Gen. Valdimir Abramov of the PVO said that he recalls another intrusion that year:

> Either on 21 or 22 August, there were three other planes that transgressed the territory of the Soviet Union, I don't remember their route at the moment, I can't remember, but they managed to go away across the Black Sea into Turkey and landed there. As a result of it quite a number of heads were chopped. Those of the Anti Aircraft batteries and one of the commanders of the air defence.[19]

After the appearance of this story in *Aeroplane Monthly* I received a number of recollections of mysterious Canberras taking-off from Wyton on secret missions either painted in black and then later in sky-blue with minimal identification. One correspondent even recalled bullet holes in a returning Canberra.

The Ministry of Defence apparently has files relating to these flights, but has indicated that these and the Sculthorpe mission files have been reviewed but are too sensitive to release. Canberra WH726 was eventually sold to the Peruvians in 1966. The USAF had been so impressed by the English Electric Canberra's performance that they had it built under licence as the B-57 by the Glen L. Martin Company. They preferred it to the U-2. In the meantime the USAF had decided it was time to do some of its own overflights.

7
'EYES AS BIG AS DOLLARS . . .'

On 8 May 1954 three USAF Boeing RB-47E Stratojets took-off from
Fairford AFB, near Oxford in Britain, and headed round the north coast
of Norway to Murmansk, on the northern coast of the USSR. The crew
of one aircraft was about to undertake one of the most secret 'peacetime'
missions of the Cold War. Nearing Murmansk two aircraft turned round
and flew back. The third dashed south, over the Kola Peninsula, deep
into the Soviet Union. The crew of that aircraft were Hal Austin (pilot),
Carl Holt (co-pilot) and Vance Heavilin (navigator).

The RB-47E, a reconnaissance variant of the B-47, had been
introduced at the end of 1953. It had a longer nose, provision for seven
cameras for day and night photography, six General Electric J47-GE-25A
turbojets and two 20mm radar-directed cannon in the tail. The 91st
Strategic Reconnaissance Wing was one of the first units to receive the
new aircraft. Hal Austin, a veteran of the Berlin Airlift, and his crew had
done several tours on England in the past few years flying the RB-45C.
They had helped to train the RAF crews for the Sculthorpe missions in
1952. Two years on they had converted to the RB-47E in the United
States. In April they were ordered with a number of other crews to fly to
Britain. Once there, Austin's crew was taken aside from the others and
briefed on its top secret mission. The purpose of this flight was to take
photographs of a number of Soviet military sites. After a practice run to
Norway at the beginning of May he received orders to undertake the real
mission. It was to prove more hazardous than expected. Austin, a tall,
thin amiable man who speaks with a deep Texan drawl, said:

> We proceeded due south from the Murmansk area. I don't recall the specific targets
> now but they were typically airfields and we were taking radar photography as well.
>
> The weather was gorgeous, we could see forever. We had been overland maybe
> 50 miles when three fighters came up, looked us over. By the time we'd been over
> Soviet territory an hour another group came up, and this time it was at least six
> airplanes. A little later on another six airplanes came up, and this time they were
> not MiG-15s. It became obvious that this group of airplanes were told to engage
> us. As we turned due west the third group of airplanes made pursuit passes on us.[1]

Much to the alarm of the crew the Soviet fighters turned out to be MiG-17s – 'Frescos', to use their NATO reporting name. Unlike the MiG-15 'Fagot', the Soviets' latest fighter had a much improved capability and could match the RB-47's performance. The 'Fresco-C' was powered by a Klimov VK-1A turbojet which, with reheat, could achieve 656mph at 35,000ft and had a ceiling of 58,000ft. Austin continued:

> Then the first aeroplane more or less flew right up our tail pipes. We knew they were armed, because I saw tracers going both above and below the aeroplane. And I hollered at my co-pilot, Carl Holt. He said, 'The guns won't work', and I said, 'Well, you'd better kick something back there and get the damn things to work a little bit anyway, or we may be a dead duck here.'

Carl Holt said:

> At one point I counted about ten MiG fighters planes, trying to shoot us out of the sky. They could keep up with us, but after they made one pass at us, then they'd have to drop down and circle back up to make another shot at us, and then they'd drop down. I managed to get a few shots off at the pursuing aircraft, enough to make them keep their distance.[2]

Austin takes up the story again:

> Well it's either the third or fourth aeroplane, I don't recall now, which then hit our aeroplane. It wasn't much, but it was enough to feel it as though you'd hit a bunch of rough air. It turned out we got hit in the left wing, and near the fuselage.

In the nick of time Austin's crew flew into Finnish airspace. Heading back towards England, Holt discovered that the aircraft was leaking and running out of fuel. Next they found only one channel was working on their damaged radio – the wrong one for the mission – as they called for a tanker. Fortunately, a friend of Austin's, KC-97 tanker pilot Jim Rigley, was on strip alert that day at Fairford and recognised Austin's voice making desperate calls for assistance. Austin remembered:

> Jim tried to get clearance to take-off but some other activity was going on, on the base, and they kept denying him clearance. So he finally told them he was going to take-off anyway. He got a couple of air operation violations for doing that, but he took-off. And Holt was worried that we were not going to be able to get the aeroplane onto a base at all. He said, 'We got no fuel left.' When I saw a glistening of an aircraft in the far distance, the weather was gorgeous in England that day too,

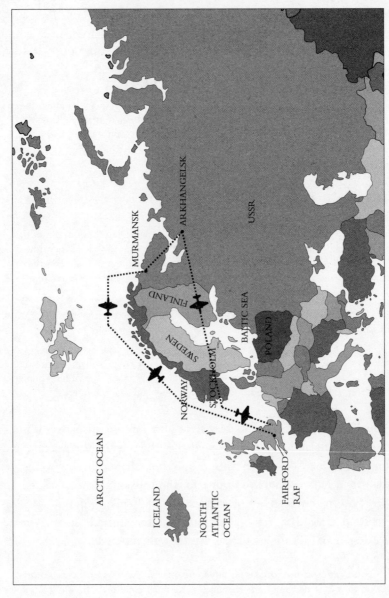

Map 3   The route of the RB-47 overflight of the Soviet Union, 8 May 1954.

you could see forever, I said, 'That's got to be a KC-97, so I'm going to head for it.' Well, we did head for it, and old Carl Holt swears to this day that when we moved in underneath that tanker, and hooked up on the boom, that we had no fuel left for the aeroplane.

The whole flight and its route over Russia was secret – including to Capt. Austin's ground crew. He recalled:

And I couldn't believe how big a crowd we had when we parked the aeroplane, the other crews had already returned sometime before. We parked the aeroplane. I've never seen so many people round an aeroplane in my life. And the crew chief sticks his head up there, with eyes as big as dollars, 'What in hell did you run into?' Well, we didn't tell him what it was. But it was not a bird, as he thought.'

Several days later a Helsinki newspaper reported an air battle between jet planes of unknown nationality over northern Finland. The Finnish Foreign Ministry denied any such fight had taken place. The paper, *Uusi Suomi*, said residents in Lapland had heard jets shooting and added, 'It is possible that American and Russian planes had been involved.' A spokesman at USAF European headquarters in Wiesbaden said no American planes had been in the area named by the paper.

The mission had shown the limitations of the RB-47, out-of-date as it went into service, as it could not outrun the new MiG-17. With a service ceiling of only 39,000ft (compared to the Canberra's 50,000 plus) it could not get above the enemy. Although it was to remain the mainstay of USAF strategic reconnaissance for some years it was better suited to the ELINT task.

Austin and his crew were summoned to meet Gen. Curtis LeMay back at Strategic Air Command headquarters at Omaha in the United States. When they arrived they were taken into a secret briefing room. Carl Holt recalls:

I said, 'General LeMay, they were trying to shoot us down.' And he said, 'What do you think they would do to you, give you an ice cream cone?' Everybody got a big chuckle out of that. But we survived. We did our piece for history, and now realise how important it was, we had done a little thing to keep the world at peace.

LeMay wanted to decorate them for bravery. Hal Austin recalls:

LeMay said, 'I tried to get your guys a silver star but you gotta explain that to Congress and everybody else in Washington when you do something like that. So here's a couple of DFCs each we'll give you for that mission.' There wasn't anybody in the room except the wing commander and us three guys, General LeMay and his intelligence officer.

LeMay had perfectly legitimate military intelligence reasons for overflights. A large part of any SAC bomber strike would go through in the vicinity of Kola. This would be mainly B-47s that could outfly MiG-15s. But SAC needed to know whether the Soviets had operational MiG-17s at any of the air bases. Austin's crew was supposed to bring back photos of these bases, and much to their consternation, they were able to bring back very clear evidence. The mission also revealed that there were no long-range bombers on the Kola Peninsula, altough it was the primary jump-off point for an attack on the US.

The mission by Austin's crew takes on much greater significance because there is no evidence that President Eisenhower was notified. All the evidence suggests that Eisenhower, like Truman, was very reluctant to approve overflights. He continued with the ban imposed by Truman, with the exception of limited permission for the U-2.

Investigating the true history of USAF overflights is still difficult, hampered by secrecy, misinformation and lack of key documents. The confusion is best shown by the memoirs of Gen. Nathan L. Twining. In 1950, Twining was USAF Vice Chief of Staff, deputy to Gen. Hoyt S. Vanderberg. He said that in autumn 1950 he was elected by the Joint Chiefs of Staff to tell President Truman about planes to fly overflights of the USSR. Twining said he took the papers and maps to the Oval Office, where Truman studied them:

> 'Chiefs all buy this?' asked the President. 'Yes, sir. We're very anxious to start on this program right away. We realise the seriousness of it, but we feel this is the only way we're going to get this information.'

By Twining's account, the President signed the authorisation and said, 'Listen, when you get back there, you tell General Vanderberg from me: *Why the devil hasn't he been doing this before?*' Twining later said, 'One day, I had forty-seven airplanes flying all over Russia and we never heard a word out of them. Nobody complained.'

Unfortunately, I have been unable to find any corroboration of Twining's account. Similarly in his autobiography Gen. LeMay claimed that at one point in the mid-1950s he flew the entire SAC reconnaissance force over the city of Vladivostok.

'It wasn't my idea,' he hastened to explain in recalling the incident. 'I was ordered to do it. They [the Eisenhower administration's intelligence chiefs] were worried about something that was going on in Vladivostok. So I laid out a mission. From Guam or the Philippines. Maybe fifty planes. Maximum altitude about 40,000ft. We picked a clear day and all of our electronic reconnaissance planes criss-crossed the area. They practically mapped the place. Two of our planes saw some MiGs but there were no interceptions. As far as I know, the Russians never said anything about it.'

There is no evidence that reveals overflights on anything like this scale from either participants or documents. The vast majority of declassified USAF documents only show border flights being flown. The USAF spy planes shot down by the Soviets in this period were nearly all ELINT aircraft flying in international airspace, or disputed airspace or just inside Soviet airspace. I obtained under the Freedom of Information Act a top secret report by the USAF research think tank RAND titled, *Case studies of Actual and Alleged Overflights, 1930-55*. At 400 pages, it makes no mention of Twining's overflights. The same applies to Soviet air defence logs I have obtained for the period, listing intrusions by foreign aircraft.

Twining's account of the president's enthusiastic response sounds suspiciously as though, when writing his autobiography some years later, he muddled the President's comments with those he cites in his letter congratulating the RAF on the first of the Sculthorpe missions.

The evidence suggests that Truman only gave permission with great reluctance. Only as recently as 1995 has it been discovered that in 1952 Truman was asked to approve two overflights of the Far Eastern Soviet Union. Truman appears to have authorised one flight known as the 'Northern run'. He had first been asked to approve flights in 1951 but the aircraft that was to undertake the mission was destroyed in a fire. Following an intelligence report in the spring of 1952 that the Soviets had begun staging bombers into Siberia, further requests were made. Truman certainly was not gung-ho about the missions. A memorandum to the Chairman of the JCS from the Secretary of Defense shows Truman refusing to sanction the second mission, 'With respect to Southern run, the President expressed concern at the length of the flight and depth of penetration with particular apprehension expressed over the fact the egress route virtually parallels the ingress route.' Details of this flight have been released by USAF historian, R. Cargill Hall,[3] in the archives of NARA, St Louis. Hall has also found and interviewed the pilot, Col.

Donald E. Hillman.[4] The mission was requested by the CIA and the Department of Defense. The route was over the Chukotski Peninsula across the Bering Strait from Alaska, where Soviet aircraft might converge and prepare for a surprise atomic attack on America.

The RB-47 had not yet entered service so the unusual step was taken of using aircraft and crews from the 306th Bombardment Wing stationed at MacDill AFB in the United States, the only unit then converting to the new B-47. Hillman was deputy commander of the wing. The mission was assigned the title Project 52 AFR-18 and was flown from Eielson AFB in Fairbanks, Alaska on 15 October 1952. The route involved flying past Wrangel Island, then turning south-west into Siberia. Col. Hillman said:

> When we had finished covering two of our five targets, taking radar and visual photography, the instruments on board announced that we were being painted and tracked by Soviet radar. A few minutes later my co-pilot, Ed Gunter, announced that he had a Soviet fighter in sight to the rear desperately climbing to intercept us. Gunter kept his eyes on the ascending aircraft but they had scrambled too late.

The exit route passed south of Egvekinot, then through the coastline of Chukotski. Hillman continued the story:

> As events transpired, we completed photographing the remaining three sites without encountering any more fighters. Altogether the mission spanned seven and three-quarter hours in the air and we had overflown some 800 miles of Soviet territory. Six months later I was assigned to Headquarters, Strategic Air Command. I was summoned to the CINCSAC's office. When I entered, Gen. LeMay arose and came round the desk, closed the door and without a word pinned on my shirt a Distinguished Flying Cross. When he saw my puzzled expression, he flashed a very slight and very rare smile and said, 'It's secret.'

There are US records of some of the numerous border flights in the period. One USAF document *Information on Operation Pieface* dated early 1953 said:

> This operation involves the use of very large camera with unusual capabilities, carried by an RC-97, for photographic reconnaissance . . . A similar aircraft operated in Europe during the summer of 1952. A special photographic mission, the only one of its kind performed to date, was performed on 16 September 1952 under the operational control of USAFE.

According to the document the aircraft flew from Wiesbaden to '13°

East 55° North' which I locate off the Danish Island of Mons, north of Rostock. The unit was the 7499th Composite Squadron.

Other documents refer to the existence of two K-30 equipped RB-50s 'in UK for a special reconnaissance mission'.[5] One of these aircraft was transferred to the Alaskan Command for 'late summer reconnaissance' off the Siberian Coast.

All the evidence indicates that the overflight ban continued through Eisenhower's presidency. Gen. Andrew Goodpaster, Eisenhower's defence aide from 1954, said, 'President Eisenhower, on a number of occasions, said that he was not going to have members of the armed forces flying over the Soviet Union. That amounted to an act of war.' This is why pilots for the CIA's U-2 overflights project, which began in 1956, were 'retired' from the USAF, 'sheepdipped' with new civilian identities. The overflight ban seems to have been total on the Western side of the Eastern Bloc, where Soviet air defences were at their best.

Former USAF pilot and historian, Robert Hopkins said:

> I've learned of a 1953 memorandum on US overflight code-names including, 'Pie face' and 'Robin'. These were all USAFE programs, and they are clearly identified as such in this memo – these US overflights were authorized by CINCUSAFE, not Ike. 'Pieface' was actually a Berlin corridor flight equipped with a camera and later SIGINT, so its status as a 'true' overflight is somewhat dubious. However, I've located other programs undertaken by not only USAFE but the US Pacific Air Force that demonstrated US military independence from presidential authorization for specific missions.[6]

There are some declassified documents that seem to refer to Hal Austin's RB-47 flight as being part of a small batch undertaken in the 1953-54 timeframe. In a memo dated September 1953 the Air Force Directorate of Intelligence asked for the JCS approval for the overflight of the Kola Peninsula. It is not stated whether this was approved or whether this was for Hal Austin's flight. But in May 1954 the Director of Naval Intelligence, in a letter to Maj.-Gen. John A. Samford, Air Force Director of Intelligence, asked for photographs from missions. He wrote:

> Information has been received that the US Air Force, in accordance with JCS authority, have completed the following reconnaissance overflights:
> a. Murmansk-Kola inlet area – two missions completed with radar scope photography being obtained in the first missions and visual photography being obtained on the second mission;
> b. Siberian area – four flights over Siberia, including coverage of Wrangel Island

and Vol; three of these flights obtained radarscope photography and the fourth obtained partial photographic coverage.[7]

According to Gen. Vladimir Abramov, former head of the Soviet Air Defence Corps (PVO) for the Kiel region in the 1950s, another overflight took place shortly after Soviet Aviation Day in August 1954, the airshow in which the US military attaché, Charles Taylor, first saw the new Soviet bomber, the Myasishchev Mi-4 Molot (NATO reporting-name 'Bison'). Abramov said:

> So he was present and was shown all sorts of new aircraft including Myasishchev's new plane. We demonstrated for him the take-off with booster rocket, so that it launched after only a few metres and soared into the skies. Three or four days later, either 21 or 22 August, there were three planes, probably RB-45s, Canberras or RB-47s. These planes intruded into the territory of the Soviet Union. I don't recall their exact routes. But they managed to escape back across the Black Sea and into Turkey where they landed. As a result quite a few heads were figuratively chopped off – those of the ground-based air defences and probably, as I recall, the commander for the air defences.

Gen. Horace Wade, a long-standing senior SAC officer, recalled two overflights in his oral history. Three RB-45Cs flying over Vladivostok after the end of the Korean War and an RB-47 flight, 'I have a feeling, that if the truth were known, there was a B-47 that was flown from Alaska across Russia and landed in Turkey.'[8] Detail is limited so it is hard to know whether these are references to identified overflights or additional ones.

In early 1956, two years after Hal Austin's flight, LeMay ordered an even more spectacular invasion of Soviet airspace. In April 1956, LeMay sent nine RB-47 photo-reconnaissance aircraft from the 26th Strategic Reconnaissance Wing, also stationed at Lockbourne AFB, up to Thule AFB in Greenland for a secret mission. The officer in charge was Gen. Hewitt 'Shorty' Wheless. The plan was to penetrate the northern region of the Soviet Union simultaneously over a broad front. In addition there were four electronic intelligence RB-47Es of the 55th Strategic Reconnaissance Wing offshore to monitor the response of the Soviet defences.

Col. Joe Gyulavics, now retired in Florida, was one of the 55th pilots:

> In 1956 we were sent up on a special mission. There were three or four crews of

the 55th SRW. I think we were sent to Alaska and landed in Greenland although it could have been the other way round.[9] Other 55th SRW pilots include Bob Hubbard,[10] Bert Barrett and Cosmo Grant. I think it was called 'Home Run'. The 26th SRW had a major, John Lappo, a flamboyant type. He was later court martialed for flying under a Mississippi bridge.

Gyulavics said that they were told they were unlikely to encounter any Soviet aircraft.

John Lappo now lives in Alaska.

In 1956 we were notified that we were going to go up to Thule, Greenland, for approximately forty-five days. I think we took nine airplanes up there. And we had the photo-recon capability, and they wanted pictures of targets to find out whether they were in exactly the same places that they thought. So we verified these by taking the pictures and getting the co-ordinates of the targets in Northern Russia. Flying out of Thule we almost always went right over the north pole and into Russia.[11]

It was Lappo who had the most exciting trip on that first mission. Because of thick cloud he overshot the target and needed to circuit again – causing a risky delay:

We went in there about 30 miles, solid overcast . . . So I asked the crew if they were with me on making that 360 degree turn and they told me, 'Well the General told us not to make a 360.' And I told them, 'Hey, if we don't get that target, he's going to have to send another airplane after it.'

The last plane out, he was closely pursued by MiGs and narrowly escaped being shot down.

I just poured the coal to it and started climbing at what we call buffet. When we were going too fast, the airplane would buffet. I just kept it at buffet. All the way and the co-pilot, of course, is the radar gunner. And he said, 'John, I got three targets back here. What should I do?' I said, 'When they get close enough, lock on them. And if they start firing, just fire back. But wait for my order for it.' And we went out there, I can't tell you time-wise, but we went out there long enough that he had them at 3,000 yards and locked on. And it was a short time after that they broke off, and went on back . . . When we got back to Thule, the General said, 'John, we told you not to make that 360,' and I explained to him why I did. And he said, 'Well you should not have, but I wish I had a squadron of you.' Consequently I felt better.

In a massive secret operation, nine SAC aircraft penetrated Soviet airspace three times in one month to take their photographs. 'When the missions were over we were given awards as a unit. It was not publicised, it was played down, because it was, at the time, it was high tension and not the time to mention stuff like that,' said another RB–47 captain who took part in the operation, Col. Richard McNab.

There is no doubt that these flights did take place. There are too many recollections by the participants to put the operation in doubt. Gen. Goodpaster was responsible for giving Eisenhower's approval for overflights. I asked him about these missions.

> I would be astounded a) that it happened, and b) that I don't remember it if it did happen. And I do think that I would have known, because that was my job. I was the Defence Liaison Officer in Eisenhower's office. And I doubt that the Air Force would have ventured into anything like that on their own. That's why I say it's astounding to me to hear reports that such flights did in fact occur.

It is possible that Goodpaster's memory is faulty. There is only one documentary reference, discovered so far, which may deal with these operations. In Goodpaster's notes of a meeting in the White House in May 1956 with the President in which General Twining was present, there is mention of a Soviet protest over the flights.[12] It said:

> The President indicated he had wanted to have this meeting in order to see just what we are doing and how we are handling the matter of special reconnaissance flights. He referred to a recent protest by the USSR.[13] He said he wanted to give the Soviets every chance to move in peaceful directions and put our relations on a better basis – and see how far they will go. For this reason, during this period, it is particularly desirable to be careful in what we do. Mr Hoover [Under Secretary] read a draft text of a reply to the Soviets.[14] The President thought a passage might be added to the effect that our Government had instructed its aviation services to be especially careful in this regard (possibility of navigational error in Arctic regions).

The President next discussed certain other reconnaissance efforts. The conversation turned to an offer by the Soviets for Gen. Twining to attend the Red Aviation Day. Gen. Twining said the operation protested about has been stopped. All actions were completed. It was set up last February and conducted in recent weeks. There are tantalising references to other spy flights that have not been declassified: Project Heart Throb, a 1950 reconnaissance operation out of West Germany, Operation 21 using B–29s, and other B–36 missions over China. By 1956 the pace of military penetration flights of the Eastern Bloc was gathering momentum. But was there a hidden agenda for these flights?

8
STRANGELY STRANGELOVE

Why did LeMay order these overflights? He had good intelligence reasons, a need for photographic and radar reconnaissance as well as hard evidence on how effective Soviet defences were. One former senior SAC General recently said the RB-47 missions were essential. He said that not only did they fly the bombing approaches, they photo-mapped the USSR west of Moscow. The Germans had pretty good photo-maps of USSR as far as Moscow but after that it was terra incognita. 'Eventually satellites showed that some SAC targets were off by four or five miles,' he said.

A more controversial interpretation is that LeMay was putting into action a secret air force plan that overflights could be used to force the USSR into a 'put up or shut up' confrontation while it was still militarily inferior.[1] Ordering the overflights, LeMay was probably the prime mover, but it is unlikely he acted alone. He probably did do these operations with the tacit agreement of at least some of the Joint Chiefs of Staff. Certainly the little documentation that does exist on these flights would make this seem likely.

To get some idea of LeMay's thinking one has to look at the wider political context. LeMay had a reputation as a first class air force officer. He was also a hard-line hawk, very conservative and an ardent anti-communist. Gen. LeMay was very careful in his public statements on US strategy not to overstep the constraints imposed on a serving military officer into the realm of the overtly political. This would have brought him into direct conflict with his political bosses. The American military have it drummed it into them that one of the national strengths is civilian control over the armed forces.

As we have seen in the previous chapter, Eisenhower's defence aide from 1954, Gen. Goodpaster said, 'President Eisenhower, on a number of occasions, said that he was not going to have members of the armed forces flying over the Soviet Union. That amounted to an act of war.'[2] There is no document that clarifies the line of command for approval of military reconnaissance missions that crossed communist borders. Research by Robert S. Hopkins III seems to suggest that the JCS and regional commanders had authority to authorise flights within the USAF.[3] Some flights certainly seem to have had this level of approval. There is some suggestion that Eisenhower let the military undertake its own missions.[4]

When Don Welzenbach was researching the history of overflights for the CIA he was told that LeMay may have exceeded his authority. He said:

> We did not see any documentation to this effect. But there was a lot of rumour and there were a lot of overflights. Well it's unclear just how many there were. There is very little record of official overflights, that is of being authorised by the President [Eisenhower]. The President was very stern and strict with authorising overflights and I believe that there must have been overflights that did not have official authorisation.[5]

Since this interview, Welzenbach's own research has led him to the conclusion that there are permissions for the overflights – they just have not been uncovered in the archives.

Did LeMay have a secret agenda for these missions whether presidentially approved or not? An important clue comes from a secret air force project. At the time the dominant view in the military was that the communists in line with Marxist-Leninist doctrine were hell bent on 'world domination' and war. They viewed Stalin's support of the North Korean attack on South Korea as the first step on this road. According to the military view it was just a matter of time before the Soviets would foreclose on Berlin, march across the Elbe River into West Germany and on to France, while the Chinese would march across the Yalu and finish the job it had started in 1950. Mao's army would also launch an amphibious landing against Taiwan. All this would be initiated by a massive nuclear attack by the Red air force.

With the arrival of Eisenhower in the White House in 1953, American national policy became the doctrine of 'massive retaliation' in the case of Soviet attack. 'Massive retaliation' was a response and therefore a passive stance in the face of escalating Soviet involvement across the world.[6] Early in his presidency Eisenhower made the now famous remark, 'The only thing worse than losing a global is winning one.'[7] The historian, Richard H. Immerman says:

Even though Eisenhower would later contradict himself on this point, I believe that he basically meant what he said. Consequently, he never considered the nuclear option viable, except in the sense that one considers suicide viable.[8]

For a country reputedly gearing for the launch of global warfare the Soviet Union's progress was slow. In 1954 the Soviets would have needed a month to deliver their arsenal of about 150 atomic bombs. By comparison LeMay's crews could deliver as many as 750 bombs in a few hours. LeMay had no interest in a graduated response to a Soviet attack. The SAC commander believed the most effective attack would be his 'Sunday Punch', a total all-out assault from all sides with everything in the stockpile.

At the time, some commentators were suspicious that LeMay and other military commanders thought Eisenhower was too soft on the Soviets and wanted to force a confrontation. By 1953 the concept of preventive war was at the height of its popularity in Pentagon and CIA circles. This was the idea that the US should launch a nuclear attack on the Soviet Union while it was still weak in the nuclear stakes and before the USSR had time to overtake the West and mount its own inevitable attack from a position of strength. The idea of preventive war emerged immediately after the end of World War 2. As Brookings Institution[9] research has pointed out, attacking the Soviet Union was being seriously discussed in the Truman administration as early as 1946.[10] It was expressed by the head of the Manhattan Project, Gen. Leslie Groves and also by Gen. Spaatz.

On 25 August 1950 at Boston Navy Yard, Secretary of the Navy Francis Matthews gave a speech which contained what was perhaps the most direct endorsement of preventive war. He stated that the United States should be willing to pay any price to achieve a world at peace, 'even the price of instituting a war to compel co-operation for peace'. The next day Secretary of State Acheson issued a complete disavowal of the remarks and said it did not represent national policy. It is said that Truman rang Matthews and gave him a firm talking to but did not fire him.[11]

Just a few days later, USAF Gen. Orvil Anderson, Commandant of the Air War College, was quoted in the *Montgomery Advertiser* in which he advocated a form of preventive war:

Give me the order to do it and I could break up Russia's five A-bomb nests in a week. And when I went up to Christ I think I could explain to Him why I wanted to do it – now – before it is too late. I think I could explain to him that I had saved civilisation.[12]

Anderson was fired.[13]

In spring 1953, Operation 'Solarium', a think-tank set up by President Eisenhower, had come up with a series of proposals for dealing with the USSR. One 'task force' was set the job of formulating the most aggressive plan. They proposed giving the Russians a two-year deadline to come to terms with the West. This required curtailing any expansionist policies. If they failed to do so they would be attacked.

Eisenhower was fundamentally against the concept of any form of preventive war. The updated Basic National Security Policy of the 'New Look' stated: 'The United States and its allies must reject the concept of Preventive war or acts intended to provoke war.' The wider conclusions of 'Solarium' were also instrumental in the new national defence policy, *NSC-162/2*, which emphasised reliance on nuclear weapons. However, according to Professor Tami Davis Biddle, despite Eisenhower's official policy, 'the rhetoric of the Eisenhower administration seemed to imply that it would chart a course of greater assertiveness in both areas.'[14]

The policy of massive retaliation was applied by SAC as 'city busting' or nation killing. The majority of their targets were Soviet cities where they could destroy industry or military sites and collect the 'bonus' of civilian casualties.

Publicly LeMay later denied that he had been in favour of Preventive War. In his autobiography he raises the subject out of the blue in two pages that appear to answer an unasked question. It is limited but still revealing:

> There was, definitely, a time when we could have destroyed all of Russia (I mean by that, all of Russia's capability to wage war) without losing a man to their defences.
>
> The only losses incurred would have been the normal accident rate for the number of flying hours which would be flown to do the job.
>
> This period extended from before the time when the Russians achieved The Bomb, until after they had The Bomb but didn't yet own a stockpile of weapons.
>
> During that same era their defences were at a low ebb. As for their offensive capacity: not one bomb or missile, in that day, could have hit the United States.
>
> We at SAC were the first to perceive this potential. We had constructed it to that point, and had our weapons ready.
>
> Certainly I never notified our President that we could do this. That wasn't my duty. The Chief of Staff of the Air Force could recognise the extend of our power, and before very long the Joint Chiefs of Staff knew it also.

. . . There are stories still current that on one occasion I called a meeting and pulled in a number of key personnel who weren't even related to SAC, and closed the doors and put this proposition up to them as a suggestion. They story goes that strong men trembled in their boots, and went quivering out of the place, white-faced at my bellicose statements.

I don't ever remember calling such a meeting. What I may have done was say to some of our own people at one time or another 'We've got this capability. Maybe the Nation ought to do it.' I might have said that, off the cuff. But never did I make any such formal suggestion.

LeMay did not like the passivity of massive retaliation. He seems to have thought it unmanly.

Always I felt a more forceful policy would have been the correct one for us to embrace with the Russians, and in our confrontation of their program for World Communism. In the days of the Berlin Air Lift I felt the same way. I wasn't alone in that regard, either. General Lucius B. Clay concurred in the belief.

I can't get over the notion that when you stand up and act like a man, you win respect . . . though perhaps it's only a fearful respect which leads eventually to compliance with your wishes. It's when you fall back shaking with apprehension, that you are apt to get into trouble.[15]

The influential and hawkish newspaper columnist Joe Alsop enjoyed a flirtation with Preventive War. He later wrote, 'I like to recall the four men I know to have advocated preventative war, simply because they seem such an improbable group. They were, in England, Sir Winston Churchill and Bertrand Russell, who was very vocal about preventative strikes until the Soviets broke the American monopoly on nuclear weapons; the ferociously tough air force general Curtis LeMay, who did not quite admit it but did nonetheless advocate it: and John Paton Davies, (a State Dept official) who does admit it, as far as I know, to this day.'[16]

Other air force commanders of the period indicated that they did not discount preventive war. In his book *Design for Survival*, LeMay's long-time deputy, Gen. Thomas Power compared the reluctance to talk about preventive war as the same that had once been experienced about cancer, sex and mental illness. 'By the same token, I consider it important for the American people to understand the implications of Preventive War and, through frank and open discussion, correct many misconceptions that exist.[17] Gen. Twining said in his book, 'I am not an advocate of "Preventive War", but believe it obvious that we must take a hard look at our political-military strategy.'[18]

While rejecting preventive war, Eisenhower did however agree to the principle of pre-emptive strike, a subtle distinction in the times of crisis. If the Russians were about to attack, SAC was authorised to attack first. What constituted an attack was not clearly laid out. A warlike action or reaction by the Soviets would have probably been enough.[19] One of the most provocative warlike actions by the Soviets would have been the intrusion of spy flights into the US.

By late 1953 LeMay was one of a handful of people aware of a radical new concept to use reconnaissance aircraft in a new role – no longer just as strategic intelligence gatherers but as tools of global-political strategy. In 1953 LeMay was in close contact with a USAF Colonel called Raymond Sleeper, then at the Air War College.[20] LeMay had known Sleeper since the Pacific War and regarded him as a first class thinker.

From 1948 Sleeper was aware that Truman's leading strategists, George Keenan and Charles Bohlen, two of the State Department's leading foreign policy advisers, had strongly expressed dissent about the policy of using nuclear bombs on the Soviet Union in time of crisis. This reaction convinced the Colonel that a serious gap existed between US military thinking and the goals that were being set by political leaders. He was looking for a new proactive doctrine whereby the air force could be used to rein back the Soviet Union without an initial nuclear attack. Sleeper had an inspiration for confronting the Soviets by refining a technique mastered in the early days of aerial warfare. It was developed from the RAF's successful use in Iraq during the 1930s of air power to keep dissident tribal populations under control.

This technique called 'Air Control' was a very cost effective way of dealing with an otherwise dangerous and difficult enemy by striking at his food supply and local support. The sequence of events was simple. If a local chieftain made trouble an RAF aircraft would fly over an area and drop leaflets saying that unless the dissidents desisted then their villages and fields would be bombed on a specific date. The RAF was as good as its word. If the chieftain had not made his peace with the British local government officer, aircraft would bomb the villages and fields on the day prescribed. After this technique had been applied a few times the tribesmen became increasingly reluctant to cause trouble. It was a cheap solution to a difficult problem.

Sleeper's idea – Project Control – was a modernisation and exponential escalation of this strategy. He explained that US forces should surround the Soviet Union, right up to the borders. This would be accompanied by a political ultimatum that would be delivered to insist that the Soviets emasculate themselves both politically and territorially. Sleeper suggested these demands could include:

- Acceptance by the USSR and her satellites of Locarno-type non-aggression pacts offered by the US and NATO; signing of peace treaties with Germany and Austria; Soviet withdrawal from Germany and agreement to unification; Soviet withdrawal from East European satellite nations.
- Acceptance by the USSR and China of a Locarno-type pact for the Far East, wherein China would abrogate her treaties with the Soviet Union and would become a recognised member of the United Nations (Formosa would retain independence); signing by the USSR and China of the Japanese peace treaty.
- Establishment of independent popularly-elected governments in the former Soviet satellite states of Eastern Europe.
- Dissolution of the Cominform.
- Acceptance by Eastern Bloc nations of United Nations plans for limitation, inspection and regulation of armament manufacture.
- Cessation of Soviet propaganda in the United States.
- Acceptance of freedom of world travel and world information.
- Release of all political and military prisoners from the Soviet Union.

Tami Davis Biddle said:

While these goals look almost ridiculously ambitious today, they do form what might have been a true 'wish list' for foreign policy-makers in 1953. In setting out such ambitious goals, Sleeper expressed his overwhelming faith in the potential of air power. He held that the terms themselves would remain consistent, while the enforcement mechanisms would gain in intensity. He wanted to insure that terms 'be clearly communicated to all groups of the enemy nations in media permitting no misunderstanding'. And he suggested that, 'Administrative procedures whereby the control groups of the enemy nations could signify their assent to US terms should be established and made known to the enemy.'[21]

The first step in moving the Soviet Union toward these goals was to be the 'persuasion phase'. This was Sleeper's new approach to combining political goals with military capability. The persuasion phase, which would begin immediately, was based on the knowledge that the US would have, 'until at least July 1957, superiority over the Soviet Union in atomic and thermonuclear weapons as well as the capacity to deliver these weapons'. The USSR would recognise and react to that fact. Persuasion was defined as 'the employment of air power in conjunction with other forces against a potential enemy to the extent that he will negotiate terms and behave politically in a manner which will accord with United States national policy.'

The explanation of the persuasion phase was filled with references to 'taking the initiative'. For example, 'The flexibility of the concept gives the initiative to the United States since it permits the direct application or political persuasion, supported by the other elements of United States power, to the core of the world problem, Soviet Russia.' Persuasion operations were to increase gradually in intensity, and were also to provide intelligence and communications information which would be useful if escalation to pressure operations were required.

The persuasion phase involved a number of operations designed to exploit the capability of air power. The first of these was a 'forward air patrol operation' which would extend the air defence of the United States against Soviet air attack from across the Arctic region – in other words to move US aerial frontiers as far forward as the northern borders of the USSR. There were two key tasks involved: establishing an airborne early warning line between Alaska and Iceland over the Polar Cap, and providing interceptor escort to the airborne early warning aircraft within range of US Arctic bases. The goals of the patrol were to extend early warning, to provide intelligence, and to force the Soviets on the defensive when faced with US surveillance of their northern air operations.

Absolutely key to this initial phase was the use of 'persuasive reconnaissance offensive', where reconnaissance aircraft would fly over the USSR to demonstrate the Russians' military impotency. The proposal states:

> By initiating persuasive reconnaissance the United States will progress from a defensive posture – which implies that it will strike back only when the enemy has already struck – to an offensive posture. United States air power will be employed in a dynamic role, since it will show readiness to take positive actions and provide knowledge of the location, disposition, and activity of the enemy air force.

If the Soviets resisted the demands of the persuasion phase, Project Control would move on to the next or 'pressure' phase. This phase was a blueprint to instigate war against the Soviets. Sleeper placed great emphasis on keeping the initiative, in terms of striking the first blow in a nuclear war.

In discussing the transition between the persuasion and pressure phases, Sleeper rejected any prohibition against the United States striking a first blow against the Soviet Union. In defence of his ideas he used the metaphor of a wild west gunfighter to explain how there might be a precedent for redefining the terms 'aggression' and 'self-defense'. Sleeper listed certain Soviet 'aggressive acts' which might assist the start of the pressure phase being presented a way as to help 'justify possible US actions'. For example, an act of aggression capable of triggering the pressure phase was considered to be 'any deployment and preparation of forces with the intent of launching weapons of mass destruction.' Thus if intelligence sources detected a Soviet preparation to launch, the US would be justified in acting first. In his proposals Sleeper made a revealing comment:

> Any nation that persists in the development and production of military force capable of threatening the existence of the Free World and whose political actions and stated national intent leaves no doubt that she intends to use that military force to conquer or subjugate free countries should be considered as an aggressor who is preparing to commit an aggressive act against the Free World.

A vital part of the pressure phase was the 'strategic atomic offensive'. The authors of Project Control assumed that because of the reconnaissance operations of the persuasion phase, they would have more targeting information available to them than would otherwise be the case, and therefore priority targets tended to be military. Soviet airfields and ports were the target set which would be concentrated on first. If the initial strike was not enough to bring about Soviet capitulation, a second target set would be chosen and hit.[22]

Col. Sleeper said that LeMay was a big supporter of Project Control and Sleeper spoke or flew to see LeMay several times a month during this period. 'LeMay told me that he carried around a summary of the plan wherever he went,' Sleeper told the author before he died in 1995.[23] The summary is still classified.

Sleeper obtained enormous resources to produce Project Control. Dozens of air force officers and civilians were involved and it is said to have cost several millions of dollars. The plan never became policy. Ray

Garthoff, then of RAND and now of Brookings Institution, was briefed by Sleeper and not impressed. He said that it was not considered in the national character to take such an aggressive pose. It was considered to have too many wrong assumptions about the previous success of Air Control. Also it was hard to see how, if the 'persuasion' phase failed, the 'pressure' phase could be anything but war and ultimately a nuclear exchange. If they behaved aggressively they would be subject to attack. Sleeper believed it would never need to go that far because the Soviets would back down.

After a series of briefings in Washington, shortly after the overflight of Hal Austin's aircraft over the Kola Peninsula, Sleeper was called to brief the Air Force World Wide Commanders' Conference at Eglin AFB, Florida, on 24 May 1954. The elite air force leadership was present – Gens. LeMay, Norstad, White, Partridge, Twining and Weyland. The Chairman of the Joint Chiefs of Staff, Adm. Arthur W. Radford, was also briefed on the concept. He believed that Project Control's proposals should be pushed all the way to the White House. The RAF's leading theoretician Sir John Slessor was briefed on the project.[24]

Sleeper's project received exposure at senior levels within the USAF, Pentagon, CIA and even in the Eisenhower administration. It never became official policy because of Eisenhower's resistance. Since then there has been a subsequent tendency to forget or play down Project Control as unlikely theory. Given the amount of interest it elicited at the time one can only assume that the military does not now like to admit that such an aggressive philosophy once abounded.[25]

LeMay's autobiography makes a clear reference to Project Control without naming it:

> It would have been possible, I believe, for America to say to the Soviets 'Here's a blueprint for your immediate future. We'll give you a deadline of five or six months' – something like that – 'to pull out of the satellite countries, and effect a complete change of conduct. You will behave your damn selves from this moment forth.'
>
> We could have done this. But whether we should have presented such a blueprint was not for me to decide. That was a question of national policy.
>
> All I can repeat is: at the time, we could have done the job as described. Whether we should have done it then or not, when you're quarterback – I don't know. You can discuss the pros and cons of such a situation from now until Doomsday. You might argue whether it would be desirable to present such a challenge to the Russians, even at this [1965] stage of the game.
>
> It is not something for the military to say. It is for our Administration to say.

Repeat: the Soviets did not possess the might to affect us in retaliation at the time.[26]

One of the most remarkable aspects of LeMay's continued fascination with Project Control is that he simply ignored one of the most damning pieces of evidence against the project. For over a year in real time in the 1954 period, Project Control was wargamed by the Air War College. The wargame suddenly ended when the 'Red' team (acting the part of the Soviets) launched a nuclear attack on the 'Blue' side (acting the US part). The attack was provoked as a result of overflights.[27] Yet LeMay had not even started his full blown and real overflight campaign at this point. The expression of the dangers of aggressive overflights could not have been more clearly spelt out.

If the project did not make it into official policy many of its elements did. One significant aspect of Project Control is that it was the first time it was fully realised that reconnaissance was no longer just a military tool but was now potentially a global strategic tool. It was a statement of power, even a means of compulsion or intimidation. Much later one of LeMay's officers. Maj.-Gen. George J. Keegan was to say of the importance of reconnaissance, 'You can have no idea how big this is. Reconnaissance and its elements have become an immense source of power and control. It's at the centre of the maelstrom.'[28]

When LeMay ordered deep penetration flights like Austin's reconnaissance missions, he must have known that they would be perceived as potential acts of war and might even be perceived as nuclear attacks. LeMay must have known about Eisenhower's reluctance over such flights. Edwin Land and James Killian discussed the embryonic U-2 project with LeMay in November 1954. They explained it would be able to fly deep into Russia. LeMay responded, 'You'll never get the President to agree that sort of thing.'[29] LeMay was also fully aware of the whole concept of Project Control. It would seem likely that Project Control was in his mind when he ordered the missions and it cannot be discounted that he was trying to force the Russians into a major hostile response.

Hal Austin's account of LeMay's comments during the pre-mission briefing is revealing:

Well, I don't know whether it is appropriate to say or not. Of course, the old man's dead now, God rest his soul. But back at the briefing at SAC headquarters he said, 'Well, maybe if we do this overflight right, we can get World War Three started.' I think that was just a loose comment, for his staff guys, because General [Thomas] Power was his hatchet man in those days, and he chuckled and General Power never laughed very much, so I always figured that was kind of a joke between them in some way or another. But we thought maybe that was serious.

If Austin thought at the time LeMay's comment might be a dark joke, over thirty years later he discovered it was not:

In the late 1980s I was involved with the Air Force Village West retirement community near Los Angeles. LeMay was the chairman of the board, and I was on the board for a while. He used to come in my office, sit down, and he'd been there a number of times before I brought up the subject of the mission we had flown. And he apparently remembered it like it was yesterday. We chatted about it a little bit. His comment there again was, 'Well, we'd have been a hell of a lot better off if we'd got World War Three started in those days.' Of course he doesn't know that the Cold War is over now but he made that comment one day. Maybe we'd all have been better off if we'd got it over with then. Well, who knows, we'll never know because history didn't go that way.

LeMay also incorporated other aspects of Project Control into his philosophy gradually tightening the iron ring on the Soviets. In June 1954 a decision was taken to establish the Distant Early Warning (DEW) Line which was designed to counter jet bombers, and which evolved into a line of radar stations from Greenland to north-western Canada. Ultimately the DEW line would give two to six hours' warning of the approach of Soviet bombers.

As soon as SAC was capable it began to increase the number of nuclear-armed bombers flying around the Soviet Union. In 1957 a proportion of SAC's bombers went onto a constant state of alert ready to take off within fifteen minutes. By the early 1960s this was to developed to the point that at any one time twelve SAC aircraft were in the air on airborne alert ready to attack the USSR at a moment's notice. SAC's missile network was also growing and ready for fast launch.

9
OPEN SKIES

While LeMay thought about Project Control, Eisenhower was concerning himself dealing with the Soviets in front of the world. At the Geneva summit conference of July 1955 he made an offer to the Soviet side called 'Open Skies'. Before the summit Ike had gathered some of his best advisers at Quantico and asked for suggestion of innovative proposals to be made. 'Open Skies' had been one of these.

Gen. Goodpaster said:

> Nelson Rockefeller established a small group down at Quantico to look into any new and innovative ideas that people might have. As I recall it, Prof. Max Millikan, of the Massachusetts Institute of Technology, came up with the idea of 'Open Skies'. Nelson Rockefeller began to have that investigated. He brought that to my attention, to bring to Eisenhower's attention, which I did.

The idea was that both sides would be free to overfly the other to monitor the other's nuclear and military developments. It was put forward as a first step towards arms reduction and was the beginnings of the idea of 'transparency'.

Goodpaster was present at Geneva:

> Well, initially, at the session Bulganin responded. Bulganin was the titular, the nominal head of the Soviet delegation, and he said something along the lines, 'Well, this is very interesting, but of course it will have to be studied carefully.' A temporising response. When we broke up to go into the tea, which always followed the afternoon meeting, I do recall that Khrushchev came up to Eisenhower and said, 'No, no, no, no, no.' I think he said it in English, but it might have been, 'Niet, niet, niet, niet, niet.' In any case, Eisenhower said, at that moment, we knew who was in charge in the Soviet delegation.

Goodpaster said they were disappointed by the response:

> But at least it was on the record, and the idea had been put forward, that it would give greater confidence to both sides if they were more fully informed of the actions of the other. But on their side secrecy is more than a fetish, it was an obsession, it was a principle with them, that they had to maintain secrecy in everything that they did, in the field of security.

Nikita Khrushchev had rejected the 1955 Open Skies proposal, according to his son, Sergei, because he believed the Americans were 'really looking for targets for a war against the USSR. When they understand that we are defenceless against an aerial attack, it will push the Americans to begin the war earlier . . . . (and) if in this fear of each other the Americans realized that the Soviet Union would become stronger and stronger, but was weak now, this (intelligence) might push them into a preventive war.' The event triggered Kremlin orders for new surface-to-air missiles and high performance fighters, and accelerated work to perfect an ICBM.[1]

In 1993 the Russian historian Col. Orlov, a former Soviet officer and historian, said the Soviets had good reason to refuse the offer:

> 'Open Skies' was rejected because in those days Khrushchev was playing a game of bluff. He made public statements which claimed that the Soviet Union was absolutely equal and not lagging behind although in reality we had to make great efforts to overtake or even to equal with Americans.[2]

LeMay and the other USAF chiefs did not like Eisenhower's 'New Look' reduced defence programme and behind the scenes campaigned against it. The main plank of their attack was the 'bomber gap', the idea that the Soviet Union was overtaking the US in the number and quality of its long-range strategic nuclear air force.

Two events had given rise to this idea that such a gap was occurring. The first was the defection in 1948 of Soviet air force officer, Lt-Col. G.A. Tokaev. He said that the Politburo was putting a high priority on a long-range air force. The second had its origins in one of the few occasions that the US military got to see new Soviet aircraft officially. At the 1947 Soviet Aviation Day Parade at Tushino air base the Soviets produced a new four-propeller bomber – the Tupolev Tu-4 (NATO reporting-name 'Bull'). This was the aircraft that had been reverse engineered from the B-29, examples of which had made emergency landings in 1944 on Soviet territory following missions against Japan, and so fallen into Soviet hands. From then on the USAF expected a rapidly increasing strategic bomber force threatening mainland USA.

According to the hawks, this would occur as soon as the Soviets had supremacy in their long-range air force (*Dalnaya Aviatsiya*). The USAF predicted this was going to occur sooner rather than later and used its own estimates to press for an enormous increase in funds. When

Eisenhower resisted this he was subjected to attacks from the media. It is generally accepted that much of this was sourced by the air force.

From his experiences in World War 2, Eisenhower understood the importance of aerial reconnaissance. After taking office in 1953 he often made a point of talking with Gen. George Goddard, the expert in the discipline. When meeting CIA analysts, Goddard quoted Eisenhower concerning good intelligence:

> Without it you would have only your fears on which to plan your own defense arrangements and your whole military establishment. Now if you're going to use nothing but fear and that's all you have, you are going to make us an armed camp. So this kind of knowledge is vital to us.[3]

The spark for the full blown bomber gap crisis occurred when the US military attaché was present at the 1954 Mayday parade when a new bomber appeared as part of the parade. This was the Myasishchev M-4 Molot, a multi jet-engined bomber, which apparently had intercontinental range, that would be known to NATO as 'Bison'. Then at the 1955 Mayday parade appeared the massive Tupolev Tu-95 code-named 'Bear'. Unlike its American counterparts it used huge turboprop engines instead of jets. It had an enormous 50m wingspan. A National Intelligence Estimate (NIE) dated 15 May 1955 put the strength of Soviet bombers capable of reaching the US at 600 by 1959 (half of them 'Bisons' and half 'Bears') but later in the year, at the Aviation Day flypast of 13 July 1955, the American air attaché reported seeing ten 'Bisons' flying-by, then nine and then another nine.[4]

A popular account is that the air force observer at Soviet Air Force Day, Col. Charles E. Taylor, had witnessed the same 'Bisons' flying over once then round in a circle out of his sight and then back again. However as Fred Kaplan has pointed out, there is no evidence for this story.[5]

Air force intelligence reasoned that the Soviets must have twice that number built, which meant that the Soviets must be turning them out at twice the rate previously estimated. Accordingly US estimates were revised upwards, to put the number of 'Bisons' alone in service by 1960 at 600. The air force promptly leaked the alarming news to the press to help force upon Eisenhower a large-scale bomber construction programme. Eisenhower was highly suspicious of the air force's estimates, but was trapped by the level of public alarm. The Pentagon fed gloom and doom prophecies to all who would listen. Its aim was to keep escalating funding. In April 1956 the Democrat Stuart Symington, who was chairman of a Senate subcommittee on air power, and an ally of LeMay, began to hold hearings on the issue. Both the air force Chief of Staff Gen. Nathan F. Twining and SAC Commander-in-Chief Gen. LeMay testified that the United States would trail the Soviets in bomber production by 1958/60.[6]

In such hearings LeMay had always liked to portray the Soviet bear as ready to strike at any moment with forces that were already bigger than the US and growing fast. As a result SAC was voted funds to maintain the most amazing armed vigilance the world had ever known.

The CIA was a participant in the bomber gap controversy. All NIEs have the Director of Central Intelligence's stamp of authority on them as the job of DCI includes assimilating and circulating intelligence produced by the service arms. SAC's Gen. LeMay was able to say that the CIA backed his findings when presenting alarmist charts on the bomber gap at hearings before Congress in 1956.[7] Defense Secretary Charles Wilson, fronting for the aggrieved Eisenhower, held press conferences to assert that US bomber capability was up to the job, but Congress and the press were helping keep the air force campaign on target. Through a series of leaks via favoured press men and senators the American public were scared into believing that the Soviets were outstripping the US in nuclear bombers. This placed a lot of pressure on President Eisenhower massively to increase the USAF budget. The eventual result was an astronomical increase of $928.5 million in the air force's FY1957 budget and Eisenhower was obliged to build more B-52s than he wanted.

Whether LeMay really believed in the bomber gap, or saw it as a way of getting funds quickly to prepare the USAF for later confrontation, it is hard to know. All LeMay's public pronouncements at the time are four-square behind the gap. But his strategy had helped to turn the air force from younger brother of the armed forces to the dominant budget player.

The lesson of Japan's surprise attack on Pearl Harbor on 7 December 1941 was deeply etched on the American psyche and none more than on the mind of President Eisenhower. On 27 March 1954 he disclosed, to a plenary session of the Science Advisory Committee, the discovery of the 'Bison' bombers. He immediately raised the question whether these new long-range bombers could be used in a surprise attack against mainland United States. Fear of a Soviet surprise attack raged among the administration and public in those years.

During his presidency, Eisenhower set up several committees to examine the surprise attack question. In late 1956 Eisenhower formed a new committee of top civilian experts and businessmen under the leadership of Rowan H. Gaither to investigate potential civil and continental attack. One of their tasks was to evaluate the possibility of such a Soviet surprise attack. It was deemed that by protecting SAC from Soviet first strike by defensive means would reduce the probability of the Soviets contemplating such an attack.

At the time it was estimated that there would be less than half an hour notice of obliteration by the Reds. SAC made a big virtue in public of their ability to react within minutes and launch a reciprocal attack on the communist world. Some months into the inquiry the Gaither committee decided to test SAC's readiness. One of the leading members of the committee, Robert C. Sprague of the Sprague Electrical Company, flew with LeMay to NORAD where a full scale SAC alert was called.

Twenty-five years later Sprague told author Fred Kaplan a remarkable story. Much to Sprague's surprise it took SAC six hours to get his aircraft off the ground. Even more surprising LeMay seemed unconcerned at this performance. Sprague confronted LeMay and was taken into a secret.

LeMay calmly replied that it didn't scare him. He told Sprague that the United States had aircraft flying missions over the Soviet Union 24 hours a day, picking up all sorts of intelligence information, mostly communications intelligence from Soviet military transmissions. LeMay explained that as he had reconnaissance aircraft constantly circling the USSR he would have a great deal of warning of Soviet preparations for an attack.[8] He offered to take Sprague into the office where this data was sent and stored. He said, 'all those statements the Soviets periodically made about American spy planes penetrating Russian airspace were true. We always said the incidents were accidental but they were not; they were very deliberate.'

This episode had one more remarkable feature. LeMay told Sprague: 'If I see that the Russians are amassing their planes for an attack I'm going to knock the shit out of them before they take off the ground.' Sprague was even more astonished that LeMay would order a pre-emptive strike against Soviet air bases. 'But General LeMay,' Sprague said, 'that's not national policy.'

'I don't care,' LeMay replied. 'It's my policy. That's what I am going to do.'[9] Jerome Weisner of MIT, who was also present, recalled the comment as being, 'It's my job to make it possible for the President to change his policy', a slightly less aggressive comment.

Either way it was a chilling remark as by 1957 LeMay was in the unique position of being able to launch a SAC nuclear strike with no outside constraints. He had wrested control of nuclear weapons from the AEC. And as defence expert Bruce Blair has shown there were no physical restraints on such a launch.[10] 'Fail Safe' devices like Permissive Action Links (PALs) did not come into service until the late 1960s.

According to Richard Rhodes:

> SAC was subject to Presidential authority. The Constitution authorised the President, not the SAC commander when to order the use of military force. But LeMay had decided at the beginning of the Korean War, if not before, that there were circumstances under which he would override the Commander-in-Chief's prerogative.[11]

10
IN THE CROW'S NEST

If LeMay was not worried about the possibility of surprise attack it was because of the intelligence coming from one key SAC unit. From the early 1950s the main electronic intelligence mission was given to the 55th Strategic Reconnaissance Wing ('the fighting 55th') who adopted the motto, 'We See All'. In the early years of the Cold War the USAF ELINT operations were a hotch potch. An early ELINT squadron, the 343rd SRS, was sent to Yokota AFB, Japan to assist in the Korean War. As well as monitoring the communist defences in Korea the 343rd flew missions for SAC. Shortly after the war SAC brought all its main reconnaissance units with an ELINT dimension under the 55th Strategic Reconnaissance Wing.[1]

On 24 February 1947 the unit had been reactivated as the 55th Reconnaissance Group (Very Long-Range, Mapping). As the unit's historian Bruce Bailey[2] said:

> The period from reactivation in 1947 till reactivation in 1950 is about as clear as an alcoholic's eyes. Official records tell one tale and another is told by orders and documents supplied by 55th members. From 1947 till after the Korean Police Action the status of the 55th was turbulent, to say the least. The group of people we associate with the early history of the 55th were bounced back and forth between four and five units due to activations, inactivation, war and transitions to different aircraft.[3]

Like USAF wings it comprised several squadrons:

> As we became more firmly established, it included the 338th squadron which was strictly weather and PR, that was the only reconnaissance they did. We were equipped with the RB-47E and RB-47K aircraft. [The latter was a B-47 modified for ELINT gathering and had a pressurised compartment for three specialists in the bomb bay.] Then you had the 38th squadron and the 343rd squadron, and these were strictly ELINT.

John 'Curly' Behrmann, a veteran of World War 2 USAF bombing missions over Germany, rejoined the USAF in 1950. He became a

'Crow' – the nickname given to the special operators who monitored the Soviet electronic signals:

> The Korean War started and there's Curly, back in the service. Well, now he's a 28-year-old, almost bald, second lieutenant, with a wife and four kids. And what are we going to do with him? So I go down to Shepherdfield, Texas, which was induction centre. I said, 'Well, I flew all the time and I'd like to keep flying.' Flight engineer?
>
> 'No, can't use you as a flight engineer, we still have a glut of them, a surplus from World War 2, so we can't put you into that, it's a commission job. You do not have specific training in that.'
>
> 'Well, what other flying jobs have you got available?'
>
> 'ECM.'
>
> 'What's that?'
>
> 'I don't know.' Hands me the book, sort of like somebody handing you a college brochure, you know, here's your courses. And ECM, Electronics Counter Measures, and it involves 14 months of school. Hey, anything that involves school, I'll go to go. So I went to electronics school.
>
> Well, what was special about the 55th, we were the only outfit in the Air Force that did what they call strategic electronic reconnaissance. Now, the Tactical Air Command had bombers that went out and looked for signals, but they were what you would call battlefield reconnaissance. Whereas the 55th were in this routine of strategic information. Basically bring as much as we can on the foreign capability, in defence, in gun laying, in everything. That's our job, find his radars, look for his radars, find out what the characteristics are, frequencies, pulse shapes, PRFs, rotation rates, all – everything that goes with it. And bring that information back. It goes to intelligence, intelligence collates it, puts it together with information from other sources, and from that hands it to the engineers to make jammers, to protect the bomber. And, this goes on whether it's peacetime, wartime or wherever, and it goes on all around the world, and we were the only squadron doing it. So you could say that way we were special.[4]

The 55th's missions were top secret. Behrmann again:

> They were secret in so far as the families, anybody we knew, other military people, nobody knew specifically what we did, and we didn't even tell them, 'I am looking for radar signals.' [If someone said] You flew secret missions, [you'd reply] 'What I'm doing is none of your business. Where I'm flying, how I'm flying, how long I fly, when I fly, all of that is none of your business.

Initially this task was relatively simple as the Russian radars of the early 1950s operated only in the VHF band (A-Band) and X-Band, while voice transmissions to fighters were in VHF only. But as ground radars proliferated they expanded into other areas of the electromagnetic spectrum and became increasing common in fighter aircraft. Behrmann:

Most of the equipment was in what had been the bomb bay; after all, these were bomber aircraft, not passenger airplanes. So they close the bomb bay and make it a crew compartment, and put electronic equipment in there with desks to sit at and work this equipment, and write your logs as you're working it. And no windows, so we could very well have been running around on a Greyhound bus, except that you were up in the air flying, but you had no visibility, nothing to look at, and you were just doing your job sitting in front of a console with a lot of electronic equipment to monitor and tune with, and run the recorders when you found a signal of interest.

And, while you were flying the missions, everybody was busy. Like, in the B-50s, we had six crows, and we had five in a row, and then the number six man was in the back compartment with one of the navigators, there just wasn't enough room, so he was put back there. It might be like a Norway mission for instance, it might be anything from an hour to ten hours, eight to ten hours, before you get to the area of interest.

By 1952 the ELINT mission had sorted itself out. The 55th was based at Forbes AFB where it was to stay for many years. The unit began to take delivery of RB-47 special ELINT aircraft. While they were not suitable for penetration flights, they were less vulnerable than Boeing RB-50s to conduct long distance border flights.

They flew their missions from forward bases including England, Turkey and Japan. Like most SAC units the 55th rotated its units to key air bases abroad, usually for about six months at a time, known as TDY. One of the key postings was the USAF base at Lakenheath near Cambridge. From there the 55th could monitor a vast area of the western and northern borders of the Eastern Bloc.

Curly Behrmann was frequently sent on TDY there. He describes a typical mission from the UK in the early 1950s:

You took-off with the tanker, usually a B-29. And you'd meet him up in Northern Norway, out over the ocean, but in that area, just before you're turning across the top of Norway. Fill up your airplane, he goes back, refuels, has crew rest, while you fly a mission along the Arctic border of Norway, around some of the islands. And then you'd come back, and again, over Northern Norway, you would catch this tanker, because there ain't no way you're going to get home without him. And then from there the tanker and you would fly back to good old Lakenheath.

'Crows' have a robust sense of humour. Curly Behrmann said:

There was a lot of kidding going on. We had naviguessers in front, and again, you didn't call them that all the time, but yes, they were naviguessers, they had to guess where they were going. And then you had the pilots, you know, the yank and bank guys. Somebody would throw a handful or corn or something, peanuts, something like that, 'and don't forget to take your pack lunch along', you know, a little bit of needling.

Bruce Bailey:

To make a Crow aircraft there was one final requirement – which is to make it excruciatingly uncomfortable. We carried so much additional equipment and tape-machines on an operational mission even crawl space or knee space was non-existent.

I was an electronic warfare officer, a 'raven', a 'crow'. And there were three ravens in the back of an RB-47, and the Raven One was the commander of the team back there, and these were the experienced people. When you went in new, you could be a Raven Two or a Three. The only distinguishing difference between a Raven Two and a Raven Three was the frequency bands that they covered. Raven Three would cover the lowest frequency bands, Raven Two the medium frequency bands, and Raven One the high frequency.

The medium frequency is where most of the intercept radars, and ground control radars and such were. Your low frequency was your early warning radars primarily, and missile guidance signals. The high frequency had the airborne intercept radars from the fighters, that was the primary function of the Raven One. But about the heaviest band was the medium band. And, as time went on, the low band became heavier and heavier, with the advent of the Tollkings, Boomrest, and several other key Soviet radars.[5]

One of the most important tasks of the 55th's ELINT crews was to find holes in the northern sector of the USSR, the route that most bombers would use during an attack. I asked Bruce Bailey whether there were many holes in the Soviet defences. His reply:

Oh, they used to say in the old days, it was just one big hole. And then they started to fill in the gaps very slowly. It seemed, even when they started to fill in the gaps, that their method was: OK, if we can put a few early warning radars up here and just get an idea that the bombers are coming, we won't worry about them until they get well in country, near the areas of interest, and at that point we'll defend against them. In the last few years of the operations, they started to beef up the northern territories more and more and more.

The ELINT missions found the Soviets had a rather unusual forward radar unit right up in the Arctic. Bailey, again:

They set up a camp there, and were operating an early warning station way out on an ice cap. And then we found another one, we found two, sitting way out there like that. So we started to photograph them regularly and watch them, and when

HQ SAC 'Peace is our Profession'. *National Archives*

General Curtis E. LeMay, Commander-in-Chief, Strategic Air Command (SAC), 1954. *National Archives*

General Thomas S. Power, Commander-in-Chief,
SAC, 1954–64. *National Archives*

General George Goddard, the father of US aerial
photography. *National Archives*

In this photograph taken in 1955, from left to right are pictured: General Nathan Twining USAF, Charles Wilson, Secretary for Defense, Donald Quarles, Secretary for the Air Force. *National Archives*

General Twining visited Moscow in June 1956, and is seen here surrounded by members of the Press Corps. *National Archives*

General LeMay (left) with Joe Charyk, Under-Secretary of the Air Force, pictured on 26 April 1960. *National Archives*

The leading US aerial reconnaissance expert, Richard C. Leghorn, seen here in 1959. *National Archives*

CONSOLIDATED PB-4Y2 PRIVATEER

The first US spyplane casualty of the Cold War was this US Navy Privateer, shot down on 8 April 1950 near Libau in the Baltic. It is pictured here at Gibraltar one month before the fateful incident. *Don Hubbard*

BOEING RB-50 SUPERFORTRESS
In the early 1950s a number of Boeing B-50 Superfortress bombers were converted to RB-50B standard for service with the strategic reconnaissance squadrons of SAC. *National Archives*

THE FIRST SUCCESSFUL AIR-TO-AIR REFUELLING OF A US JET BOMBER
An RB-45C Tornado of 91st SRW is pictured tanking from a Boeing KB-29 on 22 June 1951. *National Archives*

CONVAIR B-36 PEACEMAKER

One of the largest aircraft ever built and with a wingspan of 230ft, the B-36 was the first true inter-continental bomber, capable of striking at European targets from bases in the USA. Powered by six radial engines augmented by four turbojets, the B-36 was used in the long range stategic bombing role by SAC between 1948 and 1959. *National Archives*

Twenty-four B-36s were used in the strategic reconnaissance role and designated RB-36D. The aircraft was also used for a number of experimental programmes including the FICON (Fighter Conveyor) parasite fighter programme (GRB-36F illustrated, using a GRF-84F Thunderstreak). *National Archives*

BOEING RB-47 STRATOJET
By the mid-1950s the six-jet B-47 nuclear bomber was arguably the most important military aircraft in the West. When the Cold War was approaching its height towards the end of the 1950s, some 1,800 B-47s of all models were in service with SAC, including several hundred of the RB-47 reconnaissance variant. Assigned to the 55th SRW, 53-6245 (pictured) was an ERB-47H which was modified for oblique radar mapping and radio and radar monitoring. *National Archives*

MARTIN RB-57
Modelled on the English Electric Canberra twin-jet bomber, the Martin B-57 was licence-built in the USA and initially tasked as a tactical bomber, but was soon developed into a high altitude special reconnaissance aircraft for the USAF. Illustrated is the final high-altitude version built by General Dynamics, designated RB-57F, with a service ceiling of over 50,000ft. *National Archives*

LOCKHEED U-2

Entering service with the CIA in 1956, with a range of about 4,000 miles and a ceiling of 85,000ft (figures for U-2B) the U-2 was designed for high altitude, long range strategic reconnaissance flights over the Soviet Union. The aircraft soon acquired international notoriety with the shooting down of CIA pilot Gary Powers over the Soviet Union on 1 May 1960. *National Archives*

AVRO LINCOLN

The uprated successor to the wartime Lancaster bomber, the Lincoln was also used in a number of intelligence gathering roles. The Lincoln that was shot down on the East German border in March 1953 was an Air Gunnery School aircraft on a training mission when it strayed into the Russian zone. *British Aerospace*

ENGLISH ELECTRIC CANBERRA

An RAF Canberra is believed to have flown the overflight of the Kapustin Yar missile testing site in the Soviet Union. The aircraft illustrated is a PR7 which came into service with the RAF in late 1953. *British Aerospace*

DE HAVILLAND COMET

Crammed with top secret surveillance equipment, the De Havilland Comet 2R served with the RAF's No 51 Squadron in the ELINT role from the late 1950s. The Comet was eventually withdrawn from this role with the RAF in 1974, superseded by the specially equipped Hawker Siddeley Nimrod R1. This example, XK695, was preserved until recently at the Imperial War Museum, Duxford. *Paul Jackson*

MYASISHCHEV M-4 'BISON'
This Soviet heavy jet bomber was first seen at the May Day parade in Moscow in 1954. The 'Bison' was at the centre of the 'bomber gap', with the USAF predicting in 1955 that the Soviets would have 900 of this aircraft by 1959. In fact only 150 of the bomber version were produced. *National Archives*

TUPOLEV TU-16 'BADGER'
A Soviet jet strategic bomber that first came into service in 1954, the 'Badger' was also part of the 'bomber gap' scare. It later served mainly in ELINT, ECM and maritime reconnaissance roles. *National Archives*

TUPOLEV TU-95 'BEAR'
Most notable for its size, range and huge turboprop engines fitted with eight-bladed contra-props, the 'Bear' strategic bomber entered service in about 1954. This maritime reconnaissance version was intercepted off the coast of Alaska in 1968. *National Archives*

Wing Commander Johnny Baldwin RAF (pictured here as a squadron leader, DFC, late in the Second World War) was missing in action during the Korean War.

This was the first USAF F-86 Sabre to be captured by the Soviets during the Korean War, in October 1951. *via Russian Archives*

General Georgy Lobov, who commanded the Soviet 64th Fighter Air Corps during the Korean War in 1951–52.

Soviet MiG pilots and intelligence officers dressed in civilian clothes, Korea, 1951.

A group of MiG pilots caught in a flash-flood in Korea, 1951.

Aircrews of the 91st SRW pose for the camera in front of a RB–45C in the early 1950s.

Captain Charles E. McDonough USAF, pilot of the 91st SRW RB–45C, who was shot down and killed over Korea on 4 December 1950.

the spring thaw came, and the icecap started to thaw and break up a little, we watched it real regular, and they packed up the camp and went away and just left the old 'Kniferest' there, and when the ice melted, it fell through, it wasn't even worth you know, taking back, so they just sent them out there for the one season, to extend the early warning range, and then let them fall through the ice when it melted.

To make the communist air defences respond the ELINT crews often had to provoke a reaction. Aircraft would be flown straight at the border only turning at the last moment. Curly Behrmann said:

And occasionally we were briefed to fly a portion of the mission, and then by going low, or turning away or something, go down and then come straight in towards the border, whether it was over water or over land, usually over water. Come in very low and pop up all of a sudden to provide a sudden target for them. But this was a very seldom thing, I would say one percent, two percent of the time. It happened maybe a dozen times, that we'd do that, fly in, and hopefully come into a busy area and provoke a reaction where they would turn something on that maybe they were trying to not turn on in our presence. That was the hope you had, you know, that you'd found something new, which happened occasionally, and always made you feel very good, you know. So that was very basically the only reason and the only thing that it did, it was not a normal, everyday thing.

Bruce Bailey:

Well, we would go in a little closer. One of the best tactics is to get right on the deck at say, 200ft or less, and go in real close to the area that you're interested in, and then pop up, to 5,000 or 7,000ft right then, and you were right there, right in their lap, just a couple of miles, a few miles off of the coast or off of the installation you're looking at. And you all of a sudden show up on their radars, and this would usually cause them to turn things on that they wouldn't normally turn on. We also had tactics where if they were having an exercise, we would try to sneak in and join their bomber formations. And fly along with their bomber formations. Quite often they would turn on things at that time, that they wouldn't turn on normally, because they didn't know we were in the area.

As early as 1951 the USAF and SAC also urged the need for airborne communication intelligence platforms. COMINT was the eavesdropping of hostile radio transmissions, usually units communicating over the radio in voice messages. At the time it was hard to intercept this air-to-air and air-to-ground traffic from ground stations. A proposal was put forward to modify either a RB-50 or the RC-54 for these missions.[6] Later on C-130 (Hercules) transport aircraft were specially converted to EC-130s under the control of the National Security Agency. Bruce Bailey:

One of the ways this would work, let's say that you take an RB-47, and you run it up the Korean coast, into the Vladivostok area. And then in the Vladivostok area you make a few butterfly patterns or feints at the coast, at the city and so forth, and you stir up a reaction. You may have another EC-130 or something, a hundred miles off, or more, doing your COMINT collection. And of course, they can see that too. Well, then they come out and react to this RB-47 and either run it off or the RB-47 leaves the area anyhow, and the 130 leaves the area. This does a lot of things to them, they think that this crisis is over, and they've not had to turn on their SA-3 [NATO reporting-name 'Goa'; close-range surface-to-air missile with a slant range of nearly 20 miles to a height of 40,000ft] radar or anything. But as you leave the area, they still have fighters and aircraft of their own in the area, so then they take advantage of that, 'cos they're recovering their aircraft. By turning these radars on, and exercising them, and learning to use them. Well, when that's going on, another RB-47 comes from the other direction, from the Sakhalin Islands, Chukotsk area at low altitude, that's not been detected. And it picks all of it up right, and they pop up in order to do it. But you come in from the other direction and them not knowing you're there, they're turning on things that they wouldn't normally turn on.

The highlight for a 'crow' was finding a new signal. In the late 1950s Bruce Bailey found his:

At that time, there was suspected beam of the 'Big Mesh' radar. 'Big Mesh' was the Soviet's primary ground control intercept radar. It was a multibeam radar, and they suspected that there was low frequency beam out of it that had not been intercepted. And we went out on a mission, and I intercepted it, and I got a low enough of an intercept, and enough direction bearings and everything, that I established the signal on a single mission, and that was the first time I know that had been done.

The Soviets quickly wised up to idea that 'ferret' flights were trying to make them use their latest equipment so they could take recordings of the signals to help the development of the countermeasures for the bombers.

Bert Barrett said:

We never overflew – definite rules and the State Department had strict rules. We had to clear our missions. 12 miles from coast. ADF with radio equipment – we didn't want to make an incursion. All hell broke loose if it was thought you had. First they returned to home base – radar scope always photographed your route. Wing inspectors would look to check if you had strayed even by a mile or two. If you had, the crew was immediately downgraded from combat status. The commander would be relegated to ground crew. [7]

Bruce Bailey:

Different areas had different criteria. Sometimes a three-mile limit, but by and large we honoured the 12-mile limit. And most of our missions were planned to stay 12 miles away. There were some areas that we had to get closer because we were going between islands, or where we entered into the Baltic Sea. Then sometimes special missions and special requirements would cause you to violate the 12-mile limit, 'cos you would have to stimulate the defences and really get them active. In fact, I remember when the SA-3 surface-to-air missile system came out, we needed data real bad on that. Just about everything we tried we were unable to get them to activate the SA-3 radars. So, we started really pushing the limits in order to stimulate the SA-3s and get them on.

We would play games with the Russians. Sometimes to prevent us taking readings they would shut down all their radars except the early warning scanners.

But the crews had their own unofficial ways to stir up the Soviet defences. Bruce Bailey, again:

At first we used to throw chaff (bundles of thin metal strips) out of the aircraft. The Russians would think we were a squadron and all hell would break loose. When the bosses found out they banned this tactic and checked that we did not take chaff on board. So we came up with another trick. We used to stack all the empty beer cans on the nose wheel hatch. When we got to the Soviet border we would drop the nose wheel for a moment and all the cans would drop. Again the Russians thought we were a squadron and up would come the defences.

It was very common to have six or seven platforms up around the world at different areas, and a RB-47 in the Black Sea or the Baltic Sea gets chased off. That would cause all of the other aircraft to abort their missions, it'd go out to all the aircraft to abort. I know of many missions we flew when we're sitting there, toodling along and flat dumb and happy, where there's nothing unusual happening, and all of a sudden we get a recall and have to get out of the area in a hurry. We didn't understand it, so we get back to debriefing and say, you know, what the heck happened? Said, there was nobody bothering us, they say, oh well, the aircraft in the Sea of Okhotsk got fired at, or got run off or something, so we aborted all the missions.

Curly Behrmann recalled only one occasion when they overflew communist territory and that was a navigational error:

Well, very basically, we flew east out of Turkey, past the Caspian Sea, along the southern border of Russia. And then flew straight south, and you're flying across a really featureless desert area down there. And after flying an hour or so, we turned east, and went as far as you could go, and then were to turn north and fly along the border going west-north-west, back towards the Caspian Sea, and then break off and go home. Well, navigation error, the point is, we did intrude. It was the only violation any of my crews ever specifically made. But we did, we slid over the border and got farther up into their territory than we should have. Luckily it was in the 1950s when they weren't quite so sophisticated, or for sure our ass would have been grass. All of a sudden got a recall just about the time the navigator said, 'Hey, we are wrong, I'm sorry, get our tail out of here.' And we turned left and went home. And it was a serious enough incident that by the next morning, we had three colonels from SAC headquarters there interviewing us on what had gone wrong.

All the intelligence gathered from ELINT flights, the eavesdropping agencies and the CIA was kept behind the 'Green Door'. This opened into a top secret room deep in the SAC War Room at Offutt AFB. Only a handful of people in the United States had clearance to see this material. All the incoming intelligence was assessed and kept in this room. Each day SAC intelligence officers would produce a daily air intelligence briefing on the current state of Soviet readiness and deployment.

For instance in the late 1950s it was known that most of the Soviets' 'Bisons' and 'Bears' along with the majority of the 'Badgers' [Tupolev Tu-16s], were stationed in the southern part of the Leningrad military district. The Russians would therefore have to undertake a large-scale transfer of bombers to the Arctic bases before an attack. Any such movement would be picked up by ELINT operators.

Above all this shows the enormous importance SAC placed on the ELINT aircraft. Bob Sprague was relieved that the USA could not be taken by surprise. On the other hand SAC milked the national concern over surprise attack to get enormous quantities of money. As Eisenhower liked to point out, one B-52 Stratofortress bomber cost the same as a brick-built school in thirty US cities. SAC was able to acquire substantial numbers of further B-52s and missiles on the basis that a high percentage would be wiped out by a Soviet 'surprise attack'.

11
IN THE COMET'S TAIL

After the war the RAF's first ELINT unit, No 192 Squadron, had been disbanded to form the basis of the Central Signals Establishment at RAF Watton. But overall the ELINT role had been run down. The first signs of a revival came in September 1948 when a Lancaster and a Lincoln aircraft each fitted with a camera and modified as a Signals Intelligence (SIGINT) prototype flew to the Habbaniya British base in Iraq. From there they flew several eight-hour SIGINT sorties listening into Soviet signals traffic. In December 1949 more aircraft flew to Iraq to conduct further SIGINT sorties.[1]

Flt Sgt Bob Anstee also flew the first colonial ELINT operations, against communist insurgents in Malaya just after World War 2 in a specially adapted Lancaster bomber known as *Iris* which could listen in to the guerrillas' radio transmissions.[2]

As the demand grew for a proper ELINT unit, No 192 Squadron was reformed on 15 July 1951 flying Lincolns. Washingtons (Boeing B-29s renamed for RAF service) were assigned in 1952. These were three special RB-29As, WZ966-WZ968, given to the RAF under the Mutual Aid Program. These Washingtons had their gun turrets removed (with the exception of the rear gun position) and were designed to carry a team of between six and ten special operators.

From February 1953 the squadron was also equipped with modified Canberras. While these were capable of flying at high altitude they did not have much room. Carrying special operators was the task of the other aircraft. They carried only one special operator in addition to the pilot and navigator. It seems that the Canberras were used to stir up communist air defences. They also carried specialised radar and other equipment. Initially B2s were used, becoming the first RAF aircraft to be fitted with the new 'Green Satin' doppler. Four B6(RC)s were acquired from late 1954. These began with 'solid' noses of the usual Canberra shape, then gained T11 type pointed noses with AI Mk 17 radar and finally a bulbous nose, presumably also with radar of classified type.

The importance of the work of No 192 Squadron can be seen by the list of top brass that visited. For example the *Operational Record Book* shows that on 21 January 1953, the Secretary of State for Air, Lord De L'Isle, visited the base and was shown round Washington 966 by Flt Lt Snee.[3] The British Government still considers this unit secret and its story has never been fully told. Although it has been the subject of a number of commendations its work has always been described by the deliberately meaningless phrase, 'long-range calibration'.

Now a retired wing commander, Ron Dubock was in charge of the squadron's special operators – what the Americans would call 'crows' – from 1953. He had joined the RAF in 1941 and was involved with photo-reconnaissance Mosquitos. Mr Dubock still has his old silk neck scarf issued while he was with No 192 Squadron with a map of Russia on it. He said:

> We had some narrow scrapes. I was asked to join 192 because of my technical abilities. When I arrived on the squadron, it was not operating very efficiently, both in terms of the special equipment itself and the special operators. The special operators' leader at the time did not even know how to turn on some of the equipment on the aircraft.

He recalled his four years with No 192 Squadron as the best years of his life. 'These were exciting duties, as though being at war in peacetime.' On arrival at the squadron at Watton, the 'NCO, Special Operators' would receive an initial three months of training, including flights in a specially modified Vickers Varsity of Signal Command in which they would practise interception of British radio and radar signals.

Crews were given extensive escape and evasion training and survival training for both hot and cold extremes. They carried a lot of survival gear on board including rifles and snowshoes. Special operators were given the Soviet radio frequencies they were to scan on ricepaper. Wives and families were not permitted to know the dates and times of missions or detachments.

Sorties were usually flown at night in a ten-day window around the new moon. The squadron took care not to let its movement be known in advance as the communists would tend to switch off any new equipment if they knew ELINT missions were about. Flight plans were lodged only with those needing to know and in some cases take-off clearance was given by Aldis lamp rather than radio. The 'front office' – the pilots and navigator, engineer and signallers – were not told about the work of the special operators in the body of the aircraft. Most missions were flown from Watton, perhaps with a refuelling stop at Bodo in Norway when covering Northern Russia from the Barents Sea. While some missions were undertaken in the Far East, the only other regular operating base was Akrotiri, Cyprus, from where some three sorties would be flown during a ten-night detachment. Two regular patrols from there would be routed along the Black Sea's north coast, and run along the Iranian-Russian border and Caspian Sea.

In Germany the most used RAF forward base was Wunstorf, near Hanover. Crew members were told that Soviet agents had been observed sitting in cars outside Wunstorf watching for the comings and goings of No 192 aircraft. As a result the unit changed its German staging post to Wildenrath near the Dutch border. From here No 192 operated some of its most sensitive flights. For example the port of Baku in the Black Sea was considered to be the most heavily defended by air defences of any Soviet city. On one occasion a crew was required to fly fairly close to the port. To get a response they flew at normal altitude, 20,000ft and then descended rapidly to sea level, turned on a westerly heading, then south-east and then back up to operating altitude heading straight for Baku, turning away only at the last possible moment.

On one occasion a Washington flying along the coast of Poland and the Baltic states suddenly saw the whole coastline erupt with searchlights and gunfire. 'It frightened the life out of us,' said one crew member, 'until we realised that nothing was coming in our direction.'

Occasionally missions were flown to and from Habbaniya, the British base in Iraq – for example, Sqn Ldr Norman Hoad in Canberra 698, visiting on 20 March 1954.[4]

Recordings made from missions were handed over to GCHQ or in Cyprus to GCHQ's local station. 'On our return from a mission, all the tapes would be sent down to Cheltenham to be analysed. Then somebody from GCHQ would come up to Watton to brief the crew on what had been found.' Flt Lt A.E. Whatley continued, 'There was a squadron joke that our details were held somewhere in a file in KGB headquarters in Moscow.'

One of the stable operations of No 192 was the requirement codenamed 'Claret'. This required them to dispatch an aircraft on every occasion the new Soviet cruiser *Orzonikidize* put to sea. These trips were considered important and a plane was required to go regardless of the time or weather conditions.

In addition there were war plan exercises. In 1952 there were exercises in support of 'Mainbrace', the operational concept for the defence of Europe in the face of Soviet attack. Aircraft from No 192 would fly above the naval units in the North Sea looking for signals from attacking hostile force.

Most of No 192's missions were sensitive and simply called Air Ministry Operations and given a the title AMO and a number. No more detail than that. Dan Honley, a Canberra pilot who joined the squadron in 1957 and converted onto Comets recalled:

'Micky' Martin[5] was Group Captain (Ops) and would always brief us on operations – Air Ministry Operations. These were done at the time of no moon usually over several days. We would have very carefully laid out routes. We flew along the peripheral. We flew up to the Sea of Murmansk, often out of Bodo. For the Baltic we flew out of Watton. For the Black Sea it would be Cyprus. We would also go to the Middle East. I did some missions in the Middle East.

With the Soviets we would stand-off and one or two Canberras would come in and stir up the defence. Often they would start below radar level and pop-up near the Soviets. We never intruded into their airspace or overflew. We used to keep 20/30 miles off. We thought the Americans took losses because of their poor navigation. I had two navigators. Once we nearly went the wrong way.

One of the Russian speakers in the back would tell us what the ground controller was doing. Our ELINT equipment also told us what radar was on us. They would sometimes send MiGs up to intercept us. We could tell which radar was onto us whether it was height or tracking radar. Then as the MiG approached, [we'd see] which radar they were using. If they got their firing radar on we got the hell out. I was never shot at but I once got pursued and jinked and evaded right down to 700ft. The only time I know of a No 51 Squadron Comet being shot at was one that got warning shots from the Turkish Air Force. That aircraft was forced to land at Incirlik and stayed there for two hours. Someone had not been notified.

Flying Lincolns, then B-29s, then Comets, No 192 had notable successes including being the first to discover that MiGs were carrying airborne radar. This was extremely hazardous.

Traffic on the frequency bands to be searched during operational missions varied considerably. Therefore inexperienced personnel were initially allocated to the reasonably quiet L-Band from which they progressed to C-Band, X-Band and ultimately the busy S-Band. The twelve special operators in the pre-Breton days comprised one each on (VHF radar and voice) L- and C-Bands; two each for the S- and X0-

Bands; two supervisors and three linguists working fighter control frequencies on A–Band, there being no Soviet UHF voice transmission until the 1960s. The special operators received flying pay but were deemed worthy of their own wings.

By the mid–1950s the Russians had stopped copying Western equipment and become adept at designing ever more sophisticated radar and radio. They also became much cleverer at disguising and coding signals. The West tried to keep one step ahead with flights constantly monitoring the communist capabilities. In Europe the USAF and RAF monitored Soviet air defences. A former Battle of Britain Spitfire pilot, Geoffrey Wellum was transferred to No 192 Squadron in March 1954 to fly Washingtons.

> It was a beautiful aircraft to fly. Sometimes we would fly over Turkey and into the Black Sea. That was a hot spot and required the Prime Minister's permission. We had no reason to be there. We always flew in international airspace but the Russians didn't necessarily agree with what was international airspace. Up around the Barents Sea there were lots of Russian Islands. I didn't know much about what was going on in the back of the aircraft. I thought that best in case we were shot down and captured. There was a real risk.

The first crew to discover that the Soviet Union had developed and was using airborne intercept radar in MiG-15s was an RAF Washington ELINT aircraft of No 192 Squadron captained by Norman Hoad.[6] On this daring mission in 1955 Hoad's crew, flying a slow, obsolete World War 2 bomber, had to run at the Soviet border near the Caspian Sea and provoke the Soviet pilots into intercepting them. They narrowly escaped being shot down. Hoad was awarded a Air Force Cross for this discovery.

A month later Geoffrey Wellum also had a narrow squeak:

> The hairiest time was when I confirmed that the Soviets had airborne intercept radar. It was Norman Hoad who had discovered it. I confirmed it a month later. We were flying when the Soviets sent up a night-fighter. The ELINT people recorded his Airborne Intercept radar. Our radio operator told me that the ground controller was saying, 'You must be able to see him. You are on top of him.' I executed an emergency tactic I had devised. I dropped the flaps, undercarriage and lost height very quickly. We knew that the Soviets had difficulty locating height changes more so than direction changes. It was a very narrow squeak.

A year later in 1956, in the build-up to the Suez landings, a substantial part of No 192 Squadron was temporarily transferred to Cyprus where it ran discreet ELINT missions over the Middle East. 'We discovered that the Egyptians shut down their air defence radars just after midday each day. This was a great help when the British launched their attacks,' said Sqn Ldr Wellum. No 192 Squadron received personal congratulations from the Defence Minister, Selwyn Lloyd, for its work during the Suez Crisis.

In 1958 the squadron number changed, probably because details of the unit had been leaked by a Soviet spy in British intelligence and taking on a new number would, at least, make things more complicated for the Soviets, who were still the squadron's main target. On 21 August 1958 it was renumbered No 51 Squadron – a unit with no ELINT history. Its parent formation, No 90 Group, was renamed as Signals Command on 3 November 1958.

The three Washingtons were replaced in February 1958. The first British civilian passenger jet airliner, the Comet 1, had come into service in 1954 but its introduction was marred by a series of problems. One of the first service aircraft crashed, apparently disintegrating in midair. Following the disastrous crash, a court of inquiry reported in February 1955 that the Mk 2 – with heavier gauge metal, rounded windows and outward swept jet exhaust – was safe to operate. BOAC, who had ordered twelve, decided to switch its order to Comet 4s, leaving the Ministry of Supply with twenty-five Mk 2s in various states of completion. Ten were modified to join No 216 Squadron for transport duties.

In March 1955 the RAF ordered a special contract for three Comets using the Comet 2 airframe. This order required an aircraft with a range of 3,060 nautical miles and cruising height of 40,000ft. A preliminary equipment specification listed Marconi AB107B/114 HF radio, Marconi 7092 ADF, STR14B/15B ILS, Murphy Mk 6 200mc DME, Ultra intercom, Sperry ZLI zero-reader, a periscopic sextant and case, escape kit and smoke masks. The aircraft were to be given the serial numbers XK655, XK659 and XK663. The RAF had hoped to have the first Comet in the squadron before the end of 1955. In practice this was to prove wildly optimistic.

Two navigators were carried to increase accuracy. The emphasis on navigation was highly important because not only were accurate navigation skills required to identify the exact location of radar/radio transmitters in Warsaw Pact territory, but also for ensuring that the aircraft did not stray off course. The British approach to crewing was slightly different to the USAF. The RAF aircraft had a much larger crew, usually with at least one and more often three COMINT linguists. The 55th SRW rarely had more than one linguist aboard. If COMINT was required a separate COMINT aircraft with linguists was used.

On the Comets, provision was made for ten operators and twelve ground-crew passengers to help deploy overseas detachments. The primary operating positions, 1, 2, and 3, were provided with AN/APR-9 receivers. The Comets carried a great deal of American equipment modified with British plugs and accessories.

The delivery of the Comets was much delayed; it is believed this was due to the need to increase the number of special operator positions from ten to twelve or thirteen due to the increasing sophistication of Soviet equipment. The first to arrive was XK663 which was delivered to RAF Watton in April 1957. When all the Comets had been delivered by February 1958, the faithful Washingtons were assigned to No 23 MU and shortly afterwards sent off to Foulness Island to be used as gunnery targets.

Britain was a major centre for ELINT operations especially for the entire Western sector of the Eastern Bloc. Besides No 51 Squadron based at RAF Watton, the USAF kept a large rotating force of 55th SRW aircraft based at Brize Norton. The British and American crews co-operated as Bruce Bailey of the 55th SRW recalled:

> We worked with the RAF in developing systems for the Comet quite often. I flew on the Comet from time to time. We had RAF people, who came and flew with us from time to time. But we did have co-ordinated missions on occasions, in the Black Sea, in the Baltic Sea. We had some Chinese sorties that I can remember we had the RAF working with us on co-ordinated missions.

Wyn Shipman[7] was the Intelligence Officer for the 55th SRW:

> I had a lot of contact with the RAF Comet crews. We shared a lot of information. I only went on one or two trips. I went up to Watton a number of times. The RAF did good work but were underresourced and we would try to help. They had a lot of problems recording the signals. Long after we had stopped using them the RAF were using the old style recorders with a long thin wire which constantly broke and, when it did record, it was only a single channel – usually at the most inconvenient moment. I managed to get them one of our multichannel recorders using ferric oxide tape.
>
> One of my jobs involved co-ordinating all the missions. We would have monthly meetings of all the operators, SAC, RAF, NSA, USN. This was so we wouldn't have two aircraft in the same place at the same time.

No 51 Squadron kept in close contact with SAC. On 21 October 1961, for example, one Comet went on a liaison visit to Offutt AFB and No 544 Wing at Forbes AFB. Captained by Wg Cdr Sparrow, the plane carried a party of specialists from the Air Ministry. Led by Air Cdre J.C. Millar, DSO, the Commandant of Central Signals Establishments, it included participants from HQ Signals Command, GCHQ and the Central Reconnaissance Establishment.

The importance and danger of No 51 Squadron's work can be seen from the long list of Air Force Crosses and Medals in the *London Gazette* that its members were awarded for their 'peacetime' work.

12
THE CIA: BEHIND THE CURTAIN

From the late 1940s the West frequently penetrated communist airspace for a different set of espionage motives. Although this book is primarily concerned with aerial reconnaissance it would be impossible to get a sense of the communist mind-set without knowing about this group of penetration flights – the spy drops.

The Central Intelligence Agency was founded in 1948, based on the wartime OSS but modified for Cold War with a 'peacetime' mission. Its Office of Special Operations was assigned its initial mission against the Soviet target:

> . . . to collect secret intelligence on the Soviet Union itself, its military intentions, atomic weapons and advanced missiles; on Soviet actions in Eastern Europe, North Korea, and North Vietnam; on Moscow's connections with foreign communist parties and groups fighting for national liberation.[1]

Harry Rositzke was a member of the CIA's Soviet Division at the time. He said the Pentagon had somewhat unrealistic expectations of CIA operations and a complete failure to understand the obstacles of operating behind the Iron Curtain: '. . . during one briefing an army colonel pounded the table and demanded "an agent with a radio on every goddamn airfield between Berlin and the Urals",' he recalled.

One of the key elements of these operations was to assist and maintain contact with partisan groups in various parts of Eastern Europe. These were units that had disappeared into the forests and mountains to fight the Nazis. However, as the Red Army swept through the regions those partisans that were nationalist or anti-communist remained operating, now turning their attentions to the new communist enemy. Some of these partisan units were substantial, numbering thousands of men. In the years after the end of World War 2 they placed enormous pressure on the units of the Red Army occupying their homelands. Russian soldiers were in terror of their lives. They could not go singly around the towns. Units were ambushed. In some cases pitched battles were fought. As the dust of the war against Germany settled the Russians turned their attentions to dealing with these thorns in their sides.

Western intelligence airdrops began in late 1949 with the parachuting of agents into the Soviet Union as part of the infiltration operation codenamed 'Redsox'. Throughout the early 1950s the CIA and MI6, quite separately, trained nationals from countries that were by then in the communist sphere of influence. Once trained in espionage and sabotage they were dropped behind the Iron Curtain for special missions. As had occurred with such missions during the war, there was a poor definition between whether agents were being dropped to collect intelligence or to undertake acts of sabotage and guerrilla warfare. As one requires the lowest possible profile and the other attracts the attention of the enemy they should, in theory, not be conducted by the same people. However, matters were much more muddled.

The aircraft used to drop these agents were usually C-47 transports often crewed by émigrés to make them deniable if they crashed and were caught. The courage of those dropped in these missions must have been immense. The agents were largely recruited in displaced persons camps and trained in secret CIA or MI6 centres. The CIA had one in West Germany. These agents were then were being parachuted in at night to areas that they had not seen for up to a decade in the face of ruthless and extensive internal security services. The pilots must have been not only brave but astonishingly good fliers. They were often flying for hours at 200 metres or less in the dark to avoid radars. They were hotly pursued by MiG-15 fighters.

According to Rositzke the agents 'covered intelligence targets from the Murmansk area to Sakhalin, mostly on the margins of the Soviet landmass, some deep within.' These missions, however, were by and large a disaster. Most of those dropped were caught and executed. Some were arrested within hours of landing.

In 1995 I encountered former US Ambassador Donald Gregg at a conference in Washington. Long before his controversial appearances in the middle of the Iran-Contra affair he had been a CIA officer. During the Korean War he was in charge of getting agents. I asked him about the wider CIA operations. He declined to say anything on the subject except, 'this was not the CIA's finest hour'. Tom Bower's book, *The Red Web*, is the best account of the MI6 and CIA operations into Eastern Europe.

The Soviets often used the failure of such missions for propaganda. On 19 December 1951, TASS announced that two US-trained spies, who had been parachuted into the Moldavian Socialist Republic in the summer of 1951, had been executed by a firing squad. TASS gave the men's names as A.I. Osmanov and I.K. Sarancev. The TASS report stated they had admitted having been recruited from displaced persons camps in West Germany by the US intelligence service and that they had pleaded guilty to charges of espionage and diversionist activities. According to TASS, the captured agents said at their trial they had been dropped from a US plane under the cover of night. Open parachutes were said to have been found near the spot where the two men were arrested.

On 16 January 1953 the Polish Government, in a note to the US Embassy in Warsaw, protested against 'spying and diversionist activities on Polish territory'. An account of the protest was broadcast by the Warsaw radio on the following day. The Polish note claimed that two 'diversionists', trained in a United States 'spy centre' in West Germany, had parachuted into Poland from a USAF plane on 4 November 1952. The two men were said to have been captured by Polish security agents on the same evening. Evidently the charge had been labelled by American Air Force officers as a fake.

On 27 May 1953 TASS announced the arrest and execution of four US espionage agents who were said to have been parachuted into the Ukraine on the night of 25-26 April. According to the report, the Soviet Ministry of Home Affairs had received data that same night about overflight of the Ukraine by a foreign aircraft of unknown country of origin. Two of the agents, said to have been arrested on 27 April, were reported to have told the Soviet authorities that they had been parachuted from an American four-engine aircraft without identification marks.

The TASS report in many ways paralleled the 19 December 1951 report. The account of the case differed by including the charge that an American aircraft violated Soviet frontiers, in the specificity with which American espionage schools and teachers were named and in the specificity with which the items of their espionage were enumerated. The TASS announcement was widely broadcast by radio Moscow and was carried by most central newspapers. A month later, the story was revived and exploited for a domestic 'vigilance' campaign against imperialist spies.

During the research for this book I obtained a number of Soviet air defence logs of violations of their airspace. The earliest are the least detailed but under the heading 'Pacific Fleet 1950' it reports one such intrusion: '29 September. 3:15 a.m. Region: Sukhaya Rechka. Parachutist dropped.' In late 1952 a senior KGB officer drew up a report for Laurentia Beria, the feared head of state security. He examines all known intrusions into Soviet airspace in the previous six months. The tone is apologetic and cringing: 'I do not mean to justify the great deficiencies which truly do exist in the air defence system, which were justly pointed out at the commission meeting . . .' This Soviet document includes a map show the route of each intruding aircraft.

The report records for the evening of 2 May 1952:

> At 01.40 in the Litovizh region [25km south-west of Vladimir-Volynskiy], a C-47 enemy aircraft violated the USSR border; penetrated as far as the Rovno region, 130km into our territory. At 02.49, in the Kladnev region, (30km north-west of Vladimir-Volynskiy), the aircraft departed USSR territory heading towards Poland. The violator's flight altitude was 200-400m. The violator-aircraft was located over the USSR territory from 01.40 until 02.49, a period of 1hr 9min.
>
> Due to the flight's low altitude, radar sites did not record the violator-aircraft with the exception of one RTS [radar station] which made four fixes during the period 02.42 until 02.47.
>
> At 01.50 one MiG-15(bis) was scrambled from the Mogil'no airfield to intercept the violator-aircraft and at 02.47 to strengthen the intercept, a second MiG-15(bis) was scrambled. The fighters were scrambled in a timely manner.
>
> Intercept did not occur due to an absence of information on the target's flight and absence of radar aboard the fighters.

Two nights later a C-47 was out again flying at low level. According to the log this aircraft was over USSR territory for a period of 3hr 25min penetrating as far as the Baranovichi region. More than twenty MiGs were scrambled to intercept but they failed.

Another log reference is for the night of 12/13 August 1952. The attached note reads:

> At 00.30 according to RTS data a probable C-47 enemy aircraft violated the USSR border in the Liskovate region [56km north-west of Drogobych]. It penetrated into territory to 70km and at 01.20 departed the USSR heading towards Poland in the Volosote region [66km south-west of Drogobych]. The violator's flight occurred at low altitudes. The violator-aircraft was located over our territory for a period of 50min.
>
> Seventeen MiGs were scrambled in a timely manner to intercept the violator

from airfields: Mukachevo, Kalinuv and Mogil'no (Zhovtnevo). In three instances the fighters came within a close proximity of the target but were unable to visually detect the violator.

The intercept did not occur for the following reasons :

- the violator's flight occurred at a low altitude, which resulted in failure to obtain a fix;

- the lack of search radar aboard the MiG-15.

Fletcher Prouty, a USAF colonel permanently transferred to the CIA, ran many of these missions. In his book he recalls a Polish pilot who was recruited to fly flying boats that landed in Polish lakes and dropped off agents.

The fate of agents landing in Poland was much the same as elsewhere. In fact the Polish secret police (UB) ran a complete deception operation, maintaining an apparent partisan army. The Americans and British fed huge amounts of resources into their phoney network – very similar to the successful British deception operation against the Nazis run by the legendary XX (the double cross) committee.

At the same time the CIA became involved in clandestine operations on the Russian side of the border with Finland. Here the CIA drew heavily on the experience of the Norwegian Defence Intelligence Staff and Vilhelm Evang, whose organisation played the leading role in many of these joint undertakings. In Operation 'Uppsala', which was initiated in March 1952, the Norwegian Intelligence Staff trained Finnish agents for operations behind the Iron Curtain; although some agents went in from Norway, most of them went in from Finland. Basically this was an American undertaking initiated by the CIA, which also furnished the agents with aircraft, balloons and equipment.[2]

The British and French based in their occupation zones in Germany were also sending in agents. The British preferred dropping their agents from boats. They believed that aircraft were too noisy and detectable. Instead they used a former high-powered German gunboat captained by the robust former Kriegsmarine Capt. Klose. One of the first landings took place on 30 September 1951, along the coast of Latvia. Even by this time the partisan's war with the Red Army was in decline. The last known battle took place in February 1950. The Estonian partisan groups had been reduced to small bands. The drop by boat was reasonably discreet but on a number of occasions agents were intercepted as soon as they landed and on at least one occasion Klose's boat was attacked by

Red Navy boats. Fortunately it was so high powered it was able to outrun them.

As in the Baltic, in the Ukraine, the partisans were in decline. The British were the lead organisation in getting agents into this area. For this they used aircraft usually flying from the British base on Cyprus. In 1951 MI6 dropped three groups of agents, six agents to a group, into the Ukraine, the foothills of the Carpathians and Southern Poland. None of the eighteen was ever heard of again. It is likely that Kim Philby, the Russian spy within the British MI6, was instrumental in warning his Soviet handlers of these drops.[3]

In these countries, the chaos left after the war was slowly being eliminated and the Soviet bureaucrats and military were getting to grips with these small but pugnacious populations. The populations were closely monitored and informers to the secret police were increasing. However, these missions continued for many years.

The French also tried their hand at this game too. From 1949 to 1954, nearly one hundred agents were dropped in to Czechoslovakia, Yugoslavia, Romania, Byelorussia and Lithuania by the French SEDECE who set up a special unit called the *Matériels d'Informations Normalisées pour les Opérations Spéciales* (MINOS) to run this operation.[4]

The partisan groups in the Baltic states did inflict considerable casualties on the Red Army. Lithuanian partisans claimed to have killed 80,000 Soviet soldiers and between 4,000 and 12,000 communist officials and collaborators. The Soviets admitted losses of only 20,000.[5] Civilian casualties were high – estimated at 75,000 in the Baltic states.

It is not hard to understand what the Soviets made of all this. They certainly did not see it as the West assisting freedom fighters. They saw the West constantly illegally flying over their airspace to supply partisan armies devoted to causing mayhem in Soviet territories. To their mind it was a grossly unreasonable interference in domestic matters. Although Soviet intelligence and their satellite colleagues had considerable success, it wasn't until the mid-1950s that they finally suppressed the partisan problem.

These operations were duplicated on the Chinese borders. During World War 2 the Nationalist Chinese were assisted in their fight with the Japanese by the American pilots of the famous 'Flying Tigers' under the command of Gen. Claire L. Chennault. After the war Chennault and another American, Whiting Willauer, founded the airline China Air Transport (CAT). Nominally a commercial carrier specialising in air freight, the company served as a paramilitary adjunct of the Nationalist Chinese Air Force in the last days of the civil war. CAT's pilots fought hard and long side-by-side with Chiang Kai-shek's forces, flying troops and supplies into battle, carrying out the wounded. Following the defeat of the Nationalists at the hands of Mao's communists, CAT helped in the retreat to the island of Taiwan, from whence CAT based its operations. From October 1949 the CIA contracted CAT to fly arms to anti-communist groups in Western China. In 1950 the CIA secretly purchased CAT and involved it in its numerous covert operations in that part of the world. In 1950 CAT assisted in at least two attempts by anti-communist forces to reinvade Chinese territory.[6]

CAT engaged in numerous overflights, many being leaflet drops over the Chinese coast or Hainan. The pilots were American 'civilians' – usually adventurers or anti-communists. Escape and evasion kits consisted of several gold bars to be used for bribes in the event of being forced down.

The flights involving agents and supplies were far more difficult than the leaflet drops:

> Crews assigned these risky missions operated on precise time schedules and received detailed briefings on Chinese air defences, coastline, penetration points, ground speeds, approach corridors to drop zones, checkpoints from breaking radio silence, and flight paths for return. Because the communists had no night-fighters, evasion procedure usually meant flying in darkness and avoiding large cities.[7]

Intelligence of Chinese radar weak points and air defences was compiled from intelligence brought back by the industrious ELINT aircraft of the 91st SRS operating out of Yokota.

Long-range penetration flights by CAT aircraft began from Taiwan in March 1952. Two daylight flights, deep into Western China were made. 'Although Madame Chiang personally thanked the crew for undertaking the hazardous flight, Nationalist intelligence sources reported that the four parachuted agents had been lost.'

Later in the spring CAT was supplied with an unmarked B-17 by the air force and later a Douglas C-54 Skymaster (subsequently the DC-4). The airline promptly announced with appropriate fanfare the 'purchase' of its first modern four-engine airliner. The C-54 began routine passenger services. However both the B-17 and C-54 also conducted penetration missions. One crew flying for 14hr 21min over Chinese territory was considered to be the unofficial record by CAT. With the Korean War in full roar and with the Chinese the core enemy, CAT activities were stepped up.

One CAT flight was to attract a great deal of publicity. John T. Downey was recruited as a CIA agent in his senior year at Yale University. One of his first assignments in the field was to set up a resistance network in Manchuria. CAT was the main way to get agents in and out of occupied territory. The airline was trying out a new system of picking up returning agents, that avoided the hazard of landing. Two poles were set in the ground and a wire strung between them. Attached to the wire was a line leading to harness in which the person to be picked up was strapped. Approaching at slightly above stall speed (about 60mph), the aircraft hooked the rope and jerked the man up to flying speed, then reeled him into the aircraft. As author William Leary puts it, 'One can only marvel at the courage of those intrepid individuals who agreed to sit impassively in harnesses, awaiting possible decapitation, whiplash, or other serious injury.' CAT tried this for the first time on 29 November 1952. It resulted in a disaster that would reverberate for two decades.[8]

Downey, with another CIA officer, Richard G. Fecteau, set off on a C-47 plane piloted by CAT Capts Snoddy and Schwartz. Senior anti-communist officer Li Chun-ying had been dropped into Kirin province in October to inspect the work of a guerrilla group. He had radioed to be picked up. The new harness system was to be tried out operationally for the first time. Just as they were about to pick Li up, communist gunfire shot the aircraft down. Snoddy and Schwartz were killed. Downey and Fecteau were captured. The guerrilla group had been penetrated.

The communists kept silent for two years. Finally, on 23 November 1954, Radio Peking announced that thirteen Americans had been sentenced to prison for espionage. Eleven of the thirteen were B-29 crew members who had been shot down on 12 January 1953, while on covert mission, a 91st SRS leaflet drop, over Liaoning Province. The other two were Downey (sentenced to life) and Fecteau (twenty years). The Chinese identified Downey and Fecteau as CIA agents and released revealing details about their background and mission.

Washington denied the charges claiming the two men were civilian employees of the Department of the Army who had disappeared on a routine flight. At the United Nations, the US delegate Henry Cabot Lodge cited the sentences as another reason why the People's Republic of China should not be given a seat. The British government denounced the sentences as 'outrageous'.

In reaction Beijing revealed more information and claimed that their forces had seized from enemy agents six mortars, 998 rifles, 179,000 rounds of ammunition, 96 radio sets, secret codes, invisible ink, fake passes and gold bars. They stated that of 212 Chinese agents that been parachuted into the mainland between 1951 and 1953, 101 had been killed and 11 captured. Most had surrendered on arrival, and some had been killed by 'outraged peasants'.

As the Geneva Summit on the future of French Indochina (later Vietnam) began in the summer of 1955, the Chinese released the eleven crew members of the B-29 and several other Americans including a CAT pilot who had been captured in another incident as a gesture of goodwill. Downey and Fecteau were to remain in jail. Fecteau was released two months before Richard Nixon's visit to China in 1972. He had served nineteen of his twenty years. A year later Richard Nixon gave a press conference at which he finally admitted that Downey was a CIA agent. With this admission the Chinese released Downey.

Again, however brave, the covert operations against the Chinese had been a failure.

The *History of the CIA* said that the Korean War:

> . . . established OPC's and CIA's jurisdiction in the Far East and created the basic paramilitary capability that the agency employed for 20 years. By 1953, the elements of that capability were 'in place' – aircraft, amphibious craft, and an experienced group of personnel. For the next quarter-century paramilitary activities remained the major CIA covert activity in the Far East.[9]

According to William Leary, CAT made more than 100 perilous overflights of mainland China without the protection and benefits of a uniform, risking capture, long imprisonment, and death. 'Rewards were few for these secret soldiers of the Cold War, but they got the job done.[10]

For many years flights into China continued. Douglas A-26s, Boeing 17s, Consolidated PB-47s and, later, RB-69s, in Taiwanese markings but operated by the USAF/CIA, dropped spies and supplies. These aircraft were occasionally intercepted by Chinese MiGs.

American declassified documents also show that agents continued to be dropped into the Soviet Union. A record of one conversation shows Eisenhower approving such an agent drop in 1959. The full extent of these operations may never be fully revealed, but they were certainly very extensive.

13
THE U-2 – UNDER THE BLOOD-RED SKY

Ike was a shrewd game player. When in 1955 he offered the 'Open Skies' plan to the Soviets he knew that a secret CIA project was going to give the US the ability to overfly the USSR whether the Soviets agreed or not.

The origins of the project lay in Ike's support for an initiative that was to keep him slightly ahead of the military expansionist games of the JCS hawks. Eisenhower had set up a number of committees of non-military experts to give him independent advice on the great strategic questions. The feedback he received from them was largely critical of the CIA and military's abilities in this key area. In early 1954 he had set up the 'Surprise Attack Panel' with James R. Killian, President of MIT as the chairman. The 'Killian Panel', as it became known, had three sub-committees, one of which was responsible for intelligence issues. Its key members were Edwin H. Land and Edward Purcell.

Land had learnt that six months earlier Clarence 'Kelly' Johnson, a designer at Lockheed, had proposed to the Air Force a high-altitude single-engine reconnaissance aircraft. Johnson had even submitted a design and a few drawings. Led by LeMay, the air force laughed with contempt at this proposed single-engined, unarmed glider-like aircraft capable of only a few hundred miles per hour without a proper undercarriage.

The search for a high-flying reconnaissance aircraft began back in 1951 at Wright Field in Dayton. As we have seen, the air force had asked the Martin Corporation to start manufacturing an American version of the British Canberra jet. In 1952 an Air Force Intelligence Systems Panel, headed by Harvard's Jim Baker and including Cornell Aeronautical Laboratory's Allen Donovan had looked at the possibility of modifying the Canberra for high altitude reconnaissance. Donovan had quickly calculated that a twin-engined aircraft of air force design could never attain the necessary altitude to avoid Soviet defences.

Donovan, a sailplane devotee, drew up three criteria which he believed had to be met by any aircraft reaching altitudes in excess of 70,000ft. It had to have one engine, the plane must have a high aspect, low induced drag wing (like a sailplane) and thirdly it must be exempted from the air force's tough airworthiness standards which demanded weighty structural construction.

Land, meanwhile had decided that the air force had made a mistake when it turned down Kelly Johnson and Lockheed. He saw the potential of this aircraft for overflying the USSR to obtain vital strategic information. According to Kelly Johnson it could fly higher that any defence fighter and at the time was thought to be capable of flying above radar height. The 'CL-282' as it was known at this time, met all of Donovan's criteria and Din Land was sold on the project.

The Project Three panel was anxious to push on with the CL-282 project. According to Don Welzenbach,

> By now the panel members were aware of both the Martin RB-57 effort and a contract with Bell Aircraft to build a similar aircraft designated X-16 or 'Bald Eagle'.
>
> But its members, particularly Din Land, did not favour the air force conducting overflight missions during peacetime. Land firmly believed that overflights, which violated territorial sovereignty and international law and were conducted by military personnel in armed military aircraft, would actually risk provoking war. It was the Panel's unanimous belief that reconnaissance missions should be conducted by civilians in unarmed, unmarked aircraft. They believed the governmental unit best suited to this task was the Central Intelligence Agency.[1]

In the autumn of 1954 Dr Edwin Land wrote to Allen Dulles, the Director of Central Intelligence: 'The Lockheed superglider will fly at 70,000ft, well out of reach of present Russian interception, and high enough to have a good chance of avoiding detection. The plane itself is so light (15,000lb), so obviously unarmed and devoid of military usefulness, that it could minimise affront to the Russians even if, through some remote mischance, it were detected and identified.' The two men had a private meeting. Dulles was initially reluctant. He was not keen on the idea of CIA involvement with what he saw as military projects. An old Office of Strategic Services man, he saw the CIA role as concentrating on cloak and dagger activities involving spies. After many difficulties Land managed to bring together Dulles with Lockheed's Kelly Johnson who promised the project could be delivered quickly. He convinced Dulles who agreed to provide the costs from the CIA's secret funds.

Next on the agenda was a meeting for Killian and Land with Ike on 24 November. He listened carefully and approved the idea on the spot. According to Din Land's version, they sold it to him on the basis that this aircraft could and would find and photograph the Soviet Union's 'Bison' bomber fleet.[2] Ike agreed the aircraft should come under the control of the CIA. Another of the CIA's young whizz kids, Richard Bissell, was put in charge of making the project happen. Lockheed called the plane the U-2 and it was built in a separate hangar in California.

Knowing that the project was progressing rapidly put Ike in a remarkable position to make his offer at the Geneva summit. Eisenhower had originally approved the U-2 project on the basis that the aircraft would not be detectable by Soviet radars, and a political embarrassment. Eisenhower, ever cautious of the burgeoning military industrial complex, put the U-2 in the hands of the CIA. He did not want the USAF in charge of the intelligence gathering that would dictate the very size and funding of the air force. Ike knew of course that as soon as the U-2 was operational, the United States would be able to spy unilaterally over the USSR.

The first of the initial production orders of twenty U-2s was rolled out of Lockheed's famous Skunk Works in Burbank, California on 4 August 1955 for a successful test flight. The first operational unit was ready for deployment just eight months later.

British involvement came early on. In early 1956, the Americans requested a U-2 base in the UK. 'One or two RAF officers were cut in on the operation and a couple of senior members of the British intelligence community,' Bissell said in an interview before his recent death. Lakenheath airbase in Suffolk, already in use by the USAF, was chosen and approved by the Prime Minister, Sir Anthony Eden. In April 1956, two U-2s were delivered by transport aircraft, assembled in a discreet hangar in a remote corner of the airbase. A cover story was employed that the aircraft was for weather research for NACA (NASA's predecessor). Pilots, service crew and administration arrived at Lakenheath to form 'Detachment A'; its cover was Weather Reconnaissance Squadron (provisional).

However, test flights attracted the attention of aircraft enthusiasts and aircraft magazines. This, plus the sudden freezing of relations between the

British and Soviets over the Buster Crabbe spy affair, meant the Prime Minister withdrew permission for U-2s to operate from Britain.

Detachment A moved to Giebelstadt AFB in West Germany where the first overflights took-off in late June and early July. The cameras on the U-2 were state of the art, 36in focal length, cleverly folded up to fit into the airframe. Called the Type B camera they were built by the Hycon Corp of California and were based on an innovative design by Din Land and Jim Baker. They were capable of recording continuously for 4,000 miles of the journey with great resolution also using new state-of-the-art film. The cameras could swing from one side of the aircraft to the other shooting through seven portholes. The film format was 18in by 18in. The resolution was so good that on film taken from an altitude of 13 miles an object the size of a basketball could be identified.

While this was going on LeMay was busy with his own agenda and, as we have seen, ordering highly provocative penetrations. Fortunately the Russians did not respond militarily but they were extremely angry at the US's impudent intrusion into their airspace. Playing a wild card in the deadly game of bluff and counter-bluff, Khrushchev decided to show them.

On 24 June 1956 he invited international military chiefs – including LeMay's boss, the USAF Chief of Staff Gen. Twining – to the Soviet Aviation Day display. Twining discussed the invitation with President Eisenhower. From the minutes of the meeting it seems that Twining was going to take the Presidential Boeing 707, which seems to imply that it was fitted with secret cameras, providing an opportunity for photographs of the USSR.[3]

> The President said that if General Twining wanted to go, he saw no reason why he should say no. He could not foresee that the visit would be of any particular intelligence value, however. General Twining said there was a odd possibility that he might go in the Boeing 707, flying non-stop from the United States to Moscow. The President and the others present thought this was a splendid idea.[4]

Twining took Gen. Thomas Power with him. Khrushchev made sure the airshow was a formidable display of Soviet air power. In case Twining had not got the message, after the airshow the foreign guests were treated to a round of Russian hospitality. Red Air Force Commander, Gen. Mikhailov, was present on the podium with Khrushchev. He said:[5]

Khrushchev personally invited Twining into the park. He said, 'Oh, Mr Twining, we have shown you as you have heard all our newest aircraft, do you want to see now our rockets?'

Twining said, 'Yes, certainly, we are very interested to see.'

'But,' said Khrushchev, 'we will not show you our rockets first: show us your planes, your rockets and then we perhaps will show you ours. And by the way, Mr Twining, to you I must say quite frankly that if something like a Canberra comes in our airspace it will be shot down, all your Canberras are flying coffins.'[6]

The first overflights of East Germany took place at the end of June. This was just over a week after Khrushchev had threatened Twining about overflights at the Soviet Aviation Day. Twining returned to the US on 1 July and the first Soviet overflight took place on 4 July and included in its route Moscow and Leningrad. The Soviet leadership was at the American Embassy celebration for Independence Day. One shock was in store for Eisenhower; the Soviet radar picked up the flight. A number of MiGs tried to intercept the U-2. The aircraft's altitude protected it but the ELINT recorder on board showed that one MiG had obtained radar-ranging data.[7] The Russians thought that this flight was another damned Canberra as can be seen by their diplomatic protest which claimed they had been overflown by a two jet-engined aircraft – an error that enabled the United States disingenuously to deny that such an aircraft had been flown. Khrushchev was furious.

Gen. Mikhailov said,

And that offended, deeply offended not only the air defence, not only the Ministry of Air Defence, and the armed forces, but our government and I had the impression Khrushchev and Bulganin themselves. Because, you know, it was seen that we didn't know what the plane was, whose plane it was, but it came at a height of more than 20,000m, it flew nearly over Moscow and it was near Leningrad and then they went back. And that, let us say, gave us the impression that it was Twining who did it just to show that the Canberras as we thought at that time are not flying coffins.[8]

LeMay had underestimated the importance of the U-2. Don Welzenbach said:

There's a story told by a man whom I interviewed, when I was doing my U-2 history, a man who was sent by the Air Force to Offutt Air Force Base in Omaha, to brief General LeMay on the new U-2. And he went into the room to tell him about this airplane that didn't have guns, had only one engine, didn't have wheels, and would take pictures. And LeMay took his cigar out of his mouth, and looked at this young major and said, 'Young man, when I want a picture I don't need an airplane that doesn't have wheels or guns. When I want a picture of the Soviet Union, I'll send a B-29.' And he dismissed him.[9]

One of the first benefits to Eisenhower of the U-2 overflights of the Soviet Union was that they undermined the bomber gap scare propagated by the USAF. Don Welzenbach said:

> On one of the first U-2 overflights in July of 1956, we saw the Ramenskaya airfield, and we saw the airplanes that they had, we saw these 'Bison' bombers down there, and we could count them and there weren't that many. Now that the photograph has been released it's been published in books and it shows how many there were. Now Eisenhower immediately could put to rest the bomber gap. But he couldn't tell anyone about it, why he could put it to rest. He kept this all very secret, this was a very secret programme, very few people saw these photographs.

It appears that until the end of 1956 the CIA was willing to allow the air force's high estimates to find their way into the NIEs, even though the navy and army continually challenged the figures. John Prados has written that Allen Dulles' awareness that bombers and missiles were really in the military domain probably prevented him pressing his Office of Scientific Intelligence's arguments against the air force.[10]

The air force domination over the CIA over the bomber gap was changing. CIA agents obtained metal samples from the 'Bison's engines and a wire coathanger from an Aeroflot plane. Metallurgical analysis showed the range and payload of the 'Bisons' had to be revised downwards. In addition, the agency was also using a new method to predict bomber strength by examining the industrial capacity of the Soviet Union.

One of the smarter moves Eisenhower had made as President was increasingly using the CIA to deliver NIEs. This gradually removed the job of intelligence collection from the service which would benefit from inflated estimates of Soviet capabilities. In a National Security Council meeting in early 1954, Ike had complained that there were two things wrong with the intelligence he was being supplied. First, it did not differentiate between Russian capability and actual intentions – a very basic intelligence problem. The second was that not enough was being done to put the Russian threat into proper perspective. An overall view was not supplied at that point because the CIA was responsible for judging the Russian threat and the Joint

Chiefs of Staff were responsible for estimates of the American ability to react.

According to Ike's biographer Stephen Ambrose, what the president wanted was a 'net' evaluation, or what the military call a 'a commander's estimate'. The head of the CIA chose a brilliant young analyst, Ray S. Cline, to undertake the CIA side of this joint enterprise with the military. The military was not up to the task but gave Cline a great deal of material help. He even had access to the computer in the basement of the Pentagon. Although primitive by today's standard it was state-of-the-art at the time and was used for war gaming. When Cline fed all the most up-to-date data into the computer and war gamed he made some startling discoveries, the key one being that, 'it was a pretty desperate move for the USSR to attack us with their substantially inferior long range air force.' US tactical radar warning systems were good enough to preclude the possibility of surprise attack.[11]

With all the new data in front of him, Ray Cline then wrote the commander's estimate. What Ike had suspected was true. The military's claim of communism hell bent on world domination was not backed up by the evidence. There was no sign that the communists were either ready or able to resort to direct major military action. The JCS claim that the 'the time of greatest danger from attack is the next two years' disappeared from JCS reports.

All these factors when combined with the new evidence garnered from the first U-2 overflights led to drastically reduced estimates of bomber strength by December 1956.

By the time Congress was holding hearings for the air force's 1958 budget, projected Soviet bomber strength was officially 50 per cent down on the previous year's, and by late 1957 the projected figure for 1960 was 25 per cent down. Congress was alarmed and puzzled, interrogating the administration officials closely on the rapid changes in arithmetic. In an effort to keep the gap alive, the air force responded to the new information about the 'Bisons' by claiming that a huge increase in the Soviet aerial refuelling tanker fleet was to be expected. Despite the air force's effort the bomber gap had disappeared by 1960 and the NIE of that April put actual Soviet bomber strength at 120-185. By then, however, the air force had already been voted the funds for the fighters it 'needed' to counter the fictional figure for the Soviet bombers and the B-52s (far superior to anything in the Soviet inventory) to win equivalence in bomber strength. All the air force generals in intelligence and SAC who had managed this superlative effort to increase the number of planes in their service were promoted to higher and better posts.[12]

The Soviets issued three sets of diplomatic protests over U-2 flights after 10 July 1956. Washington denied all three. Other quieter protests trailed off, almost as if the Kremlin had decided to resign itself to the violations until it could down a plane. It was as if the humiliation was so great they did not want to make it public.

As Michael Beschloss said in his book *Mayday* about the U-2 affair:

> Both Eisenhower and Khrushchev had ample reason for public silence about the flights – Eisenhower to preserve the secrecy essential to U-2 operations, Khrushchev to keep his nation from learning that under his leadership Soviet armed forces were too weak to close Soviet skies to enemy planes bearing, for all anyone knew, nuclear weapons.[13]

Eisenhower read Khrushchev's silence as a partial acceptance of intelligence flights. However, Eisenhower was not prepared to allow numerous overflights of the Soviet Union. After the realisation that the U-2 could be tracked by radar, its overflights were severely curtailed. Chris Pocock said, 'the limited scope of operations and the highly restricted dissemination of U-2 derived intelligence meant Eisenhower and his policy makers never did acquire the means to unequivocally disprove the widely held notion that the Soviet Union was achieving strategic military superiority over the US. Ike intuitively knew that the tables would turn if a U-2 were shot down. As early as 1955 the President had told the U-2 team, 'Well, boys, I believe the country needs this information, and I'm going to approve it. But I tell you one thing. Some day one of these machines is going to be caught and we're going to have a storm.' Welzenbach said:

> Eisenhower believed that overflights were not really worth the antagonism that it caused to the Soviet Union. He did not see that the intelligence being gained warranted the jeopardy to détente. And this, despite the fact that the early U-2 overflights had put an end to the bomber gap controversy. He was reluctant all through his term to authorise overflights. He did so only under great duress.

All the declassified U-2 documents that have been released tend to confirm Goodpaster's statements. They show Eisenhower as being very reluctant to sanction even overflights by the U-2 which was theoretically immune to the Soviet Air Defences. There were also a number of U-2 SIGINT and telemetry flights to observe Soviet rocket tests. A priority of the U-2 flights was the missile-testing sites. One mission in September 1957 flew over Kapustin Yar. Another a year later over the Semiplatinsk site also discovered Tyuratam, the Soviet Union's centre for long-range missiles.

But by 1958 the CIA was having difficulty persuading Eisenhower to approve many overflights. In fact, between March 1958 and July 1959, Eisenhower did not approve one single flight over the Soviet Union. What to do?

14
THE U-2 – THE BRITISH STORY

In July 1958 Flt Lt Robert Robinson of the Royal Air Force was flying his Canberra B2 back from a special mission at the H-bomb test range at Christmas Island in the Pacific. Approaching England, he received an unexpected radio message : 'Flt Lt Robinson. Upon landing you are to report immediately to the Vice Chief of Air Staff at the Air Ministry.' Robinson, who retired as a wing commander to Sussex, said his reaction was alarm. 'You were never called by name over the R/T. I thought, "My God, what have I done?"'[1]

He needn't have panicked, Robinson had been chosen to lead a special detachment of British pilots flying the American U-2 spyplane. His work over the next two years was so secret that the British government still refuses to admit its part in the U-2 overflights of the Soviet Union which came to an abrupt end when Gary Francis Powers was shot down on May Day 1960.

The British still consider the project so secret that even the CIA cannot mention their involvement. In the 1980s retired CIA historian Don Welzenbach wrote the agency's own official history of the U-2 project but it has never been able to make the book public. The following exchange took place when I interviewed him.

PL: And will your book ever be published?
DW: My book has been published. It hasn't been released, it's still secret.
PL: And why is that?
DW: We cannot get authorisation from a certain foreign country, to admit that it participated in the programme.
PL: Is that the British government?
DW: It is.[2]

The British Government also refuses to release its files of the U-2 programme into the Public Record Office although they are over thirty years old.

In 1958 the U-2 programme was one of the most highly classified operations in the world. Flt Lt Robinson was a natural British choice for flying the U-2, having specialised in high altitude flying. He had joined the RAF in 1946, first flying Meteors and then as a test pilot at Farnborough.

In spring 1958 he had been at Christmas Island as part of a special two-aircraft unit flying Canberra B2s modified with double Napier Scorpion liquid-fuelled rockets to propel the aircraft up to the altitude needed for nuclear fall-out sampling. One of these aircraft had set a new world altitude record of 70,310ft on 28 August 1957 (although the U-2 had been secretly reaching these heights for two years). Unfortunately at the time of the Christmas Island nuclear tests the Scorpion of B2 WT207 exploded at 56,000ft. The crew ejected and survived but it put paid to Scorpion-assisted high altitude work.[3]

Back in England, the Vice Chief of Air Staff told Robinson to go to America forthwith. 'The Vice Chief would only say that I would be flying an aircraft at very high altitude and ultimately operating in Europe,' said Robinson. He was also promoted to squadron leader.

At the CIA headquarters in Washington DC Robinson was briefed for the first time on the U-2. He was joining the project at a key moment. The British were again helping out their American intelligence allies who were having a spot of bother with a President who was increasingly ambivalent about the U-2 project.

Since World War 2 British and American intelligence co-operation had been close, the core of the 'special relationship'. The British had nurtured American intelligence through infancy. Now fortified by Cold War funding, the American prodigy had outgrown the parent.

Despite the reluctant eviction of Detachment A from Lakenheath, the British received intelligence information gathered from the U-2 programme. This was particularly helpful during the Suez crisis, when photographs were routinely made available. The U-2 overflew Cairo during an RAF bombing raid on an air base. The CIA made the photographs available so quickly that they got a return cable exclaiming, 'Warm thanks for pics, quickest bomb damage assessment we have ever had.'

As a result of the successful testing of the British hydrogen bomb at Christmas Island in the Pacific in 1957, the Americans began to treat the British much more seriously as a partner once again. The schism over the

Suez fiasco on which the British and American governments had split, was pushed into the background. To the Americans Christmas Island was a test in more than one way, it was also a test of commitment. The Americans began to treat the British equally and initiated joint war plans. A new nuclear attack plan was drawn up in which the RAF dealt uniquely with specific targets.

The British were invited to join other top secret projects. By 1958 it was becoming increasingly difficult for the CIA to get permission for overflights. (It now transpires that most US overflights of USSR were flown from 1956 to early '58.) Bissell came up with the idea of bringing the British operationally into the programme so the number of flights could be increased. He said later:

> My theory was to set up a system whereby there would be another chief of state who could give consent, namely the British Prime Minister. So I approached the RAF, and needless to say, they were eager to be in on the act.

American flights could be approved by the President, the British flights by the Prime Minister. This would increase the number of possible flights.

On this occasion, British Prime Minister Harold Macmillan agreed the plan, and four RAF officers were elected and sent to Laughlin AFB in Del Rio, Texas for training in May 1958. They were Sqn Ldr Christopher Walker and Flt Lts Michael Bradley, David Dowling and John MacArthur. All were instructor pilots with A2 ratings, unmarried and in their late 20s. Navigation and health were the key to the project and two navigators and a specialised flight surgeon were assigned to the special British unit.

On 8 July 1958, Sqn Ldr Walker was killed when his U-2 crashed near Wayside, Texas. It was concluded that the aircraft had broken up at high altitude, probably resulting from loss of control after an autopilot malfunction. It was at this point that Sqn Ldr Robert Robinson, quietly flying back from the Pacific, was brought into the project. In the two weeks following his arrival in the United States, Robinson travelled all around the country. First to the Lovelace Clinic, USAF's aeromedical laboratory in New Mexico, for medical tests. Then to the firm of David Clark in Massachusetts to be fitted for a pressure suit. Next he was sent to a CIA training camp in Virginia where he was trained in using and assembling a variety of Russian weapons. The camp contained a simulated section of Soviet border, complete with minefields, watchtowers and guard dogs. Robinson was taught to sneak through undiscovered.

Finally he was sent down to Laughlin AFB to learn to fly the plane.

It was quite a lengthy training before you stepped inside a U-2. This was organised by SAC, therefore as you can imagine it was extremely thorough. There was no two-seater version of the U-2 at the time so we were trained in civilian two-seater aircraft that had similar characteristics. I had been a test pilot all my life really, so I had flown about 100 different types of aircraft. This one was different, mainly because of the bicycle undercarriage arrangement. It's not easy to land. Unless you land on both wheels exactly at the right speed at the right time you start bouncing around. And the other thing, of course, is that it has no wheels on the wings, you're balancing the aircraft for landing. Landing and take-off were not easy, particularly in a crosswind. I must admit that the first flight, I wouldn't exactly say I got a fright, but it was much harder than I had expected. After a while you got the hang of them but you can see why there were so many accidents during training.

Robinson said it was an ideal aircraft for the job at hand if rather vulnerable at low altitude:

It flew very nicely, but being structurally light and really quite a weak aircraft, it was very, very subject to turbulence and there were many accidents where the aircraft did disintegrate or break up in flight either because of weather conditions or just hitting too much turbulence or having to fly through a thunderstorm. It was designed to do a job and that it did extremely well, but from a pilot's point of view the handling qualities were secondary in many ways.

But long operational flights were uncomfortable for the pilot:

You were wearing a pressure suit which is very cumbersome and difficult to move around in in the cockpit. For ten hours you couldn't eat, you couldn't drink and you couldn't even scratch your nose because once the visor was down it was sealed down and you could not open it until the end of the flight. If you had the misfortune to have a hair sticking down the front of your nose you were gonna have a troublesome flight. You could have a pee but that was quite complicated.

In January 1959 Robinson was sent to Incirlik AFB in Turkey where the CIA's Detachment B was based. The other members of the British contingent had arrived some months before. Det B was now the only permanent U-2 detachment in Europe, since Det A had been withdrawn in 1957 after frequent scares over communist spies watching the base. Det

B consisted of four aircraft, seven US pilots and about 200 support personnel from the CIA.

Incirlik was a Turkish air force base with a USAF unit handling transport and intelligence-gathering flights. It was effectively a key forward base in operations against the Soviet Union. Conditions were basic and the U-2 unit lived in trailers. Outside the base the presence of the British was only known to a few Turkish government officials.

The official cover story for the British was that they were temporary employees of the Meteorological Office in London. The real British chain of command was from Robinson as unit commander to Grp Capt. Bingham Hall at the MoD in London, who in return reported to Sir John Grandy, the Assistant Chief of Air Staff (Operations).

The Americans paid their 'civilian' pilots three to four times USAF pay. Robinson said they were paranoid about pilots being bribed and wanted to pay high rates. They demanded that British paid their pilots the same amount. This was against all the principles of the RAF where all flying is paid at the same rate. He said:

> So a typical British compromise ensued. We were paid three and a half to four times what our equivalent rank would have been in the Air Force. As a lowly squadron leader I was paid more than the Chief of the Air Staff.

By the time Robinson arrived at Incirlik the number of Soviet overflights had slowed to a trickle. However, the British were involved in constant spy flights over the Middle East and other trouble spots.

According to Robinson, American intelligence always knew in advance when the Soviets were about to launch a test missile. A U-2 loaded with special electronic listening and telemetry devices was always on alert. It would be sent up three hours before the shot to fly along the nearest border. Many missions were flown across Iran timed to be overhead Masshad when the missile was launched from Tyuratam 600 miles away to the north.

The U-2 programme was primarily for overflights of the Eastern Bloc, but the total number of overflights is still regarded as a secret. When I interviewed Don Welzenbach in 1993 he refused to be specific.

PL: How often did Eisenhower authorise U-2 flights over the Soviet Union?

DW: Well not very often, I can't tell you that, because it's still secret.

PL: Thirty times?

DW: Oh less than that.

PL: In the entire four years?

DW: In the entire four years. Less than thirty.

PL: And that's still secret, the actual number.

DW: That is still secret. Hopefully it'll be declassified some day.

The former enemy tried to be more forthcoming. In 1993 Gen. Mikhailov, the Deputy Chief of Air Defence for the Moscow region said, 'I know exactly, about eighteen, during these years, until Powers was shot down.'

The Soviets clearly failed to identify a number of flights because in the autumn of 1995 the CIA finally declassified the number of U-2 overflights of the USSR. The official US figure is twenty-four.[4]

But the number of overflights flown by the British remains a secret and so does whether they are included in the total of twenty-four. This is one area where retired Wg Cdr Robinson remains coy. Some authorities say that the number is between two and four, all personally approved by the Prime Minister. But my understanding is that in 1959 Sqn Ldr Robinson flew over Tyuratam and the medium-range ballistic test site at Kaputsin Yar near Volgograd. Flt Lt MacArthur flew another in early 1960. According to Chris Pocock's excellent history of the U-2:

> On one of the overflights, Flt Lt John MacArthur flew round the target twice, and on the other, Sqn Ldr Robert Robinson pressed on through a mission despite leaving a contrail behind him – the Agency pilots had been told that both these deeds were strictly forbidden.[5]

The U-2's ability to fly so high protected it from Soviet aircraft. Robinson said:

> You were always looking behind, and you would see many, many aircraft all lined up below you but with the inability to reach you. The only concern we had was if the engine failed or if you had a hydraulic failure which brought you down to about 55,000ft when you became more vulnerable. A lot of people think that a single-engined aircraft flying at that height all the way over Russia, sounds fraught with danger. In fact we had great faith in the equipment. It was a very reliable aircraft and the engine was a magnificent engine. Pratt & Whitney J75. I mean it never hiccuped, it just kept on going.
>
> The middle eastern flights came up once or twice a week on a shared rota basis.

Those flights were all done from Incirlik and all landed back there. But overflights of Russia tended to take place from other airfields and this was because the Russians were monitoring Incirlik. There was a radar station in Syria which could see us taking-off.

The most popular airfield was Peshawar in Pakistan and this had many attractions. It was well to the east, it was quite close to the southern border of Russia where the radar was not very good. They didn't expect any threat from Pakistan or that area so it was possible to get through the radar chain and into Russia without being spotted on radar. Now this was vital. If you got into the country nobody knew you were there.

Once the target list was approved the pilot was flown to Peshawar, where the U-2 had already been delivered. Take-off was usually at 05.00. The pilot had to get up at 02.30, followed by a special breakfast and then two hours pre-flight breathing oxygen.

The routes avoided known SAM-2 anti-aircraft missile sites. The flights were long and tough; it took 9 hours from Peshawar to Bodo in Norway. One of the best accounts is contained in a CIA history paper based on one of the early flights detailing the flight of U-2 pioneer Hervey Stockman and written by Don Welzenbach.

The British pilots could select a survival kit of their own choosing. In addition they were given a silver dollar on a chain to hang round their necks. Hidden inside the dollar was a needle coated in cyanide. The British cover story, if shot down, was that they had the aircraft on autopilot and the pilot had blacked out because of an oxygen failure and the aircraft had strayed into Soviet airspace accidentally. 'The Americans didn't have a cover story and in fact it was the British cover story that Gary Powers used,' said Robinson.

One of the Robinson flights resulted in photographs of a new type of Soviet bomber. He said:

The picture I was most proud of was of an aircraft factory. The CIA told me to fly exactly down this road through a town. They didn't normally have maps of the town but they did of this town. It was essential to go down this road because on one side of the road was the airframe factory, on the other side was the engine factory. I was able to film both sides.

Eisenhower's increasing reluctance to permit U-2 missions comes in a series of White House minutes. For example, on 7 April 1959 President Eisenhower called in Secretary for State Neil McElroy and Richard Bissell. He told them that he had 'decided not to go ahead with certain

reconnaissance flights for which he had given approval the preceding day.'
He gave them reasons:

> First we now have the power to destroy the Soviets without the need for detailed
> targeting. Second as the world is going now, there seems no hope for the future
> unless we can make some progress in negotiation (it is already four years since the
> Geneva meeting). Third we cannot, we *cannot* in the present circumstance afford
> the revulsion of world opinion against the United States that might occur . . .

In summary, the President said he did not agree that this project would
be worth the political costs.[6]

The U-2 project became headlines across the world when a mission
from Incirlik was shot down with a SAM-2 missile on May Day 1960. As
Eisenhower had promised, a storm was unleashed by the Soviets.

The urgent need for this flight was that the CIA had received
information that the Soviets were operating a major ICBM facilities at
Plesetsk in the north of the USSR. This flight was to be the first
complete overflight of the Soviet Union from border to border. It was
also unusual in that the route was almost a straight line. Taking-off from
Peshawar, it was to overfly missile testing sites at Tyuratam, Sverdlovsk
and finally Plesetsk. The mission had been scheduled for the end of April
but bad weather delayed the flight. Secretary of State Christian Herter
had banned the flight from taking place less than fourteen days before the
Paris summit between Eisenhower and Khrushchev on 14 May. Just
outside Sverdlovsk a SAM missile exploded just behind the aircraft
sending it into a dive.[7] Robinson said:

> I knew Gary Powers extremely well. We were on the same unit. We'd see each
> other every day and he was the most pleasant, self-effacing, quiet American and a
> most likeable man.
>   He didn't eject which again was unusual. I spoke to him afterwards and his story
> was that when the missiles went off he in fact had his straps loose in the cockpit.
> When the missile went off, and presumably blew the tail off, he was then pushed
> forward and he couldn't operate the ejection seat to get out, he was far too far
> forward. So he literally let go of the canopy and climbed out at some enormous
> altitude. But in doing that he possibly sensed he did not operate the destruct
> system. This required two switches. One you armed the system with; the second
> one when you pressed it gave you 70 seconds before it blew up. So the Americans
> thought he should have killed himself.

Robinson had warned the American detachment commander that
May Day was not a good day to fly over the USSR:

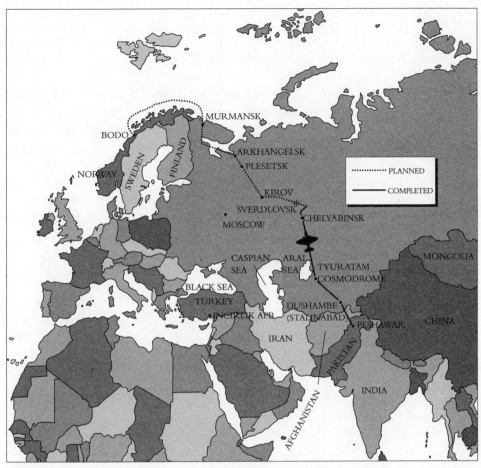

Map 4   The planned route of Gary Powers' overflight, 1 May 1960.

There'd be a maximum alert and it was a very dangerous thing to do, highly provocative, as it turned out. It was getting very close to Moscow and I would think they were very nervous. They knew that something was happening and clearly the order was given it must be destroyed.

The detachment commander ignored Robinson's advice: 'I don't think he really understood the significance of May 1st as much as we do. It didn't really mean so much to him, but it was not a prolonged conversation.' After three days of uncertainty, the news that Powers had been captured meant the British unit quickly packing up and leaving Turkey. Robinson:

As soon as it was known that he'd been captured the pilots left immediately. This was really to save the embarrassment with the Turkish government because they didn't know we were there anyway and it was best we left.

The pilots were all called to a meeting at the Air Ministry with Sir George Ward MP, Secretary of State for Air. He wanted their opinion on whether Powers would reveal the British U-2 involvement to his Soviet interrogators. Hints had already emerged in the British press and parliament that there was close co-operation. In the end Ward decided neither to confirm nor deny.

Robinson said that he talked to Powers after his release from Russia and Powers said that he had never been asked by his interrogators anything about British involvement.

The British contingent from Detachment B was instructed to 'vanish' for a while, until things died down. Robinson went off to Spain for some months. Robinson said:

The shooting down of Powers brought the use of aircraft over Russia to a premature end. It was always known or became increasingly known that it was only a matter of time before the missiles or the latest versions of supersonic jets with pop up missiles would make life untenable for us. The aircraft itself couldn't go much higher. There were other developments but really aerodynamically that was it. You were operating within really two knots between stalling and compressibility so you couldn't force it any higher, but at the same time they were developing the supersonic successor to the U-2 which was the Blackbird.

Initially it was certainly intended that the Blackbird would take over from the U-2 for Russian flights. This didn't occur and I think there were also technical problems with the aircraft, but it did bring it to a premature end. I think if someone had authorised further missions after that it would have been considered extremely provocative. The U-2 itself is still in service, it's still used as you know and has been used really for many missions. It's used now over Bosnia because it's just one of those useful aircraft.[8]

However, a limited version of the CIA's U-2 programme was resuscitated after some months, although there were to be no permanent overseas units. Nationalist Chinese pilots flew the U-2 regularly over China and it was a CIA U-2 that photographed the missile sites that sparked the Cuban missile crisis in 1962.

British involvement continued. In 1961 another British contingent was sent to join the CIA programme. It included two pilots, Sqn Ldr Ivan Webster and Flt Lt Charles Taylor. After training they joined the headquarters squadron at North Base, a remote and secure facility at the northern edge of Edwards AFB in California.

In August 1962 three U-2s returned to the USAF base at Upper Heyford in England for a short stay. Their presence stirred up much excitement amongst the tabloids. Their commander, Col. Arthur Leatherwood, assured the public that his planes would not be used for spying over Russia. The *Daily Worker* reported that the Scots miner's leader had written to President Kennedy demanding that he remove the U-2s.

Further modifications to the U-2 occurred including in-flight refuelling capability and the ability to land and take off from aircraft carriers. Using that capability a U-2 from Edwards AFB in California photographed the French nuclear test site at Mururoa atoll in the South Pacific in 1964.

British pilots did not participate in any of these operational missions although they were allowed to ferry U-2s to the overseas deployment bases. After a three-year tour, Webster and Taylor were replaced in 1964 by Sqn Ldr Basil Dodd and Flt Lt Martin Bee. However, Webster lobbied to stay in the U-2 programme and in an unprecedented move as a British citizen he resigned from the RAF and was hired as a civilian by the Lockheed Corporation to continue flying the U-2 under contract.

Immediately prior to the outbreak of hostilities in the 1967 Arab–Israeli War, a U-2 was based at Upper Heyford. But the actual spy missions never took place.

Two further RAF personnel were assigned to the CIA's U-2 programme. Flt Lts Richard Cloche and Harry Drew replaced Bee and Taylor in 1967. They flew an enlarged and improved version of the aircraft designated the U-2R. They participated in a deployment to RAF Akrotiri from August to December 1970. They flew along the Suez Canal monitoring the cease-fire between Egypt and Israel.

15
SHOOTDOWN

Gen. LeMay's nose had been put out of joint by the assignment of the U-2 programme to the CIA. Despite his initial antagonism to the U-2 project he and the senior USAF commanders realised that it would control the flow of intelligence vital for USAF budgets. At the time Eisenhower asked the CIA to develop the plane, the SAC commander had reputedly said, 'We'll let those sons of bitches get in and then we'll take it away from them.'[1] LeMay's biography gives an account of the struggle for control of the project. 'The CIA fought him from the start and finally, Gen. Nathan Twining signed an agreement accepting a subordinate role for SAC in the U2 program.'[2]

After 'Open Skies' and into 1956 LeMay continued with his overflight operations. The uprated American version of the Canberra was now in service – the Martin B-57. The main reconnaissance variant was the RB-57D which had a massively increased wingspan – from about 65ft to over 109ft – and two 9,700lb thrust Pratt & Whitney J75-P-5 turbojets. The first batch was assigned to the 4080th Squadron, a reconnaissance unit that was later to be the first SAC unit to use the U-2.

It is hard to get from Western sources exact details or confirmation of the flights undertaken at this time. Again in some ways it is easier now to get them from the former Soviets. Retired Air Defence General Vladimir Abramov said that he personally can recall three flights in this period:

- On 9 July 1956 three RB-57s entered Kaliningrad and separated at Kaunas. One flew south-west toward Poland. Another flew west toward East Germany and then to Kiev. The third flew north to Leningrad and then turned south to fly toward Minsk. The aircraft were in the air for 3hr 30min.
- On 10 July 1956 one B-57 or B-66 entered at Peremyshl Yary and flew over Chernovety to Odessa.
- On 10 September 1957 an aircraft flew from Iran to the Caspian Sea, Krasnovodsky, Grozny and Tbilisi. It was in the air for 4hr 2min. Eighteen Soviet planes were sent to intercept but failed.

It is likely that some of these flights were U-2s, although details of U-2 flights have still not been released. I have not been able to get corroboration of the other flights or find out to which nationality these aircraft belonged. Other RB-57D flights followed. According to Robert Hopkins, Eisenhower discussed overflights with his military advisers: 'SAC overflights continued after 1956 in the form of Black Knight RB-57D high altitude missions over the USSR and Red China.'[3]

Hopkins said Black Knight overflights could be authorised by the four-star theatre commander. My own suspicion is that that was a technique used to keep the operations under the USAF's hat, which was fine as long as the Russians did not complain. Hopkins believes that Eisenhower was lax in monitoring military overflights and allowed the air force wide latitude in planning and conducting these missions. It appears that Eisenhower was not fully and properly briefed.

In September 1956 a detachment of the 4080th SRW, flying RB-57Ds, was sent to Japan, where they commenced a series of operations under the codename 'Sealion', which apparently involved penetration of Communist airspace. The pilots had the impression that these missions were not only sensitive in terms of the Communists but that Washington was also unaware of them. On 11 December 1956 LeMay sent three RB-57 aircraft over Vladivostok. The Soviets went public and complained bitterly. The protest was picked up and carried by the *New York Times*.[4] The Department of State's reply was:

> . . . a thorough investigation has revealed that the only authorised US Air Force flights in the general area of Sea of Japan were normal training activities. If, however, USSR would offer information to enable positive identification of aircraft allegedly involved, or otherwise establish proof of allegation, US Government would be pleased to conduct a further study of the matter.

According to a reliable source, a still unreleased White House minute shows that Eisenhower was furious and rebuked the USAF. It was not the first time the President had caught the USAF exceeding its remit. From 1951 the USAF had run a series of balloon operations against the Soviet Union. The unmanned balloons, each with a camera, were sent across Russia and picked up. The operations suffered from severe problems and cock-ups. Many balloons fell short into Soviet hands sparking major diplomatic incidents. Despite Eisenhower's protests the USAF continued to exceed its permission, finally leading him to cut off the project finances.

Gen. Goodpaster recalls :

He authorised the [balloon] flights with the proviso that there would not be a time set for them to come down. Some of the Air Force people decided the President really didn't understand the problem, and didn't understand how sure they could be that these balloons would not come down in the Soviet Union. Well, the history is different. They did come down in the area of the Ukraine, as I recall. We got a blistering protest, and I had the unenviable job of bringing this to the President's attention. And out of that came his instruction, which I passed on to the Pentagon, no more balloons.

Don Welzenbach said:

After the end of the first balloon flight, Eisenhower ordered a complete stand-down on the balloons, he didn't want any more built, he wanted all the money returned that had been authorised for this. The second balloon flight, which was a little over a year later, I think came as a bit of a surprise. Now he authorised the flight but when it went awry also, and we got a note from both the Soviet Union and Poland complaining about this, he was irate. He wanted all the money returned. He didn't want any more balloons. He made this very, very clear. There weren't any more balloons after that. But his first stand-down orders seemingly had very little effect on the Air Force. It proceeded to develop this other programme.

By 1957 the skies were beginning to fill up with Western spy flights. The USAF began operating seven Lockheed RB-69 multi-purpose spy planes for the CIA from Wiesbaden AFB in West Germany. The CIA had first asked the US Navy to purchase the aircraft and operate them on the CIA's behalf. In his book *The Secret Team*, L. Fletcher Prouty wrote that the USN did not wish to become involved in the project. They were worried that if any of the aircraft were shot down the navy would have to shoulder all the blame. The USAF was less scrupulous. The RB-69s were used across the world and are reputed to have conducted numerous penetration missions into communist territory. Prouty wrote that they were the first operational carriers for a sideways-looking radar system (SLAR) with which the Iron Curtain could be penetrated under all weather conditions.[5]

On 25 April 1958, Eisenhower temporarily suspended 'reconnaissance flights, by military or other aircraft, over the territory of the USSR or other Communist countries.'[6]

LeMay later said that although Eisenhower had authority over the CIA overflights, 'that didn't mean that we [at SAC] didn't do some of our own. We did in those days.'[7] In this interview LeMay said that 'it became difficult to get permission to overfly Russia to take these pictures.'

An incident in May 1958 in Asia caused political intervention again from Washington. Secretary of Defense Neil McElroy wrote to the JCS in July 1958 that existing instructions were explicit on the limitations of all reconnaissance flights operating on the periphery of the Sino-Soviet borders. Recent violations of these instructions by RB-47s had placed the United States in a serious position with respect to the Soviet Union. The Secretary announced that the violations would be investigated.[8]

At the 25 May 1960 National Security Council meeting Twining told Eisenhower that the 1960 congressional inquiry into U-2 operations might reveal the extent of military overflights of the Soviet Union. Twining feared that 'if the investigators probed CIA [overflights], they would want to investigate JCS operations as well.'[9]

Overflights had made flying missions near communist airspace a tense affair. Interception by MiGs and other communist fighters was a regular occurrence for crews flying ELINT missions around the communist bloc. As we have seen, both British and American ELINT crews maintain that they didn't intrude into Soviet airspace, except by accident. However, intrusions into communist airspace seem much more frequent than just the penetration and overflight missions. It is not hard to see why they were so angry.

Gen. Vladimir Abramov, former head of the Soviet Air Defence Corps (PVO) for the Kiel region in the 1950s:

> The job of the PVO was to prevent intruders from trespassing into Soviet Air Space. Unlike the international standard which is 3km from the country's borders, the USSR standard was 25km. Our instructions were to force land the plane if it came within the restricted area and to take the pilots captive. If that proved impossible we had to shoot them down. There were severe punishments if we did not and medals and promotion if we succeeded.[10]
>
> Everyone knows that the territory of the Soviet Union was about 22 million square kilometres plus the territories of the Warsaw Pact. And the length of the border line was about 22,000km. Our task was not to let one single intruder aircraft into our territory. We were also to rebuff any attack on any spot like hydroelectric stations, atomic energy sites and so on. We also had to keep out foreign spies. At that time in the 1950s we were at our most vulnerable. In the first place there were central parts or different spots in Siberia, the Far East, North and Polar regions. That's where the development of air defences was having to grow fast. I don't feel like giving the names because I feel hurt for the Soviet Union, for Russia, because at the time we had practically no air defences in these areas. We had to reduce to a great extent the intruders flying through our skies.

Following the RAF overflight mission of 17 April 1952, the Soviets set up a high level commission. Its official, K.A. Vershinin, reported to top Kremlin leaders including Beria, Bulganin and Vasilevski. Over the following six months he carefully logged and examined every border and intrusion flight. In his eight-page summary he cites that in the area of the Liaotung Peninsula and Far East, the Soviet radar detected 'at a distance of only 60km from our shores, 429 flights, which judging from their characteristics, could have been used for reconnaissance of our radar system.' Of these flights 'there were nineteen border violations'.

Vershinin's conclusions on the air defence system were damning. He examined the interception rate:

> Every violation of our state borders, regardless of whether an interception took place or not, was investigated by special commissions, established in the European part of USSR territory by order of the War Minister and in the Far East, as a rule, by the Commander of air defence forces of the Far Eastern Border. In individual instances, the incidents were resolved by the Regional Commander of air defence forces.
>
> According to the results of the investigations, it has been established that the reasons for our fighters not completely destroying or not intercepting enemy aircraft are the following:

A. The nineteen incidents which took place in the daytime

> • In five interceptions only two enemy aircraft were shot down.
> The other three violators, judging from the pilots' reports, which are confirmed by gun-camera photos, were at least damaged.
>
> Inaccurate shooting by the pilots appears to be the reason for not completely destroying three of the intercepted enemy aircraft. This is due to a lack of practical knowledge in the use of the ASP-ZN automatic gunsights.
>
> Lack of practical skill in the use of the ASP-ZN sights appears to be a common flaw in the training of all pilots within VVS [Air Force] fighter aviation.
>
> This in turn appears to result from the fact that, up to this point, the question of developing three-dimensional targets to enable the actual utilisation of the ASP-ZN has not been resolved, and pilots do not receive the necessary training in firing on airborne targets.

> In the remaining fourteen incidents, interception of the violators did not take place for the following reasons:

> • In one incident the enemy fighter pilot, hit in the Antung region, after violating the borders of the Liaotung peninsula treaty zone, parachuted before being intercepted by our fighters from Port Arthur air defence;[11]
> • In one incident, also in the region of the Liaotung peninsula, our fighters did not take-off because of bad weather;

• In five incidents in the Sakhalin-Kurile region, the piston-engined fighter aircraft which were launched —three pairs of P-63s and two pairs of La-11s – were not able to attain enough speed to catch the violator, which was capable of faster speeds;

• In two incidents in the area of Liaotung peninsula due to the short time between receiving the information that a violator had been discovered and the violator leaving the bounds of the treaty zone border, our MiG-15(bis) fighters were not able to gain the necessary altitude and cover the 110km distance between the airfield and the point of the border violation;

• In one incident in the region of the Liaotung peninsula, where action occurred under jamming conditions as a result of indiscretion on the part of the pilots and poor control exercised by their command point, one of our fighters was shot down and the violator aircraft was not destroyed;

• In one incident in the Kavkaz region the violator was in the area of a fighter airfield. The violator escaped unpunished as a result of unsatisfactory work on the part of the regimental VNOS [aircraft warning service] post in reporting, and the disorganisation of the division command post duty officer.

B. Violations which occurred at night

• In three incidents in the Sakhalin-Kurile region fighters did not take-off due to poor meteorological conditions. Furthermore, the violation occurred within a month after the organisation of this area of air defence and fighters were poorly prepared for night actions.

• In three incidents fighters were guided to the target by ground radar, but were not able to visually locate the violator.

• In three incidents fighters took-off but were unable to come close to the violator because the target was only intermittently fixed on.

The principal deficiencies are as follows:

• The length of time to send a report on the first detection of a violation from the radar station to the fighter aircraft command point. This deficiency directly affects the timely launching of fighters.

• There are significant breaks, lasting two, three and even four minutes, in the transmission of messages from the radar station to the fighter aircraft command point in tracking targets. [These breaks] greatly affect the accuracy of navigational calculations, since a jet aircraft travels no less than 12km/min. Large mistakes are possible in calculating future points [of aircraft]. If the target changes course, then the mistake in the calculation becomes almost impossible to correct.

• In certain cases there are serious inaccuracies in the contents of the messages reported by the radar station. These inaccuracies are committed by radiotelegraph operators and radiotelephone operators as a result of insufficient skill and, sometimes, because of negligence. In practice, one or two inaccurate messages in tracking quick-moving targets can entirely preclude interception.

• These three deficiencies basically depend on the training, efficiency, and co-ordination of staff, especially of radiotelegraph operators and radiotelephone operators. However, a deciding role is also played by the technical imperfections in the methods of sending messages, in which there are certain unavoidable transmission echelons. As a result, the message is passed through several hands, and this lengthens the time required and does not preclude inaccuracies.

As a suggestion for the elimination of this deficiency, I consider it absolutely essential to take the most decisive measures to expedite the completion of the system of direct images transmitted onto the radar screen suggested by the designer, Comrade Shorin from MPSS.

The implementation of direct guidance for our fighter pilots is greatly affected by the fact that the message from the radar station is sent by radio, telegraph or telephone, which, in addition to the delay, leads to great inaccuracies.

In order to correct this deficiency permanently, I believe it to be of the highest importance that we quickly resolve the problem of widening the distance of the 'Periscope' remote radars within 300m of the command point.

In order to improve the quality of flight crews' weapons training in firing at airborne targets, it is urgently necessary to create, in the shortest time possible, three-dimensional targets to provide for utilisation of the ASP-ZN gunsights.

The measures provided for in the draft resolution – along with intensified training of staff, completion of a system of decentralised notification of fighter aviation command points by immediate transmission of messages from radar stations, and the creation of a radio bureau in the command points of air defence regions – will fundamentally improve the effectiveness of border air defence troops.

[signed] Vershinin K.A.
19 December 1952

During my researches I also obtained Soviet documents listing intrusions on the Soviet far eastern sector during the period of 1952-55. Although only a partial list, it lists dozens of incursions by Western military aircraft. In 1972 a Soviet author published data stating that from 1953 to 1956, USAF violated the borders of the USSR 130 times and of the other socialist countries 211 times.[12] Many violations lasted for just a few minutes and involved a few kilometres. Every so often they were more serious.

The result of the commission and Vershinin's work was a shake up of the air defence system and a speeding up of the supply of better equipment to the PVO. Even so the PVO was unable to stop any of the 1954 missions. Gen. Vladimir Abramov said:

The commanders of air defence in this area were reprimanded or punished though the PVO chiefs knew that it was impossible to guide our own planes in the dark. Later on we were equipped with new airplanes like the MiG-19 with just over supersonic speed. My air defence division in the Ukraine was the first to receive those planes. Later on others received these aircraft. These aircraft were equipped with onboard radars.

From 1955 on it was usually the 'crows' or special operators in the ELINT aircraft listening to radar frequencies who were the first to realise the MiGs were on the way up. Curly Behrmann said:

> You would tell the front end, the pilot and co-pilot, 'I've got MiG signals.' And the co-pilot would probably look around and he would confirm, 'Yes, I see MiGs coming in.' And you continued to fly your mission and look for other signals, and tune back and forth and double check MiG signals regularly, to see that they were still there and what they were doing.
>
> The MiGs came in, in a search mode; it was always pip-pip-pip, pip, pip, pip-pip-pip, pip, pip, you know, it just didn't matter which angle they came at you from the tail, that's what their search radar sounded like. And when they got lined up behind you they'd be going, pip, pip, pip-pip-pip, pip, pip, pip-pip-pip, brrrrrrrrrrrrrrrt.

In 1960, Lt John McKone was the 28-year-old navigator of a USAF RB-47H Stratojet of the 55th Strategic Reconnaissance Wing on temporary duty at Brize Norton in England.[13] Three months after the U-2 incident his crew was assigned a mission to Murmansk. McKone said that little had prepared him for what happened on that July mission:

> Now we were used, of course, to flying these missions, that the Soviet fighters would come up and fly escort with us, as we call it. And they were rather unpredictable.
>
> We were briefed beforehand that this was supposed to be a milk run and nothing to happen on this mission. That it was very quiet up in this particular area that we were going into, the northern coastline of the Soviet Union near the port of Murmansk. At the mouth of the White Sea we were to make a 90 degree left turn to maintain track towards Novaya Zemlya, and then back to Brize. That mission was about 12 hours in those days and we were at no time to get closer than 50 nautical miles to any of the Soviet landmasses.
>
> We were two minutes early at the turning point. I told the aircraft commander, 'Okay Bill, start your left turn now.'
>
> I'd already given him the heading to take. As we start the left turn I heard over the intercom the co-pilot say, 'check, check, check, right wing.' I heard the aircraft commander, Bill Palm, say, 'Where in the hell did that guy come from?' Like it was a surprise. Suddenly we had a fighter off our wing.
>
> As we were taking this left turn, without any warning whatsoever, he started firing on us, pumping cannon shells into our number two and three engines, they caught fire and seized and that threw our airplane into a flat spin. I could hear the cannon shells hitting the airplane and the airplane shuddering.
>
> I was already strapped into my parachute and I was ready to go in case we really

ran into trouble. I can remember that the aircraft commander said, 'Wait a minute, wait a minute,' which to me, said don't bale out yet. So I didn't. And then I remember a second burst of fire, and I saw some holes opening up around my position in the airplane, that were about the size of cannon shells coming through there. Then I heard the aircraft commander say, 'Bale out, bale out, bale out' and I heard alarm bells ring and red alarm lights coming on for baling out. I heard a couple of explosions behind me, which sounded like ejection seats and the canopy going off. And I figured it was time to get out of there. So I baled out.

Of the RB-47's crew of six only two men survived. Lt John McKone and Lt Bruce Olmstead were fished out of the sea by a Soviet trawler crew. They were then sent to Moscow where they were paraded for the public and press. The Soviets tried to duplicate the outrage of the U-2 but as the aircraft had technically been in international airspace the shootdown only succeeded in stirring up anger among the American people. They were held in Lubyanka for seven months before being returned to the US.[14]

The possibilities for fatal misunderstandings during border flights can be seen in the case of the RB-47 shootdown. At the point McKone and his colleagues were attacked they were just beginning to turn away from the Soviet mainland. The intercepting pilot Lt Vasili Poliakov, now retired, said that he believed that the RB-47 was on a photographic reconnaissance mission and was heading straight towards a new secret Soviet nuclear submarine base.[15] In fact this was not the task of the RB-47 as the crew knew nothing about it.

Gen. Abramov admits there was a lot of pressure on the pilots during these interceptions. 'There was a lot of pressure from above and I suppose pilots might tend to shoot down an aircraft rather than being accused of letting it escape,' he said.

Communist attacks on aircraft started in 1947 and did not end until 1983. The first ELINT aircraft to be shot down was the US Navy Consolidated PB4Y-2 Privateer shot down in April 1950 in the Baltic. Inevitably as these converted bombers were sitting ducks for MiGs they took the heaviest casualties of the Cold War. The 55th alone suffered eight losses in as many years.

In March 1996 veterans of Strategic Air Command attended the SAC Chapel at Offutt AFB to commemorate those who lost their lives during the Cold War. Over 2,000 members died to keep SAC at the peak of professional readiness. Over 200 were killed by communist air defence.

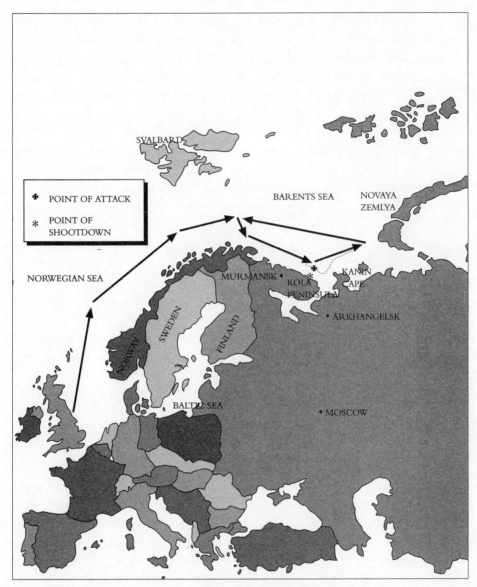

Map 5   The planned route of RB-47 and the shootdown area, 1 July 1960.

On the chapel wall a plaque was dedicated on which there are additional spaces. Further names will be added when the secret missions these crews were lost upon are declassified.

The West always claimed after these shootdowns that the communists had been unprovoked and generally the flights were in international airspace (if only just). Sometimes they were over disputed areas like the Sakhalin or Churls Islands. But sometimes Western aircraft really did stray. The communists tended to vent their anger at the more vulnerable aircraft. What they were really furious about were overflights.

In many cases the route of these flights remained in dispute. The Americans saying they were in international airspace and the Soviets saying that they were in their airspace. Forty years on it is possible to examine many of the cases in detail. In the National Archives in Washington are the files of Sam Klaus.[16] He was a legal officer at the State Department from the 1940s to 1960s. It was his job to make claims for reparation at the International Court of Justice. The United States would usually attempt to sue the communist government responsible for any such shootdown. He was given access to classified information about routes. It appears that in most cases the Soviets caught these aircraft in airspace recognised by the West as international.

The British took far fewer losses than the Americans for their involvement in the aerial espionage war.[17] But in March 1953 an RAF Lincoln, an updated version of the Lancaster bomber, strayed from the British zone in Germany into the Russian zone. The Russians claimed that it penetrated 125km into their airspace. Documents in the Public Record Office released thirty years later confirm this. The aircraft appears to have strayed completely off course. It seems that the crew suddenly realised what had happened as it executed a sharp 180 degree turn. But it was too late. PVO MiGs caught up with it and attacked, shooting it down on the border. Five crew members died immediately, the remaining two died of their injuries shortly afterwards.

How the aircraft strayed remains an open question. The captain was a highly experienced pilot who had flown many bombing missions over Germany during the war. There has been speculation that as the aircraft was a Lincoln it was engaged in an ELINT mission and that the claim that it was on a training mission was just a cover.[18] However, the documents show that this was an aircraft from the RAF's gunnery training school. It was one of two over Germany that day, both of which were carrying no ammunition. The other Lincoln, flying along the border 75 miles to the south, was buzzed by MiGs but was not attacked.

It remains possible that while these were not ELINT aircraft that they had a secret brief to provoke the Soviet defences which were recorded from the ground. But as yet there is no evidence.

Other nations also engaged in spy plane missions against the USSR, some in conjunction with the US and some on their own account. In particular Sweden flew CIA-supplied DC-3 ELINT aircraft. One was lost in the Baltic on 13 June 1952 after being attacked by MiGs. None of the eight-man crew from the aircraft was ever found. The incident was further exacerbated when MiGs attacked and shot down a Swedish Catalina rescue aircraft with further loss of life.

The Swedes continued the game they had played during World War 2 of playing neutral while helping the British and Americans. In January 1949 the British Naval Attaché in Stockholm forwarded a report to Washington, based on Swedish intelligence, which supplied important information about Soviet radar chains on the east coast of the Baltic and in northern Germany.[19] As a result the Swedes had a number of cat and mouse run-ins with the Russians. The Soviet Ministry for Foreign Affairs admitted in notes that it had overflown the fortified Swedish area of Karlskrona. The notes were dated 28 August 1946, and 25 September 1947 but the actual dates of the overflights were not known. The Soviets claimed they had occurred because of bad weather.

Later, the Soviets claimed that Swedish military aircraft had violated their airspace on the 17 and 26 July 1951. During the exchanges following the shooting down of the two Swedish planes the Swedish Ministry of Foreign Affairs confirmed that two violations had taken place and that the Swedish government had conveyed its regrets at the time. The only known Swedish statement that the first accident had involved 'a Swedish military aircraft which came by mistake to a point north-west of Libau about 2.2 nautical miles from the coast.' Regarding the second, 'a Swedish military aircraft had been in the area north-west of Vindau and at one moment came to a point somewhere more than five nautical miles from the coast.'

The story of the 1952 Swedish shootdowns has been documented by the Swedish journalist Roger Älmeberg.[20] His father, Alvar Älmeberg, was the captain of the DC-3 and for thirty years Roger had no idea what work his father was really engaged in. Retired Soviet Air Force Gen. Fjodor Sjinkarenko said that the aircraft had intruded over communist territory near Riga.[21] Roger Älmeberg believes that at least some of the crew were captured and he has reports that some were later seen in the Soviet Gulag.[22]

In 1993 Swedish TV also released the 1963 interrogation of convicted Soviet spy Stig Wennerstrom, a former Swedish military attaché. His testimony details US efforts after World War 2 to build a chain of radar and radio listening points around the Soviet Union. The missing link in the chain, he said, was the area between northern Germany and Norway. The problem was solved in 1949 when the Swedish and US defence personnel agreed to work together. The Americans provided state-of-the-art technical gear to the Swedes, flying them into Swedish air bases at night to keep the arrangement secret.

Casualties mounted as the number of operations undertaken by western ELINT aircraft grew. Towards the end of the 1950s further agencies were getting in on the ELINT agenda. The secretive National Security Agency, like its British counterpart GCHQ, had rapidly developed huge sophistication in eavesdropping Soviet communications. Their aircraft were aimed at different targets to the ELINT aircraft of the 55th complementing a mushrooming network of NSA and GCHQ bases. The had no interest in radars or air units, they were more interested in other military and political and even industrial communications of the Soviets. Their aircraft had different types of equipment on board and often carried a complement of 'COMINT' operators. These were language specialists who could understand Soviet radio conversations and record what sounded like the most interesting. The NSA's operations were carried out by Lockheed EC-130 Hercules aircraft based in Germany under the anonymous title the 4028th Composite Squadron. This unit lost a C-130 on 2 September 1958. It had crossed the border into Soviet Armenia, taking a short cut, and was caught by MiGs. The slow and cumbersome aircraft was easy prey and was shot down near the village of Sassnaken. Officially it was listed as a 'transport'. Of the seventeen crew on board the EC-130, six bodies were later returned to the American Government.[23]

There were allegations that the EC-130 was pulled off course by false navigation signals. At the time aircraft used the signals from radio beacons placed on friendly territory to guide themselves. The communist technique of falsifying beacon signals and luring aircraft over the borders was called 'mekoning'. In retrospect it is unlikely that is why the EC-130 had ventured over the border. But various spyplane crew members have told me that the Soviets used 'mekoning'.

Between 1947 and 1960 the West lost over twenty aircraft shot down in peacetime by Eastern Bloc countries. Only one CIA aircraft is listed. It is expected that after future declassifications more will be added.

Two months after the U-2 fiasco Eisenhower told Twining to increase the level of supervision over military reconnaissance flights by establishing the Joint Reconnaissance Center at the Pentagon to 'monitor all reconnaissance operations conducted by' the military. Approval authority for future military reconnaissance missions, peripheral or overflights, was assigned to the Joint Chiefs.[24]

For the Soviets, the U-2 shootdown was a triumph after years of failure.

16
RED BEARS

When the Soviets finally shot down a U-2, Khrushchev, by all accounts, was in a heady mix of anger and elation — at last the chance for some revenge. For over ten years the Kremlin had felt impotent because of their inability to stop overflights. Whatever the wrongs of the communist regimes, they must have perceived themselves as being taunted by the West.

Just shortly before, in remarks made to the Czechoslovak embassy in Moscow in 1960, Soviet Premier Khrushchev had bitterly complained that in 1956 a US reconnaissance plane had flown as far as Kiev, 250 miles inside the Soviet border.[1] In his memoirs he said, 'When Stalin died we felt terribly vulnerable . . . The Americans had the Soviet Union surrounded with military bases and kept sending reconnaissance planes deep into our territory, sometimes as far as Kiev. We expected an all-out attack any day.'[2]

The Politburo was only too aware that these spy flights showed that they were technologically compromised. That went a long way to explaining why the Soviets made so little fuss publicly about overflight missions at the time and instead made most complaints about peripheral flights. They were trying to make the Eastern Bloc look invincible. It would not have helped to have admitted that Western aircraft were violating their borders with impunity on a daily basis. Now they had turned the tables. The shootdown was to destroy Eisenhower's ambition of an East–West summit leading to a nuclear test ban treaty, his legacy for peace in the last year of his presidency. But the writing was already on the wall. After Powers' U-2 had disappeared, Allen Dulles maintained the hope and belief that the crash had been unobserved and undiscovered by the Russians. Dulles suggested to the administrator of NASA, T. Keith Glennan, that he release a pre-prepared cover story. Glennan told the media that a high altitude weather research aircraft on a flight from Adana, Turkey was missing and that, 'it might have accidentally violated Soviet air space.' He said that the U-2 was a high altitude aircraft, vital for the space programme. It was assumed that this frankness would take some sting out of the Russians' tail should they find the remains of the crashed aircraft somewhere in their territory.

This was what Khrushchev had been waiting for. On the 5th, five long days after the plane had disappeared, he reported that an American plane had been shot down over Soviet territory. He gave no more detail than that but took the opportunity to harangue the Americans as warmongers. The American public was angered, in the collective belief that this was another innocent aircraft shot down.

Immediately afterwards Lincoln White, the official State Department official, repeated Glennan's story and again claimed innocent action on the part of the 'disabled' pilot.

On the same day the US Ambassador told Washington that he had picked up cocktail-party gossip that the American pilot had been picked up and was in good health. Then on 7 May Khrushchev went for the kill:

> Comrades I must let you in on a secret. When I made my report I deliberately refrained from mentioning that the pilot was alive and safe and that we had the remnants of the plane. We did this deliberately, because had we given out the whole story, the Americans would have thought up another version.

He then went on to give the whole story in some detail. He concluded, 'We are so close to the summit and to peace. I am ready to accept that this was a cruel and terrible provocation made by others without the knowledge of the American President.'

He challenged Eisenhower to say he had no knowledge of the U-2 flights and to fire the CIA executives responsible. That was the price of Eisenhower's long sought-after summit. Eisenhower did know and had approved the flight. He did not fire Dulles and his U-2 team, even if it would have been a sacrifice for the summit. He agreed Secretary Christian Herter's statement on 9 May:

> In accordance with the National Security Act of 1947 the President has put into effect since the beginning of his administration directives to gather by every possible means information required to protect the United States and the Free World against surprise attack and to enable them to make effective preparations for their defence. Under these directives, programs have been developed and put into operation which have included extensive aerial surveillance by unarmed civilian aircraft, normally of a peripheral character, but occasionally by penetration.

Eisenhower's action was unprecedented. He was admitting that the United States was spying. He admitted that he had lied in the past about this. From Khrushchev's point of view, Eisenhower admission of spying and refusal to apologise upped the ante of the whole affair.

Khrushchev's son, Sergei, recalls his father's anger:

> For Russians and my father, it was the sign that the American do not really want to negotiate the political question. They want to show their military strength and show their fist.[3]

For domestic and international face Khrushchev had to be tough.

When Khrushchev arrived at the Paris summit a few days later he used the occasion to launch into one of the most vitriolic public denunciations of another country that the world has ever heard. The Soviet delegation then walked out. The summit had ended. Eisenhower's great crusade for peace was dead. There was to be no thaw in the Cold War. The East-West tensions were about to escalate into a new series of confrontations that were to come perilously close to all-out nuclear war.[4]

Insight into Khrushchev's thinking comes from a recently released memo taken during a 1986 meeting between the Soviet Ambassador, Anatoly Dobryin, and George Shultz, the Secretary of State. One guest, Paul Nitze, asked Dobryin why it was that U-2 flights did not disturb relations until one was shot down and then it became a big issue. Dobryin said that initially Khrushchev was furious at the Soviet military because they could not shoot down the U-2. When they did, he tried to pursue the public fiction that Eisenhower was not responsible (since he wanted to continue to deal with him). He did not expect Eisenhower to disown the flights, but thought he would understand that he should not state publicly that he authorised them. When Eisenhower did the latter, however, Khrushchev was unable to continue dealing with him because that would have meant a public loss of face. (He said that Khrushchev later commented he would gladly entrust the education of his children to Eisenhower because he was 'truly an honest man,' but that he wondered if he understood the responsibilities which go with political leadership in international affairs.)[5]

The Soviet military does not seem to have been angered as much about the U-2 flights as the politicians. In 1993 Gen. Mikhailov said,

> At the time it didn't seem so very provocative from the military point of view. We thought this was just intelligence work because all the flights were just over sites

that other intelligence sources couldn't reach. These were test sites, launching sites, airdromes, airbases, naval bases and so on. At first we thought it was the air force but then we realised it was something special – probably the CIA.[6]

Following the U-2 crisis Eisenhower stopped all penetration flights over the Soviet Union. The Taiwanese took over U-2 flights over communist China, four aircraft were lost over the next few years and there were waves of anti-American protests from Beijing. The remains of the aircraft went on display in the Chinese capital. Peripheral flights were suspended to be resumed several months later. As we have seen, one of the first in July 1960 was shot down by the Soviets and attempts to turn that into another U-2 propaganda coup were not as successful.

From 1960 the Russian strategic aerial reconnaissance operations began to expand. Up to this point it had been largely a one-way traffic from the West. Then a growing number of Soviet 'Bear' and 'Bison' aircraft began to make long-distance reconnaissance missions. The 'Bison' and 'Bear' bombers that were considered to be the great threat of the bomber gap were considered too vulnerable by the Russians for attacking continental America. Of the 125 'Bisons' built many were converted from bombers into maritime reconnaissance and electronic countermeasures platforms. It was these aircraft that patrolled the coasts of Europe.

I have not been able to authenticate one single instance of a substantial penetration of American or British airspace by Russian aircraft. There is no doubt that Russian aircraft flew along coastlines of the USA and the UK trying to provoke the defences into action. They may have even flown over remote parts of Canada, Alaska and the Arctic. But it was never on the same scale as the Western effort. They simply did not have the equipment. I am not saying that the communists would not have done them if they were able. But they didn't.

According to a press dispatch from Copenhagen on 9 September 1952, observers on the Danish Isle of Bornholm reported repeated violations of Danish sovereignty by Soviet military planes that day. Scores of Soviet bombers and fighters were said to have flown over Bornholm all morning. Russian warships were also observed in the area. Danish reports were ridiculed by Soviet radio broadcasts as 'mischief-making rumours'. Danish islands in the Baltic were subject to a number of overflights in the following years.

On 16 March 1953 a USAF spokesman stated that vapour trails from engines of unidentified planes had been sighted occasionally over the far northern approaches to the North American continent. The most recent report of such activity, he stated, had come from an airborne observer over Alaska on 10 March; it resulted in a brief 'yellow alert'. The USAF spokesman apparently queried an AP dispatch quoting the Fairbanks *New Miner*, which reported a 'yellow alert' there the night of 7 March.

On 7 March, the Alsop brothers, with their close intelligence contacts, had written one of their syndicated columns about Soviet strategic air reconnaissance. They asserted that Soviet air reconnaissance of the Western hemisphere began in the summer of 1948 and that the earliest sighting of such flights was over Alaska and north-western Canada. Detection of unidentified aircraft (presumed to be Soviet reconnaissance planes) had been made mainly by visual sightings of contrails; few had been made by radar.

Approximately twelve sightings had been confirmed as undoubtedly resulting from Soviet reconnaissance missions of which two had occurred in early March 1953 one in northern Canada and the other in the vicinity of the important US base in Thule. No Soviet planes had been intercepted. Subsequent to the Alsop brothers' statement on this subject, authoritative sources in Washington disclosed essentially the same information regarding at least twelve Soviet overflights within the previous year over the polar area of the North American continent and Greenland.

In an article entitled, 'Russian Planes are raiding Canadian Skies', in *Colliers* magazine on 16 October 1953, William A. Ulman reported an eyewitness account by US jet fighters of the Alaskan Air Command to intercept an unidentified aircraft 'almost certainly a Russian' which had been picked up by radar stations on the west coast of Alaska. Ulman did not explicitly state whether the unidentified plane in question had actually violated US territory or territorial waters, but added the following statement: 'Almost every day, at least one unidentified airplane violates (sic) our continental borders.' A general in the Alaskan Air Command was quoted as saying: 'They [Russian planes] come in at all times and places and some have even penetrated deep into north central Canada.'

The frequency of the Soviet air violations in this region reported by Ulman contradicts the previous reports. From the context of Ulman's story it seems likely that most of the violations detected by US Alaskan coastal radar defences refer to a type of Soviet air reconnaissance which had not been previously disclosed. The almost daily incursions reported by Ulman appear to be, for the most part, instances of border reconnaissance of the Alaskan coast by Soviet reconnaissance aircraft. As Ulman points out, such planes are difficult to intercept since they can quickly return to international airspace or, given the proximity of Soviet territory to Alaska at some points, to their own territory as soon as US fighter-interceptors take to the air; 'Their mission apparently is to feel out our radar defences and photograph our coasts. When our jets go out to meet them they run.'

Again on 13 December 1952, USAF disclosed that contrails of an unidentified aircraft had been spotted from a USAF aircraft over Greenland on 10 December 1952. Although the North-east Air Command Headquarters in Newfoundland, the Air Defense Command and the Pentagon were at once notified, no general alert was sounded because no pattern was established. The radar network covering Greenland did not pick up the unidentified plane. The direction of the contrails indicated the plane making them was flying away from the United States.

Early on in the Cold War the United States had begun installing early warning and defensive radar networks to identify Soviet aircraft as soon as possible. At first the plan was limited to the radar net *Lashup* which by June 1950 consisted of forty-nine stations in the United States and Canada. The Joint Chiefs of Staff set up the Continental US Defense Planning Group (CUSDPG) in 1948 and this group was the basis for the enormous defence network built over the next decades.[7]

In August, Soviet aircraft based in the Kuriles began to make flights over the northern Japanese island of Hokkaido. The frequency of the flights soon reached a level which indicated deliberate violation of Japanese airspace. In a public statement on 13 October after the RB-29 Superfortress incident of 7 October, Brig.-Gen. Delmar T. Spivey, Commander of the US Air Defense Force for Japan, declared that: '. . . by purpose or accident, Russian planes from time to time fly over Japanese waters . . . Sometimes our planes take-off on alerts and sometimes we just sit tight to see what will happen.'

An overall Far East Air Force summary of 'confirmed' and 'suspected' overflights of northern Japan in the three-month period 1 September to 29 November identified thirty-four confirmed violations and thirty-eight suspected violations.

The reasons for these flights puzzled the Americans although they did consider it possible that the Soviets were engaged in a number of objectives, including testing the radar defences. The worst clash over this occurred on 7 October 1952 when an unarmed ELINT RB-29 Superfortress was dispatched on a 'duly authorised flight mission over the Island of Hokkaido, Japan'. This aircraft was attacked by two Soviet fighter aircraft from the Island of Yuri – the nearest Soviet territory. The RB-29 was shot down, hitting the water at some point between Akiyuri Island and Yuri Island in Japanese territory.[8]

Yuri Island is part of the Habomais territory and was contested by the Soviets and Japan. The Soviets were well aware that the US and Japanese authorities never recognised that the Habomais, which were occupied by the Soviets following World War 2, were part of the Kuriles awarded to Russia at Yalta. The Japanese government had taken the position that no peace treaty was possible with the USSR until the status of the Habomai and Shikotan was clarified. This problem has continued to the present. The US Government issued a claim in the World Court for $1,620,295.01 in 1953.

Ten days later the US warned the Soviets that it was going to take a tougher approach to air defence over the Hokkaido area. After the warning Soviet intrusions continued for a while. As the US counter-action started to shape up, the Soviet flights began to decline. A year later they were down to one every two weeks.

In April 1958 the Japanese air force took over the responsibility for the air defence of Hokkaido. In the first nine months Japanese F-86F Sabres were sent up 426 times. In the future the number of scrambles for unidentified aircraft would average 380 per year.[9]

The Soviets gradually developed their own ELINT aircraft. Both the Soviet long-range bomber force and the naval air service used the four-engined Antonov An-12 – NATO reporting-name 'Cub-B'. Usually a transport in the same mould as the C-130 Hercules, the 'ferret' version was identifiable by its antennae and spherical radomes under the fuselage.

After the U-2 affair there were a number of reports in the American press claiming that the Soviets had been penetrating US airspace. In a trailer to a larger article on US missions a smaller additional note headed 'Alaska Flights Reported' carried a claim by an Alaskan State senator that aircraft presumed to be Soviet made 'monthly flights over Alaska in recent years.'[10] Shortly afterwards in a UN Security Council debate, following the downing of McKone and Olmstead's RB-47 Stratojet in July 1960, US Ambassador Henry Cabot Lodge raised Soviet flights near Alaska. He showed a map on which were drawn the flightpaths taken by each of the six Soviet 'ferret' flights in 1959 and 1960. In each case the Soviet aircraft had flown less than thirty miles from the Alaskan coast.

In March 1963 two 'Badgers' – Tupolev Tu-16s – probably due to navigational error, flew over the Alaskan coast. Both quickly turned when the Alaskan coast became visible.[11]

As historian Robert Hopkins has observed, the Soviets took a different approach to intelligence gathering:

> If the Soviets wanted target data, for example, which the United States had to acquire by deep overflight, all the Soviets had to do was buy a roadmap from a local gas station, showing the location of Carswell AFB in proximity to Fort Worth, Texas. There was simply little direct need for Soviet overflights because of the ease of collecting against US installations through open sources or other covert means. Do not forget that Soviet aerial reconnaissance, especially against US fleet operations, was extensive, just as much so as ours against them. Also, look at Soviet aerial reconnaissance over Western Europe and other locations. A substantial amount of Soviet ELINT, primarily COMINT and to a lesser degree SIGINT, came from the Soviet trawler fleets that ringed the US coastline.[12]

Soviet airliners, particularly the regular Ilyushin Il-62 flight from Moscow via Shannon to New York for UN support, or even regular Aeroflot flights when the United States and the Soviet Union still had a bilateral air service agreement, conducted covert overflights. The difference was notable between the way the United States sent aircraft like the RB-47s deep into the USSR and how the Aeroflot flights took place, but they were intended to achieve the same purpose.

The Il-62s were configured clandestinely with cameras and other reconnaissance gear, enabling them to overfly regions and take photos or record ELINT. Such flights typically traversed legitimate airways along the northeast US, but the Soviet airliners would often 'stray' from these airways, and stray quite a distance. As an example, Robert Hopkins said:

> We in the air force received daily intel briefs on Aeroflot 'missions' that strayed hundreds of miles off course over New England to overfly Pease AFB, New Hampshire, Plattsburgh and Griffiss AFB, New York State, and other air force installations. Photos of these areas showed B-52 alert deployments, and gathered ELINT relevant to this mission. Most of these sorties complemented Soviet satellite recon, and provided yet another glimpse of what the United States was doing.

The Soviets relied on satellite photography during the 1960s more than aerial reconnaissance. Although this is later than the key period in which this book is primarily interested, it reflects a Soviet long-term commitment to new technology and space early in the 1950s at the expense of aerial platforms, much like the Soviet commitment to ballistic missiles rather than long-range jet bombers during the so-called bomber gap and missile gap.

Robert Hopkins said,

> Curiously, LeMay was adamant in his opposition to satellite reconnaissance in lieu of aerial reconnaissance. He told the CIA and air force briefers who informed him of the CORONA satellite program that he wasn't interested because it was still unproven technology. The difference is important but subtle – the United States would rely upon airplanes because they had them and they worked, and the Soviets would eventually rely on satellites because they didn't have the airplanes and couldn't make aerial reconnaissance work.

Colonel John R. Lovell, an intelligence officer who was flying as a passenger in the RB-45C piloted by McDonough, also died when the aircraft was shot down.

Four RB-45Cs in RAF markings but minus their serial numbers, lined up behind their RAF aircrews and USAF groundcrews at Sculthorpe, *c.* 1952.

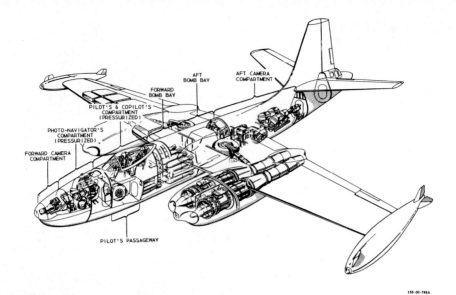

Two diagrams showing the distribution of vertical and oblique cameras in the RB–45C. Flash-bombs were carried in the bomb bay.

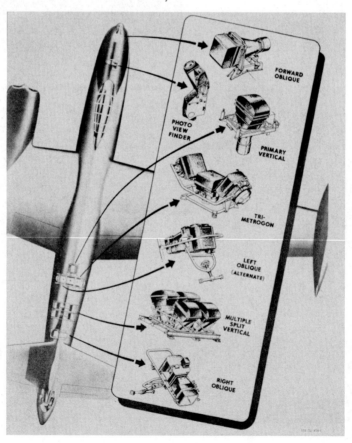

The addition of British roundels to their RB–45Cs was the source of great curiosity to the USAF crews at Sculthorpe. Here two members of the 91st SRW are photographed under the tail of one such RB–45C.

RAF aircrew pose in front of an appropriately embellished RB–45C.

Two views of RAF-marked but unserialled RB-45s at Sculthorpe, with large finned tip-tanks prominent.

Members of the 322nd Reconnaissance Squadron, including two members of the RAF Sculthorpe secret unit, photographed in front of Detachment Ops at Sculthorpe during deployment in 1951. *Sam Myers*

RAF aircrew and a USAF officer in front of the 323rd Strategic Reconnaissance Squadron operations section building at Sculthorpe. John Crampton is standing at centre, left.

Robert Robinson, photographed in the mid-1950s.

Robinson with U-2 team members in the late 1950s.

Jim Barnes, one of the Incirlik U-2 pilots, pictured in
retirement at his California home in 1993.

On 8 May 1954 three RB-47Es flew towards Murmansk where two turned around. The third flew a deep
penetration mission into the Kola Peninsula. The crew of the aircraft were Hal Austin (pilot), Carl Holt
(co-pilot) and Vance Heavilin (navigator). They are pictured here with the author at a reunion for the
Lockbourne AFB in September 1993.

An RB-47F refuels from a KC-97 tanker aircraft in 1954. A KC-97 from Fairford in Gloucestershire saved Austin and his crew when they ran short of fuel on their return flight to England.

Joe Gyulavics was an RB-47K pilot with the 55th SRW who participated in the April 1956 incursion into Siberia.

Richard McNab of the 26th SRW was another RB-47E pilot who flew on the special penetration missions into Siberia in 1956.

McNab's 26th SRW crew pictured at Thule AFB, Greenland, in the spring of 1956.

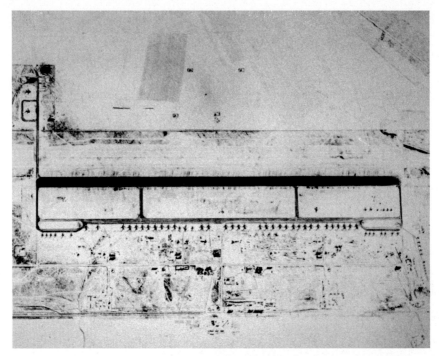

This photograph of Engels Field in the Soviet Union, taken from a U-2 in 1957, showed US intelligence just how few long range bombers the Soviets actually possessed, thereby destroying the myth of the 'bomber gap'. It is one of only four CIA U-2 photographs to have been released to date. *National Archives*

Also photographed from a U-2, this view of the Soviet missile site at Tyuratam helped to disprove the 'missile gap' myth. *National Archives*

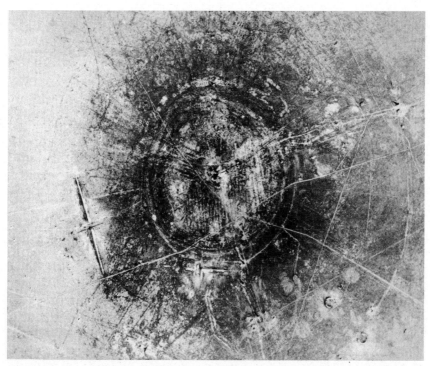

A Soviet nuclear test site 'somewhere in the USSR'. *National Archives*

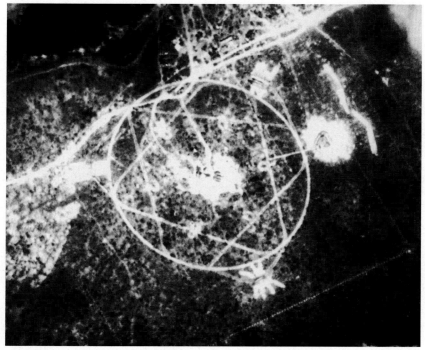

The first photographic proof of Soviet surface-to-air missile (SAM) deployment in Cuba, obtained by a CIA U-2 on 29 August 1962. *National Archives*

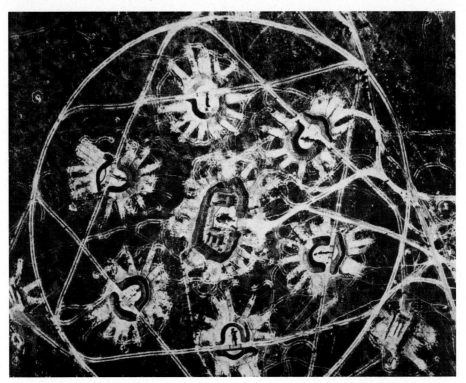

Newly arrived Soviet SA-2 'Guideline' SAMs on a site in Cuba, photographed from a CIA U-2 in September 1962. *National Archives*

The Soviet freighter *Volgoles* en route to Cuba. Four missiles can be seen under tarpaulins on the deck. *National Archives*

Volgoles berthed at Casilda Port, Cuba, 6 November 1962. The vessel was photographed from low level by a Tactical Air Command RF-101 Voodoo reconnaissance aircraft, whose shadow can be seen at bottom right. *National Archives*

A low-level photograph of the Soviet Medium Range Ballistic Missile (MRBM) site at San Cristobal, Cuba. Five MRBMs are apparent together with the missile ready tent in the foreground. *National Archives*

A Soviet Intermediate Range Ballistic Missile (IRBM) site in Cuba, photographed from a USAF U-2. *National Archives*

No 192 Squadron air and groundcrews at Watton, Norfolk, 1956. On 21 August 1958 No 51 Squadron was reformed by redesignating No 192 Squadron, then at Watton operating as a Special Duties unit in RAF Signals Command. *Geoff Gardiner*

No 51 Squadron aircrew pictured at RAF Wyton in August 1966 in front of Comet XK671.
Geoff Gardiner

A mid-1950s photograph of pilots and navigators of No 540 Squadron at RAF Wyton. Fourth from left in the front row is Flight Lieutenant Monty Burton, who, with navigator Don Gannon (on his right), flew the squadron's Canberra PR3 WE139 in the 1953 London–New Zealand air race.

This photograph of Baku in the Russian Caucasus was probably taken in November 1956, by either an RAF or USAF reconnaissance aircraft operating from Cyprus or from one of the NATO bases in Turkey. *Public Record Office Air 34/717 via Roy Nesbit*

17
SATELLITE WARS

In spring 1957 LeMay was appointed the Vice Chief of Air Force Staff under Gen. Thomas White. LeMay's crusty deputy Tommy Power was appointed head of SAC. Provocative overflights by SAC also slow up at this point. LeMay's pugilistic approach was now to be used to box for the entire air force. In later interviews LeMay always maintained that he understood his clearly subordinate role to the President and Congress and he understood that his job was only to provide military advice. It was, he said, for the politicians to make political decisions. But LeMay and his colleagues immersed themselves in Washington politics fighting the USAF corner, and they could fight rough.

After the bomber gap much the same pattern was repeated shortly afterwards over the missile gap. And again the missile gap capitalised on public fears. At first, it seems that LeMay was not a proponent of missiles, despite his prophetic 1946 speech. An old bomber man, he believed his manned B-52 Stratofortresses were better weapons than missiles. Gradually, being no fool, he could see that the unmanned missile was eventually going to be central to Western defences.

With the help of German scientists, both the Americans and the Soviets had been pressing ahead with rocket technology. LeMay was USAF Research & Development director 1946-47. He claimed he suggested launching a satellite into space but was told it was too expensive. But by 1951 the Atlas project had been given the go-ahead for SAC's first generation of American intercontinental ballistic missiles. The Soviets were doing the same with their SS-6 'Sapwood' rocket.

In 1957 American national prestige took, perhaps, its greatest postwar blow when the Soviets launched the first space satellite, *Sputnik*, successfully into orbit outside the Earth's atmosphere. It had been launched on top of the enormous SS-6 rocket. Many American civilians, politicians and military officers saw this as evidence that the Soviet Union was pulling ahead in rocket technology. If the Russians could send a rocket into space, then firing a missile at their home was a horribly real threat. US intelligence was abreast of Soviet developments and contrary to popular views, was fully aware of and had correctly predicted the launch of the SS-6 rocket.

Don Welzenbach described the depth of knowledge the CIA had:

> The Tyuratam missile test centre in the far reaches of the eastern Soviet Union was accidentally discovered by a U-2 which was going somewhere else, and happened to fly over it. It was a big discovery, very, very important. But again, this was an era in which Eisenhower could not discuss with the general public, with the Congress, with the armed forces committee. He had to keep these facts very secret. And again he had to cover his knowledge by evading direct questions in press conferences and, again, sort of playing the fool. You know, talking in these incomplete sentences. Eisenhower was not a stupid man, but he did have to keep something secret, and he did it by indirection.[1]

But the CIA did not know how many ICBMs Russia was building.

Development of ICBMs then came to be perceived as a matter of survival for the United States, in that destruction of the US by the USSR could be anticipated if Moscow was first with ICBM capability. Eisenhower and anybody else with access to the intelligence knew it did not matter who got there first, the US would not be far behind and, in any case, the ability of the Russians to hit the US with a nuclear bomb did not mean it could protect itself from US retaliation by bomber-delivered weapons.

Eisenhower continually found himself unsuccessfully trying to lower the temperature of the air force, public and congressional concern on the issue. The first National Intelligence Estimate giving the Soviets a large missile arsenal was released in November 1957 and projected that the Russians would have 500 ICBMs by the end of 1960, or 1,000 by the middle of 1961. According to Fred Kaplan, there was no evidence for this estimate:

> All earlier intelligence assumptions had led to the conclusion that the Soviets could have 500 intercontinental bombers by that date. When the projection proved false, Air Force intelligence essentially changed 'bombers' to 'ICBMs', but retained the original number 500.[2]

The huge figures, however, were the responsibility of the air force staffed by the same intelligence people who gave America the bomber gap. Tommy Power took over the day-to-day running of the missile gap campaign, leaving LeMay to make the high profile interventions. It seems clear that, in some attempt at compromise, the Director of Central Intelligence was letting air force figures into the NIEs, even though his own staff did not believe them. The apparent Soviet missile build-up was creating a situation of near panic on Capitol Hill. The situation was exacerbated by a leaked report showing that America would have a mere thirty ICBMs in 1960, seventy in 1961.

The picture was further complicated by the reappearance in August 1958 of Joseph Alsop, the newspaper columnist who had spearheaded the bomber gap controversy with air force leaks. 'At the Pentagon, they shudder when they speak of the Gap, which means the years 1960, 1961, 1962 and 1963.' Who his sources were is not known for sure, but it looked like the Air Force again. His copy angrily accused the government of lying down and letting the Russians soar ahead in the nuclear stakes.

In January 1958, the administration announced that three Ballistic Missile Early Warning Systems (BMEWS) were to be built at sites in Fylingdales in England, Clear in Alaska, and Thule in Greenland. These would give the United States at least 15 minutes warning of a surprise attack by Soviet ICBM and SSBN missiles. This was given a top priority.

The panic caused by Soviet ICBM development and the *Sputnik* was played upon deliberately by Khrushchev, who boasted in 1959 that ICBMs were coming off the production line 'like sausages' and that one factory could produce 250 of them in a year. The Kremlin saw this deception as the best protection against the US. And it was bought by the US intelligence community. The Kremlin was able to build on the US fear of its capabilities in a precise fashion, aided by the provision to them of NIEs through Col. W.H. Whalen, a KGB spy on the JCS staff who was finally apprehended in 1968.

Under heavy pressure from the air force and the military contractors, Ike tried to stand his ground, although he had already authorised the construction of dozens of ICBMs. His failure to go completely over the top on missile construction was severely disliked by the air force. Meanwhile, the air force and the CIA's OSI argued continually about the deployment of the SS-6 'Sapwood', *Sputnik*'s launch vehicle. Through 1959 the Russians accelerated the tests of the SS-6, but there were quite a few failures. There was also no evidence of its deployment outside the Tyuratam launch centre. The rocket was massive and the Russians had problems siting it, but nothing compared to what followed.

The air force said the Russians had done enough testing, but the CIA was saying the hiatus in Soviet tests through the last half of 1958 was due to serious technical problems. U-2 photography did not help. To the air force, one CIA man said, 'every flyspeck was a missile.' Air force intelligence claimed that the Soviets were hiding ICBMs in buildings, grain silos and any substantial structure.

Quite incorrectly, American intelligence continued to identify the United States as the main target of the Soviet weapons, when in fact it was Europe. Nearly all of the bombers and missile systems then being built by the Soviets were of medium or intermediate range. The NIEs overestimated the ICBMs that could put fear into the hearts of every American yet, remarkably, seriously underestimated the number of MRBM and IRBMs.

In his memoirs, Khrushchev said:

> What you have to remember is that when I faced the problem of disarmament, we lagged significantly behind the US in both warheads and missiles, and the US was out of range for our bombers. We could blast into dust America's allies in Europe and Asia, but America itself . . . was beyond our reach.[3]

Despite LeMay's diverse pressure on Eisenhower, the President did not confront or fire him. Gen. Goodpaster said:

> President Eisenhower thought that LeMay was a very strong and effective military commander. And really had a lot of respect for what LeMay had done in putting the Strategic Air Command in shape, and training them to a very high level of proficiency. At the same time, Eisenhower had a very strong feeling that [to paraphrase Clemenceau], the issues of military posture were too important to be left to the generals, that this was a matter for his determination. And as a result there was a jockeying back and forth, Eisenhower trying to play down the hysteria over a military threat, or the likelihood of war, which he himself was convinced was not going to happen unless we made serious mistakes.
>
> On the other hand, he very well recognised and commented on this with great asperity from time to time; that the services had an interest in trying to build up the idea of a military threat, and the imminence of possible attack.[4]

LeMay and Power continued to get their way. From 1960 the introduction of a mixed force of long-range B-52 Stratofortress bombers and Atlas, Titan and Minuteman missiles paved the way for a truly intercontinental SAC. The B-47 was being phased out. No longer would it be dependent on vulnerable forward bases and potentially untrustworthy allies. The need to have aircraft in Britain was reduced and this was accelerated by the acquisition by the British of a mixed force of their own consisting of V-bombers and the medium-range Thor missiles.[5]

Meanwhile, the Soviet ICBM programme suffered a major setback. In August 1960 the commander of the Soviet rocket forces and hundreds of scientists and technicians were killed in a colossal explosion during the fuelling of a rocket.[6] An eight-month halt in testing occurred, but the setback was probably greater than this hiatus indicated, in that probably some of the best missile brains in the Soviet Union had been killed.

The NIEs had been steadily reducing the projected size of the Soviet missiles force in any case, and the CIA was getting good information to back it up from photos taken by the new Corona satellite. The Army and Navy were projecting very low numbers for Soviet missiles, even none at all in the case of the Navy. For the Air Force the sky was still the limit. The differences were reflected in the NIE of April 1960 which projected Soviet ICBM strength by mid-1963 at 200 to 700, the huge spread revealing the inter-agency disputes.

Even on those figures the US was way ahead. Eisenhower always tried to restrain the industrial military complex but how successful he was is open to question. When JFK took office, some 1,100 American ICBMs had been budgeted for, evidence that the Air Force's astute management of public opinion, the widespread hysteria about Soviet intentions, internal dissension in the intelligence community and unscrupulous politicians had all conspired in preventing accurate intelligence assessments from being heard.

The missile gap remains a dramatic demonstration too of how increased and better intelligence does not necessarily make for better decisions, or is not allowed to get in the way of ideology. Corona photographs showed virtually the entire rail network, the only conceivable means by which the SS-6 could be transported. On this evidence the Soviet Union had no ICBMs at all. The CIA was also getting intelligence from Penkovsky on the deficiencies of the SS-6 and the Kremlin's decision not to use it at all as an ICBM.[7]

With a Presidential ban on overflights following the Gary Powers shootdown the emphasis for gathering overhead reconnaissance shifts to the new satellite technologies which were to be vital in the emerging missile gap arguments.

The U-2 shootdown was the end of an era in aerial reconnaissance.

The beginnings of the transfer of the strategic overhead photography from aircraft to the new satellites began in the last years of the 1950s. The arrival of satellites was to open the whole of Russia to scrutiny. The first was the Corona project, a proposal for an imaging satellite system meant to take pictures of Earth from space. Ultimately Corona took over aerial espionage from 1960 to 1972 and involved ninety-five satellites. It had been named by an official who took inspiration from his Smith-Corona typewriter. The decision to go ahead came a few days after the United States orbited its first satellite, *Explorer 1*, into space from Cape Canaveral, on 31 January 1958. The *Explorer* flight discovered the Van Allen radiation belt.

The satellite's key architects were many of those who had made such a success of the U-2 programme. Key figures included Dr James R. Killian, President Eisenhower's science adviser, Dr James G. Baker, and Dr Edwin H. Land of the Polaroid Corporation who headed a panel of CIA consultants that advised on the potential of space reconnaissance.

The top secret project was carried out by an industry team at the forefront of aerospace research. Lockheed Missiles and Space built the spacecraft. Itek and Fairchild made the cameras. Eastman Kodak made the film and General Electric made the film-return pods. Douglas Aircraft made the rockets.

The whole project was given a cover story that spacecraft were being launched to examine the hostile climates of space.

The Corona programme was not without its problems. A dozen missions failed before the one in 1960 finally succeeded. One rocket exploded on the launching pad. Three failed to get into space. Two satellites did not make it into space. Two satellites went into unstable orbits. Three cameras failed. Exposed film was expelled from the satellite on a regular basis from outer space in a pod. In the earth's atmosphere a parachute would open and the pod plucked out of the sky. Most didn't make it, including one gold-skinned pod which landed back in the Russian forest, where lumberjacks hacked at it with axes.

Gen. Goodpaster said that Eisenhower backed satellite reconnaissance:

> There were a lot of failures, but Eisenhower was very steadfast. He said we are going to stick with this. He was convinced it was going to succeed. He saw it as necessary as the time of the U-2 was about to run out.

The first major triumph came in August 1960 on the fourteenth mission (coincidentally on the same day that Gary Powers was sentenced in a Moscow court). It was known as KH-1, or Keyhole 1, after its first-generation camera. More than a half a mile of Kodak film weighing 20lb was recovered by an air force Fairchild C-119 Flying Boxcar. Among the photographs was a Soviet bomber base at Mys Shmidta, on the extreme northern coast of the Russian Far East. The base was only 400 miles from Nome, Alaska and was of great strategic importance. The first successful mission covered more than 1.6 million square miles of Soviet territory – far more than the U-2 missions had obtained in their twenty-four flights. The intelligence gap filled quickly. A greatly improved camera known as KH-3 was first used in August 1961 and featured a faster lens and finer focus. Its ground resolution was 25ft. This compares with 40ft in the KH-1 camera.

In September 1961, after five successful Corona missions, the CIA cut sharply its estimate of Moscow's long-range missiles, to between ten and twenty-five launchers from 140 to 200 launchers. The Corona KH-4 satellites which first flew in February had two cameras for stereo vision. This was an enormous help to the photo-interpreters like Dino Brugioni to extract a great deal more information from photos. Although the programme success rate improved there were still failures. One frequent problem was the fogging of film. This was believed to be a result of the sudden discharge of static electricity that had built up in the spacecraft – ironically a phenomenon known as corona. By 1984, Corona had mapped all twenty-five of Moscow's ICBM missiles. In total the Corona programme produced photographs of more than 750 million square miles of the Earth's surface.

The political scene had also changed. In 1961 Eisenhower had served his maximum number of terms. It was not his Republican replacement, however, that took over but the Democratic candidate, John F. Kennedy. As Robert McNamara entered office as Secretary of Defense a major debate was in progress about how many of the new Minuteman ICBM missiles should be built. Some in the NSC thought 250 would be more than enough. The Joint Chiefs of Staff wanted 1,600 and, true to form, Tommy Power at SAC wanted 10,000. These were also based on varying estimates of the Soviet missile build-up. Kennedy and McNamara knew the Soviet had virtually no ICBM offensive capability, but since the missile gap had been central to JFK's presidential campaign, their hands were politically tied. 1,200, later reduced to 1,000, were built.

The Russians saved JFK and his colleagues from having to climb down on the missile gap fiction, because they began testing a new missile, the SS-7, which would be known to NATO as 'Saddler', in December that year. They still had no ICBM, but tougher-than-thou politics and Cold War hysteria were now running the arms programme in the US.

In June 1961 the CIA estimated Soviet missiles at fifty to one hundred, while the air force came in with three hundred and the navy, getting the prize for accuracy, ten, if any. (The estimate was produced immediately before the first good photographs from Corona were received.) As the Berlin Crisis led JFK to seek new estimates, they started to fall. The September NIE admitted that the June figure of fifty to one hundred was 'probably too high', adding that although Moscow had the capability to deploy a large number of ICBMs, it had deliberately opted not to.

The new Corona satellite reconnaissance was showing that Soviets had hardly any SS-6s in place.[8] Events like the 1961 earth-orbit of Yuri Gagarin had no real impact on the Soviet ICBM programme, but a very significant impact on US arms programmes. By the end of 1961 the warning of SAC was becoming less and less credible. After JFK ordered a review of SAC's evidence by the CIA and other analysts to explain the discrepancy between its views and theirs, SAC found itself with few Washington supporters. The only missile gap was the enormous lead in missiles the US had over the Soviet Union. Thus was set the scene for the nuclear arms race; the Kremlin's fear of Washington's intentions began to rise to the proportions Washington's fear of the Kremlin had. The truth concerning Soviet hostility was rather prosaic. All the intelligence showed that the Soviets were not ready for war. But the placing of American intermediate-range missiles in Turkey was to provoke a series of events that were to take the world close to war.

President Lyndon B. Johnson once remarked:

> We've spent $35 billion or $40 billion on the space programme and if nothing else had come of it except the knowledge we've gained from space photography, it would be worth ten times what the whole programme has cost. Because tonight we know how many missiles the enemy had and, it turned out, our guesses were way off. We were doing things we didn't need to do. We were building things we didn't to build. We were harbouring fears we didn't need to harbour.[9]

A 360-page CIA declassified folio shows that the spy system destroyed the idea that the United States has fallen far behind the Soviet Union – the much vaunted missile gap. The satellites revealed that in 1963

Moscow was building anti-missile defences, in 1964 that China was about to detonate its first atomic bomb and discovered in 1967 that Israel had destroyed around 250 aircraft of their Arab foes during the Six-Day War.

James W. Plumber, Corona's industrial manager, said the wave of innovations behind the system not only illuminated a multitude of foreign enigmas but also helped US programmes such as the Apollo programme to put men on the moon.

18
CUBAN HEEL

Aerial reconnaissance was to play a key role in the Cuban Missile Crisis – the moment of history when the world came closer to nuclear war than any other. By this time Gen. LeMay was Chief of Staff of the Air Force having taken over on the retirement of Thomas White. SAC was still being run by his old friend and deputy Gen. Thomas Power.

Shortly after the United States reconnaissance Corona satellite showed that a Soviet advantage in the missile gap did not exist, Paul Nitze, the Assistant Secretary of Defence, warned the Soviet Ambassador over lunch that the missile gap favoured the United States. After the collapse of the Paris summit, tensions had multiplied. The Berlin Crisis had resulted in the construction of the Berlin Wall. Following the abortive 1961 CIA-backed invasion of Cuba, the Bay of Pigs fiasco, the Soviets believed the Americans were going to invade Cuba sooner or later as they interpreted much of America's foreign policy as aggressive. The Americans had already placed intermediate range ballistic missiles in Turkey, effectively in the USSR's backyard. In this climate Khrushchev ordered nuclear missiles to Cuba.[1]

The first clues the American intelligence community received of the movement of Soviet missiles into the southern hemisphere came in mid-August 1962, when agents and refugees began reporting the sightings of missiles in Cuba with sizes and shapes resembling the SA-2 surface-to-air missile. US intelligence watched with interest as the Cuban minister for industry, Che Guevara, arrived in Moscow for a six-day visit.[2] At about the same time a number of Soviet passenger ships arrived in Havana from which disembarked a substantial number of young Soviet men whom the CIA suspected of being military and technical advisers.[3]

On 29 August a CIA U-2 was dispatched to photograph Cuba. Although the flight covered the entire island, clouds obscured portions of the eastern end. Although overflying Cuban airspace was illegal under international law, the United States had no hesitation. According to Dino Brugioni, within minutes of the developed and printed film being put on the table, a photo-interpreter shouted, 'I've got a SAM site.'[4]

An unrelated U-2 mission pushed tension up a notch. On 30 August 1962, a USAF U-2 on an air sampling mission in the Far East intruded into Soviet airspace over the southern end of Sakhalin Island. The pilot had been navigating by the wrong star. The USAF watched on the radar with growing alarm this intrusion and called the pilot back over the open airwaves.

The Soviets protested on 4 September. The diplomatic note states that this was a 'gross violation' of the Soviet frontier and was 'obviously provocative in nature'. The note repeated previous threats of retaliatory action, including the destruction of bases of other nations used by the United States to stage flights over the Soviet Union. Britain, West Germany, Turkey and Japan were named as countries where the U-2 had again appeared since the May 1960 Powers shootdown.

The next day there was a meeting of the United Nations General Assembly where the Soviets again vigorously complained. The United States admitted that 'an unintentional violation may in fact have taken place'. The issue was left hanging, unresolved.

On 5 September the CIA sent another U-2 over Cuba and although the island was largely obscured by cloud, some successful photos showed further substantial newly arrived Soviet military equipment. It was becoming clear that the Soviets had sent numerous SA-2 'Guideline' missiles, 'Komar' class guided missile patrol boats and MiG-21 'Fishbed' fighters to Cuba. A new wave of concern swept through the US intelligence community. Also under construction seemed to be installations for missile sites different from the SA-2.

At the White House an intelligence forum on Cuba was convened. During the Special Group on Cuba meeting of 6 September, Col. Ralph Steakley, an air force aerial intelligence expert at the White House, gave a briefing on aircraft-reconnaissance flights gathering electronic intelligence. RB-47s and F3D ELINT aircraft had been drafted in, and Navy Constellations and SAC U-2 ELINT configured planes were flying around Cuba. These aircraft began to pick up signals associated with the SA-2.

Speculation began to grow within the US intelligence community that the Soviets were installing MRBMs and IRBMs. CIA Director John McCone would later testify to the House Appropriations Committee: 'On 21 September, we received our first agent report that there was the possibility and that report and other information led us to the conclusion of the fact that the missiles, the first missiles, probably arrived around 8 September.'

For fear of provoking a major Soviet reaction with further U-2 overflights there was no aerial reconnaissance of Cuba for over a month. On 17 September a peripheral mission was authorised by the President. By the time the flight reached Cuba from Edwards AFB the weather had turned bad and the mission aborted. New rules for U-2 and other reconnaissance missions had been formulated for Cuban airspace. None were to fly closer than twenty-five miles, the range of the SA-2. Brugioni said:

> Confident and cocky, General LeMay sent several SAC RB-47 photographic planes along Cuba's coast. The results were disappointing with poor quality photographs. LeMay then sent several B-52 bombers, configured for reconnaissance, aloft. The results were equally disappointing.

The USAF borrowed an army 100in focal length still camera. This was placed into a Constellation aircraft and flown around Cuban waters pointing at the island but produced another failure. LeMay then asked that a longer focal length camera, the 'Boston' be used.[5] There were only two such 240in cameras in existence. One was installed in an RB-57 which was designed to photograph deep into East Germany and Czechoslovakia while flying along the border. The other camera was in a C-97 aircraft used for similar purposes. This aircraft was usually flown from Rhein Main airfield in West Germany and was reassigned to the United States. But because of technical problems the camera was very hard to get good photographs from and when the C-97 was run along the Cuban shore the results were typical. 'The camera malfunctioned and the limited photography obtained was of little intelligence value,' said Brugioni. Navy reconnaissance flights were having greater success.

Another U-2 peripheral mission on 27 September spotted a further SA-2 missile site at Banes on the Cuban coast. A second peripheral mission was flown on 29 September and covered the Island of Pines and the Bay of Pigs area. Further missions followed into early October.

Also present were units from SAC's 55th SRW which had been deployed to MacDill AFB near Tampa, Florida. Their PR aircraft were to photograph all ships coming to and going from Cuba. They recorded a growing traffic in Soviet merchant ships. In addition ELINT missions were flown three times a day around Cuba recording all the signals being emitted by radars. By late September these aircraft noted that they were being 'painted' by SA-2 missile radar. There was no actual reaction to the flights either from aircraft or missiles.

As the Cuban crisis was developing from an intelligence into a political and military issue the White House decided that SAC should take over the U-2 missions from the CIA with their own aircraft. They didn't want CIA 'spies' captured. On 12 October, Gen. Power was called to Washington and ushered into the office of the Secretary of the Air Force, where he was asked if SAC would take over U-2 missions over the island. Power agreed.

Two experienced SAC U-2 pilots, Maj. Richard S. Heyser and Maj. Rudolf Anderson, were assigned to fly alternately the new U-2F model over Cuba. Heyser undertook the first SAC overflight on 14 October. It was to be the most crucial reconnaissance flight of the entire crisis. He brought back two rolls of films which were quickly processed. Photo-interpreters found hard evidence of medium-range ballistic missile sites rapidly being prepared especially near San Cristóbal.

The Cuban crisis went into top gear. What action should be taken was the subject of a great deal of discussion among the Kennedy administration. A special emergency team of administration thinkers called ExComm was set up to manage the crisis. The Joint Chiefs of Staff held daily meetings and advocated military action, primarily bombing the missiles sites and possibly invading to wipe out the sites in their entirety. Again, Gen. LeMay was to take a central and aggressive role.

Kennedy preferred a graduated response. On Wednesday 24 October Kennedy's naval exclusion zone was implemented round Cuba – the first pressure and confrontation with the Soviets. Ships approaching Cuba were to be intercepted, searched and either turned round or impounded.

At SAC Headquarters in Omaha, Gen. Power had, without consultation, uprated the state of alert, 'Defcon', up from 3 to 2 – the first and only time it was ever done. By this time SAC had every available aircraft and nuclear weapon available – a total of 2,952 nuclear weapons in bombers or missiles ready to attack the Soviet Union and China as need be. At any one time more than fifty SAC B-52 aircraft were flying constant airborne alert – clearly ready to fly on to their Soviet Union targets. General Burchinal, LeMay's deputy chief for plans and programmes, said: 'We got everything we had in strategic forces . . . counted down and ready and aimed, and we made damn sure they saw it without anybody saying a word about it.'[6]

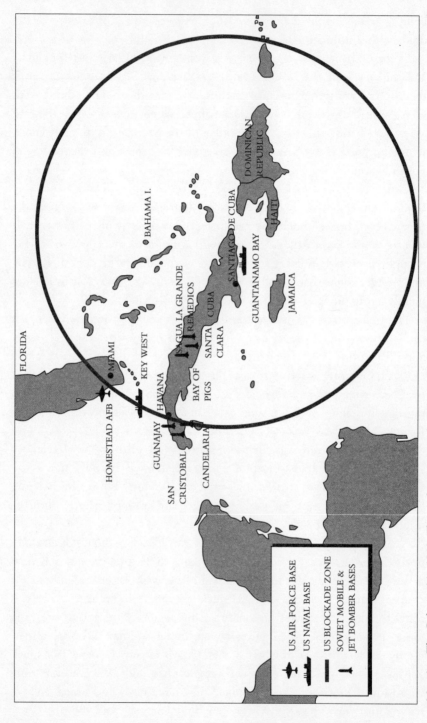

Map 6   The Cuban crisis, 1960. The circle represents the US–imposed quarantine zone.

Power issued the initial alert orders in plain language over SAC's world-wide communications system to all bomber wings. It was ghost-written for dramatic effect:

> This is General Power speaking. I am addressing you for the purpose of re-emphasising the seriousness of the situation the nation faces. We are in an advanced state of readiness to meet any emergencies and I feel that we are well prepared. I expect each of you to maintain strict security and use calm judgment during this tense period. Our plans are well prepared and are being executed smoothly. Review your plan for further action to insure that there will be no mistakes or confusion.

His broadcast was clear to the Soviets – who monitored these transmissions.

SAC also undertook another controversial move. It launched an Atlas ICBM from Vanderberg AFB in California across the Pacific to the Kwajalein test range, in the Marshall Islands, on 26 October at the height of the missile crisis. The Atlas, which was unarmed, had been scheduled for testing; it was launched on its pre-crisis schedule. It was potentially risky and threatening action to take, easily capable of being misunderstood by the Soviets. No one at SAC asked the President whether they should be rescheduled for after the crisis.

Aerial reconnaissance was still playing a key role with intermittent overflights and constant ELINT and sea lane missions. As a result of the poor quality photographs obtained by the C-97 and other, non U-2, reconnaissance platforms Gen. LeMay called Gen. George Goddard back from retirement. The 73-year-old Goddard arranged for his cameras to be fitted to a RF-101 Voodoo reconnaissance aircraft of Tactical Air Command. Unlike the U-2, this converted fighter was able to go in at low level to get photos, 'so clear you could see the rivets on the missiles'.

High level U-2 photography continued. On 27 October one of the SAC U-2Fs was shot down by a Soviet SA-2 missile battery and the pilot Maj. Rudolf Anderson was killed. The president, the JCS and ExComm discussed retaliation, including taking out the SA-2 battery. But Kennedy decided to bide his time.

Perhaps the most tense day of the crisis was 27 October. According to the historian Scott Sagan, another incident involving a U-2 'which could have produced a false warning of an attack', occurred when a Strategic Air Command U-2 spy plane accidentally flew into Soviet airspace . . . New information reveals, however, that the incident was even more dangerous than was previously believed.'[7]

The U-2 was from the 4080th SRW deployed at Eielson AFB in Alaska. It was on a High Altitude Sampling Program (HASP) mission, testing the Arctic atmosphere for radioactive debris from Russia's nuclear weapons testing sites. The U-2 detachment flew at least one sortie per day throughout the crisis. The pilots had orders not to fly closer than 100 miles to Soviet airspace. On the night of 26 October, U-2 pilot Maj. Charles Maultsby took-off and followed a new route over the North Pole. Maultsby strayed off course when the aurora borealis prevented accurate star sighting and he flew well into Soviet airspace above Chukotski Peninsula.

Soviet MiG interceptors based near Wrangel Island were scrambled to shoot him down. Realising his error, Maultsby immediately established radio contact, in clear radio conversation, with a US Command Post in Alaska and was told to turn due east and return to US airspace as quickly as possible. Scott Sagan says that US Convair F-102A Delta Dagger interceptors armed with GAR-11 Falcon air-to-air nuclear missiles were scrambled to protect him. So for a time the decision whether to use nuclear weapons, during a period in the crisis, lay in the hands of fighter pilots.

On arrival back Maultsby was flown down to SAC Headquarters where he briefed Gen. Power and the SAC staff on the incident. According to Maultsby, Power did not reprimand him and said that he only wished that the U-2 had not been on a HASP mission, since if it had been equipped with photographic or electronic intelligence devices, SAC would have learned even more about Soviet military forces as their air defence systems reacted to the overflights. HASP missions were suspended for the rest of the crisis.[8]

The Soviet warning system could have misidentified the U-2 as a SAC bomber. This was Nikita Khrushchev's specific complaint when he protested to Kennedy the next day:

> The question is, Mr President: How should we regard this? What is this – a provocation? One of your planes violates our frontier during this anxious time we are both experiencing, when everything has been put into combat readiness. Is it not fact that an intruding American plane could be easily taken for a nuclear bomber, which might push us to a fateful step . . .

Scott Sagan said, 'It is unlikely that Khrushchev's expression of alarm was disingenuous.'[9]

The most difficult and crucial decisions during the crisis lay with President Kennedy. If he made the wrong decision it could spark Armageddon. He took note of his adviser's view and it is fascinating to see who advised what course of action. All the JCS and many of the administration staff believed that military action, including invasion, should be taken against Cuba. This was based on the concept that the Soviet Union was placing the missiles as a prelude to an attack on the United States. But none were more aggressive than the Chief of Air Staff, Gen. LeMay, who pressed Kennedy to up the ante and to bomb Cuba and take out the missile sites. LeMay was of the hard school of poker playing, total win or total loss.

The CIA analyst, Dino Brugioni, who was present, said LeMay argued at one Pentagon briefing during the crisis that, 'the Russian bear has always been eager to stick his paw in Latin American waters. Now we have got him in a trap, let's take his leg off right up to his testicles. On second thoughts, let's take off his testicles, too.' LeMay was pushing Kennedy into attacking Cuba. If necessary he would launch a full scale strategic nuclear attack on the Soviet Union and China if they showed any sign of retaliation. The historian Ernest May talked to Gen. LeMay a decade later: 'It was his belief that at any point the Soviet Union could have been obliterated without more than normal expectable losses on the US side.'[10]

LeMay said later, with obvious contempt:

> The Kennedy administration thought that being strong as we were, was provocative and likely to start a war. We in the Air Force, and I personally, believed the exact opposite . . . We could have gotten not only the missiles out of Cuba, we could have gotten the Communists out of Cuba at the time . . . During that very critical time, in my mind there wasn't a chance that we would have gone to war with Russia because we had overwhelming strategic capability and the Russians knew it.

LeMay had viewed Kennedy as a coward since the abortive Bay of Pigs invasion which had failed because Kennedy had not provided air support.[11]

Kennedy ignored LeMay's advice. Robert Kennedy later wrote:

> When the President questioned what the response of the Russians might be, General LeMay assured him there would be no reaction. President Kennedy was sceptical. 'They no more than we, can let these things go by without doing something. They can't after all their statements, permit us to take out their missiles,

kill a lot of Russians and then do nothing. If they don't take action in Cuba, they certainly will in Berlin.

The President's judgement was fortunately more astute and better than LeMay's. Khrushchev backed down and LeMay was furious at the lost opportunity. Secretary of Defense Robert McNamara remembers that LeMay made his feelings known to Kennedy:

> After Khrushchev had agreed to remove the missiles, President Kennedy invited the Chiefs to the White House so that he could thank them for their support during the crisis and there was one hell of scene. LeMay came out saying, 'We lost! We ought to just go in there today and knock 'em off.'[12]

Author Richard Rhodes said that what neither Curtis LeMay nor Thomas Power knew, and no one in the US Government knew until 1989, was that contrary to CIA estimates, the Soviet forces in Cuba during the missile crisis possessed one to three megaton hydrogen warheads for some twenty medium-range ballistic missiles that were targetable on US cities as far north as Washington DC. While these required Moscow's consent for use, there were also seven tactical nuclear weapons that were available at the request of the local commander. There were also 43,000 not 10,000 Soviet military on the island. If the Soviet field commanders had launched their missiles as well, millions of Americans would have been killed. Seven thousand megatons would alone have been enough to cause a lethal nuclear winter over the northern hemisphere.[13]

After the Cuban Missile Crisis, Gen. LeMay found it increasingly difficult to work with the Kennedy administration, especially Robert McNamara. They fell out over McNamara's refusal to authorise the new bomber, the B-70 Valkyrie into production. After JFK's assassination, Lyndon Johnson kept on both McNamara and LeMay. But retirement loomed. LeMay was to remain the hawk to the last. When efforts were made to get a nuclear test ban agreement with the Soviets, Congressional hearings were held. Both LeMay and Power spoke out against a test ban, advocating instead that the US developed a 100MT thermonuclear device — a weapon of unimaginable power. Power retired in 1964 and LeMay in 1965. In his autobiography published shortly afterwards, LeMay showed he had lost none of his enthusiasm for the philosophy of using strategic bombing as a threat. In what proved to be a highly controversial remark he advocated massive strategic bombing of the

Vietcong if they didn't do what they were told in language reminiscent of Project Control.

> My solution to the problem would be to tell them frankly that they've got to draw in their horns and stop their aggression, or we're going to bomb them back into the Stone Age. And we would shove them back into the Stone Age with Air power or Naval power – not with ground forces.[14]

In 1968 he teamed up with George Wallace to run unsuccessfully as an independent candidate for Vice-President of the United States. Wallace, as the Governor of Alabama, was famed for his white supremacist beliefs. This was a move that baffled even LeMay's closest acolytes and LeMay later recognised as a mistake. Gen. Curtis Emerson LeMay died in 1990 in Los Angeles. Thomas Power retired in 1964 and died in 1970.

19
ENDGAME

I hope this book reveals that spy flights played a much greater and more central role in the early Cold War than previously believed. During that period, aircraft reconnaissance was to reach its apogee. Developed into a vital tactical aid in World War 1, aerial reconnaissance became an indispensable strategic tool in World War 2. But in the Cold War it developed an even more profound additional role, as a global political tool. The impact of that new role was to leave its mark over thirty years later.

By using their superior aerial reconnaissance capability during the 1946-1963 period the Western allies were kept apprised of the capabilities of the Eastern Bloc. In contrast the communist inability to conduct reciprocal reconnaissance left them badly uninformed of western capability. They had to rely on other methods of espionage to get intelligence on which to base their policies.

As I researched the material for this book and became aware of the previously undisclosed volume of Western spy flights over the communist bloc, I began to realise the impact they had. Soviet sources confirmed that the Kremlin had been angered by the arrogance of these flights. I began to suspect that there was more to these missions than just intelligence.

As the reader will have seen, the presence of Gen. Curtis E. LeMay looms large in this book. As a main user for this intelligence he set the tone for nearly two decades. He exemplifies the tensions between the military 'hawks' and the Presidency. LeMay was to be a senior air force commander during the office of four presidents. But it is his relationship with Eisenhower that is crucial in the understanding of Cold War history. The watershed is the U-2 affair. It was the culmination of a series of policy decisions. Its consequences were to rack up the stakes in the Cold War.

Eisenhower believed that Khrushchev was genuine about his policy of 'peaceful co-existence'. He had turned away from Stalin's conviction of a presumed capitalist attack. Khrushchev summarised his stance in a 1959 speech to the XXIth Party Congress:

We hold the view that relations between the states with different social systems should be based on peaceful co-existence . . . We shall never renounce our views and have no illusions about our class opponents changing their ideology. But this does not imply that we must go to war over our divergence in views. In every country, it is the people themselves who shape their own destiny and choose their own course of development.

Khrushchev believed that Stalin's 'inevitable' war between communism and capitalism would result in global annihilation. By 1956 Khrushchev stated that such a war was no longer 'fatalistically inevitable'. Additionally he realised that the West shared his fear of nuclear war:

On the one hand, these circles [capitalist elites] have an interest in the arms race because it brings them profits. On the other hand they cannot but see that the arms race increases the danger of a war whose flames would devour all their fortunes, including the profits made from the arms race.

Khrushchev was relying on 'peaceful co-existence' for furthering his own political aims. These included reducing the size of the military budget to realise more money for foreign aid to help broaden Soviet influence in the Third World.

This strategy had left Khrushchev dangerously isolated domestically, and a great deal rested on it success. The Soviet military-industrial complex (in many ways a mirror image of the American one), epitomised by Marshal Rodion Malinovsky, viewed his plan to reduce heavy industry and the armed services as madness. Stalin's old allies were out of power but were waiting in the wings for an opportunity to regain control. Even the senior Presidium leaders voiced concern over Khrushchev's innovations.

As we have seen, Eisenhower was very conscious throughout the U-2 programme that the potential for sparking confrontation was very high. During 1959 he was particularly hesitant because of the state of the Cold War. This is spelt out in Gen. Goodpaster's meticulous records of Eisenhower's meetings. For example the note of the meeting between the president, Secretary McElroy, Secretary Quarles and Gen. Twining on 12 February 1959:

The President is reserved in the request to continue reconnaissance flights on the basis that it is undue provocation. Nothing he said, would make him request authority to declare war more quickly than violation of our air space by Soviet aircraft. He stated that while one or two flights might possibly be permissible he is against an extensive program.[1]

As the group was leaving, the President pointed out the close relationship between these reconnaissance programs and the crisis which is impending over Berlin. As 27 May[2] approaches, the President believes it would be most unwise to have world tensions exacerbated by our pursuit of a program of extensive reconnaissance flights over territory of the Soviet Union.

It is fascinating that the US felt justified in overflying the Soviet Union yet by Eisenhower's admission nothing would have provoked them more quickly than a Soviet spy plane overflight. Eisenhower's private cautious comments jar with the reality of military overflights. Either he did not understand the impact of aggressive military flights or he was not fully informed.

With the further discovery of the Project Control archives I began to see where LeMay's agenda of aggressive airpower had come from. I have concluded that under LeMay and then Power reconnaissance missions transcended their usual use as an intelligence tool; they had became a global political tool. Apparently using a covert air power doctrine derived from Project Control, LeMay put a great deal of pressure on the Soviet Union. These missions were a systematic provocation in a game of hard nosed poker. There was concern after some overflights that the Soviets might respond by attacking a reconnaissance air base. There can be no doubt that if the Soviets had retaliated LeMay would have been prepared to launch his 'Sunday Punch' against them. He was not a man to suffer from indecision or doubt.

The SAC War Plan could be launched if there was an 'unambiguous Soviet threat' of attack. Even long after he retired he would not say what would have constituted such a threat.[3] He would say nothing more than that he would have known what it was. In a discussion with the White House analyst Dan Ellsberg in the early 1960s, LeMay said he did not see why the President needed to be in the loop for the decision to launch a nuclear attack:

He said that it seemed wrong that a person who may have just have been in office for a couple of months should make the decision when there were people like himself that had spent their entire lives preparing for such a judgment.[4]

As Bruce Blair of the Brookings Institution has said there was no physical restraint to stop a SAC commander launching a full bomber attack. The East-West aerial spy war was never just about intelligence. It was also a game of bluff and counter-bluff. As this book shows reconnaissance became a Cold War weapon in its own right. SAC officers were playing their own game dependent on the inferiority of the Soviet Air Force. This consisted of rubbing Soviet noses in their own impotency. If you can fly reconnaissance aircraft with some impunity in the enemy's airspace, it is a good way to show them that you could fly your bomber there too. The risk is that you may provoke the other side too far. In a nuclear world the stakes are raised exponentially.

Rhodes points out that if LeMay had ordered a nuclear attack in 1954, he could have delivered enough nuclear weapons to cause Eastern Bloc casualties of 60 million dead and 17 million injured. In 1963, under LeMay's orders, Power was prepared to deliver enough nuclear destruction to kill 100 million.[5] Daniel Ellsberg said that in 1961 the USAF had calculated that if it launched its War Plan, there would be 520 million casualties in the USSR, China and their satellites.[6]

Eisenhower miscalculated exactly how much the Soviets were offended by the constant spyplane intrusions into their territory. When finally Gary Powers' U-2 was shot down Khrushchev fully revealed and demonstrated the anger the Soviets felt about spy flights. The disintegration of the summit into Soviet recriminations spoiled what Eisenhower planned to leave as his legacy – the beginnings of peace between the superpowers. He thought that Khrushchev might be sympathetic to the idea that U-2 reconnaissance was ultimately peaceful and Eisenhower's method of constraining his military-industrial complex. He was wrong. Khrushchev was genuinely angry. The Soviets had had to put up with years of overflights, penetration and peripheral flights. Many were in armed aircraft that were indistinguishable from bombers. They did not look peaceful. Khrushchev later said:

> This latest flight, towards Sverdlovsk, was an especially deep penetration into our territory and therefore especially arrogant of our sovereignty. We were sick and tired of these unpleasant surprises, sick and tired of being subjected to these indignities. They were making these flights to show our impotence. Well we weren't impotent any longer.[7]

Eisenhower's gamble had failed. Even now it is not possible to tell whether Eisenhower did not think that military intrusions would cause major ill feeling or that he simply did not know the scale and audacity of them. This leaves the last unanswered questions over Eisenhower's relationship with the military. Did he constrain them or did he approve of their more aggressive activities, wishing to be perceived as the soft cop to their hard cop? A school of historians has portrayed Eisenhower as being in a constant discreet conflict with budget-busting generals like LeMay and the military industrial complex. But he did not fire LeMay and neither did Kennedy. It might be that LeMay and the JCS did not tell Ike of the extent of their aggressive reconnaissance missions.

My own belief is that Eisenhower did not have a tight control on the military. He thought that they needed a little play, but that ultimately he controlled them. This loose grip was to result in the loss of his dream of an early accommodation with the Soviets. Was the intelligence gained by such flights worth the loss of the summit?

After a 'decent interval' of national outrage and indignation against the USSR, the Democrats made political capital out of Eisenhower's discomfiture. In the run up to the presidential elections the Democratic Advisory Council, endorsed by Adlai Stevenson, Harry S. Truman, John F. Kennedy and Stuart Symington, unleashed a vitriolic attack:

> All Americans resent the manner in which Mr Khrushchev treated the President of the United States in Paris, Mr Khrushchev killed the meeting. He thereby did incalculable harm to the cause of peace. But the Eisenhower-Nixon Administration handed him the opportunity to do so by embarking on a policy which it knew and had decided was unsound (going to Paris without an agreement worked out over Berlin), and by handling the incident of the American U-2 plane in a manner for which there is no precedent . . . The foreign policy of the Eisenhower-Nixon administration is in shambles. It has become obvious that the operation of the government of the United States in its most important areas is chaotic. The integrity of the word of the United States has been put in doubt. The danger of an all-destructive nuclear war has been increased.[8]

In this climate it is not surprising the lessons of the U-2 affair were not learnt. The distrust between the two superpowers grew over the next years. The Cold War mentality dominated the Kennedy administration. When the bomber gap was discredited the USAF deftly jumped horse and claimed that was because the Soviets had shifted their resources into building missiles. So then there was the missile gap. LeMay's deputy and then SAC Commander Gen. Power did most of the work on creating the figures. At the time he was demanding that Kennedy budget for 10,000 ICBMs it transpired that the Soviets had a handful.

If this book shows the possibilities of aerial reconnaissance it also shows that, like all intelligence, it can be distorted to fit an argument. From 1949 up to McNamara's decision to scrap the B-70 project, the USAF and in particular SAC generally won every budget battle they went into. The air force's success severely dented the army and navy budgets. LeMay used the intelligence gained from reconnaissance missions to claim repeated evidence of Soviet build up and therefore the need to increase SAC's funding. One of LeMay's greatest claims to fame within the air force was that he was the man who bust the one-third ratio of budget distribution to each of the armed services. The air force budget grew to half of the defence budget of over $40 billion a year in 1960.

Gen. LeMay realised that whoever had control of intelligence had control over the defence budget. But he misjudged the potential of the U-2. When the CIA's U-2 programme began to show that the Soviets were not building up to the extent the air force claimed, LeMay and his colleagues waged a clever publicity war in the media working on public fear of a surprise Soviet attack. In Congressional hearings he unequivocally stated that the Soviets were ahead in the arms race. Yet, he must have known they were not even contenders at that point.

Despite his public assertions over the threat of Soviet aggression LeMay knew that during his tenure in the air force the Soviets were never in a position to 'win' a nuclear exchange. Yet LeMay maintained that the Soviets were ultimately going to attack. One of the limitations of aerial reconnaissance is that it can show capability but it cannot reliably determine an enemy's intentions, only infer them.

Even when the first Corona satellite photographs showed that the Soviets had just four SS-6 'Sapwood' ICBMs nobody stopped to think. As Ray Garthoff of the Brookings Institution has pointed out, when the Corona satellite photographs showed that the Soviets only had four SS-6s, no one in the White House asked the obvious question. The US ICBM programme was based on the idea that the Soviets would have hundreds of SS-6. But no one asked whether the new satellite intelligence merited a total re-evaluation of the defence policy. As former White House staffer, Daniel Ellsberg (later the man who 'leaked' the 'Pentagon Papers'), said:

> When I look back I think this is one of the biggest mistakes we made. When we got that intelligence no one said, 'Hold on; wait a minute, perhaps this is a good moment to talk about an arms treaty before things get out of hand.' All we could

say was, 'Great, that means we are way ahead.' The machine had gathered a momentum of its own. It is possible at that point that a serious arms ban treaty could have been implemented.

The U-2 affair stopped Khrushchev's 'peaceful co-existence' policy dead in its tracks, exacerbating his domestic problems. The diplomatic analysts William Hyland and Richard Shyrock have written that 'from roughly the time of the U-2 incident onward, Khrushchev seems to have been confronted with increasingly effective opposition.'[9] American writer Michael Beschloss in his seminal 1986 book on the U-2 affair suggests that Eisenhower failed fully to comprehend the impact of the resumption of U-2 flights. A decade on when it is possible to get some idea of the history and sheer scale of spy flights, of which the U-2 was just a small part, Eisenhower's misjudgement looks much more serious.

There are some questions about the British involvement in the whole affair. After 1956 the British seem to play a smaller role in aerial reconnaissance missions against the Soviet Union. We have seen RAF involvement in the U-2 programme and No 51 Squadron kept flying its ELINT missions. If there were other RAF overflights they are unknown to me – although that does not mean there weren't any. Many questions remain over the flights that did take place. How did the Soviets know that overflights were not nuclear attacks? What was the assessment of the risk? Were they deliberate provocations or was the intelligence vital? Did Churchill approve the earlier RAF flights at the request of Truman and Eisenhower to take the heat off the Americans? Or did Churchill approve them behind the presidents' backs? Was the impact of overflights ever fully assessed? We do not know. We are not allowed to know. The British do not seem to have any major policy problems with the United States overflights, the U-2 affair or Cuba. If there were discussions over reconnaissance overflights they have not been released into the Public Records Office. In effect, by 1961 RAF's Bomber Command was all but integrated into SAC's strategic plans.

During the Cuban missile crisis, Bomber Command's V-force went on alert alongside SAC. The C.-in-C. Bomber Command, ACM Sir Kenneth Cross, put the V-force on alert without recourse to Whitehall or No 10 Downing Street. Again during that crisis aerial reconnaissance was to play a key role. The United States felt justified in overflying another country, albeit one that, like Turkey for the Russians, was harbouring nuclear missiles in the backyard.

LeMay and Power were prepared to carry the crisis all the way to a full nuclear exchange with the Soviets. There were even a series of clear threats at the Soviets. Also, as Scott Sagan has pointed out, any one of a number of acts, including the U-2 intrusion into the USSR on 27 October, could have been misread and accidentally triggered Armageddon.[10] Again LeMay and Power were prepared to play a harder game of poker than their President.

Gen. LeMay always maintained that he was not a politician, despite having come close to spending a year as a Republican senator in 1945 and at the end of his career standing as vice presidential candidate along with George Wallace on a third party ticket in 1968. It looks as though his agenda was far greater than just a military one. This book raises a question: did the lax control of LeMay and his colleagues by successive presidents lead to a much colder Cold War than was necessary?

It was in this period that a voice of dissent grew in both America and the West, that was concerned about the actions that had been taken since 1945. In an editorial for the *Saturday Review*, shortly after the U-2 shootdown, Norman Cousins voiced growing moral concern:

> An uneasiness is settling over America. It goes deep down. There is a feeling that we are under going a moral shrinkage in the eyes of the world. The bigness of our history seems to have been interrupted. The large image of America created by our past seems less clear than it was once a short time ago. And we are sensing a mood of disconnection – disconnection between ourselves as individuals and those who speak and act for us as a nation.
>
> Another question of right and wrong has now come up – but this time we ourselves are wrong. We dispatched jet planes on military reconnaissance over Russian territory. In doing so, we took appalling risks. The main danger of nuclear war today comes not from a definitive policy by any nation to launch such a war, but from an act of carelessness or hideous miscalculation. An alien, military reconnaissance plane taking photographs over any country . . . is a specific and volatile act of provocation that could ignite war fuses.[11]

The relationship between superpowers nose-dived. McNamara put a brake on the air force budget, stopping it from getting all its own way. But it was too late. By the mid-1960s the United States industrial military machine was so great that the Soviets decided that they had to match it. The real arms race began. In the next twenty years it was to consume an enormous part of the wealth of the West, and may have more than a little to do with the decline of Western economies in relation to the Pacific rim. By the mid–1960s a full–scale arms race was under way that diverted a high percentage of the resources of all the nations involved.

Despite the advent of satellite reconnaissance it was many years before the USSR and China were extensively covered and risky overflight programmes were continued into the 1970s to obtain what could be considered strategic or tactical intelligence. Eisenhower had approved the 'replacement' programme for the U–2, the SR–71 Blackbird aircraft, perhaps one of the most remarkable looking aircraft in aviation history. This black–painted, sleek, manned rocket could travel at three times the speed of sound. It had its uses. Satellites were essentially passive and could not, for instance, test communist air defences. US efforts to get the Soviet air defences to activate the large Pechora radar were unsuccessful until a SR–71 provoked it into doing so at some time in the 1970s. A report which noted that Soviet SAM missiles had been fired at an SR–71 in 1983 added that: '. . . since its entry into service and the start of high altitude reconnaissance missions, more than 900 SAMs . . . have been fired at the SR–71 without success.'[12]

This is surely an extraordinary admission of a hidden war taking place in peacetime. Again, we are lucky that it never tipped over into all out war.

The 55th SRW also continued its activities eavesdropping and provoking communist defences in conjunction with the RAF's No 51 Squadron. From the late 1960s the RC–135 became the workhorse of the wing. Based on the Boeing 707 it looked like an airliner on radar. It was the activities of these aircraft that was to lead to the worst disaster of the spyplane war, the shooting down in 1983 by a Soviet Sukhoi Su–15 of the Korean Airlines Flight KAL007.

It is very likely that 747–200B HL7442 was shot down because the Soviets thought it was an RC–135 spyplane that frequently operated in the area. It was a monumental blunder by the Soviets: 269 innocent people were killed because a deadly intelligence game had gone wrong.

My own assessment is that the RAF and USAF spy flights over and around the Eastern Bloc were courageous, provocative and illegal. I have nothing but admiration for those who flew them. They played a greater part in early Cold War politics than has been previously acknowledged.

How close did spy flights bring us to war? I believe it was 'a damned close run thing' and the experience has much to teach us. This is increasingly shown as the senior officers of the old Soviet Union reveal their contemporary thinking.

The communists were not benign. Their air force took a very aggressive stance. It was not until the mid-1950s that the Soviet air defences were capable of intercepting some penetration flights. This meant that most interceptions took place on the borders against slow lumbering ELINT aircraft. The communists usually claimed that the aircraft were in their airspace. From the material I have seen this was rarely true in the case of shot down aircraft. They were usually in international airspace or, sometimes, disputed airspace. The Soviets maintained borders further out than was internationally recognised. Given the opportunity, they would have been more aggressive and shot down every spyplane intrusion into their territory.

The Soviets were continually misread and vice versa and thus poor decisions were made by both sides. The Soviet Union was a totalitarian state, but it was also a federation that had suffered enormously from World War 2. It may not have been bombed strategically but it had suffered the German 'scorched earth' policy. I believe the failure to grasp this fully and the consequences of suffering 27 million war dead, as well as the Soviets' desire never to see a reunited Germany if it was under Western dominance, were never fully taken into consideration by the United States. This in turn led, as in the cases of the Korean War and Cuban missile crisis, to misunderstandings of the other side's intentions that nearly tripped into World War 3. By their own admission Western military observers overestimated Soviet capability and intentions. 'We saw the Soviets as ten feet tall,' said one SAC general. Military men will always argue that they need the equipment and intelligence to fight war should it come. But if they are given their head there is ultimately the danger that excessive arming becomes an arms race and impertinent intelligence gathering becomes a provocation. I have heard it said many time by its veterans that SAC won the Cold War. One of the points they make is that the Soviet Union bankrupted itself trying to match SAC. This is a strange form of economic determinism.

It is good, on the one hand, that military men follow orders and are prepared to obey their commander-in-chief when the time comes. On the other hand, it is worrying to see a group of people who are so without doubt as to the right of their cause that they are prepared to kill 500 million civilians and leave the world a smoking irradiated ruin. Bombing detaches the perpetrator from the fact they are killing children. LeMay once remarked, 'there are no innocents in war'. I disagree.

It all argues for the strongest possible civilian control of the military and more openness where possible. But we will always require people of courage to defend their nations.

If history has one overriding purpose it is to stop us making the same mistakes again. Yet there is a reluctance to be forensic about what the Soviet capabilities and intentions really were in the Cold War. Most participants do not want their own beliefs challenged. It has served their purpose for fifty years; why challenge it now?

I suspect that when the definitive history of the Cold War comes to be written at a more objective time in the future that it will not be seen to be as one-sided as, for forty years, we once believed. 'SAC won the Cold War' is the belief of many in the West but I wonder whether the beginning of the end might have started thirty years earlier if SAC had not flown all those overflights. Perhaps, had we been better informed and less misled, the Berlin Wall might not have been built instead of standing for nearly thirty years before it was pulled down.

Appendix 1
NOT FORGOTTEN

Of the forty US military aircraft shot down between 1947 and 1977, over 350 crew had been on board: 187 men had survived, 34 bodies were recovered, but the fate of some 135 had never been explained. Families of the missing men were usually told that they had been on routine training flights and that there was no chance that they had survived. But some relatives had always harboured a suspicion that their loved ones had been captured by the Soviets or Communist Chinese and taken to the Gulag. Over many years the United States government requested information about crew members reported to be in camps. But during the Cold War there was a blanket denial from the Communists that any such prisoners had been held.

Then, in June 1992, President Boris Yeltsin admitted that it was possible that American aircrew had been held in Soviet prison camps and promised to open Soviet records. In a remarkable act of post–Cold War co-operation a joint US–Russian Commission was set up to find out what happened to the lost fliers.

The Joint Commission investigated nine main cases where crew members might have survived. One of them is that of the RB-50 Superfortress of the 55th SRW shot down on 29 July 1953 by Soviet fighters after straying over their waters near Vladivostok.

Until the Commission started work, only one account was public: the official censored version of the sole survivor of the seventeen-strong crew, co-pilot John Roche, who together with his captain, Stan O'Kelly, parachuted and landed in the sea.

The more detailed debriefing was recently declassified. It reveals that Roche and O'Kelly heard other survivors : 'As we were together during the course of the morning, I and Capt. O'Kelly both heard sounds of a voice yelling far in the distance through the fog bank. '

Eventually, the two men were separated by a rough sea. O'Kelly was drowned. Two bodies were later washed up on the coast of Japan, the other fourteen crew members were posted missing.

New evidence of other possible survivors is slowly emerging. On an island near Vladivostok back in 1953, there was an anti-aircraft gun battery. Its crew witnessed the whole shootdown. One was Lt Georgi Kravchencko. He said :

> The battle was not very long but it was quite intensive fighting. The aircraft started to smoke. The moment the smoke appeared there the parachutists started dropping down very fast. We counted about seven of them as the plane started slowly going down.[1]

Bess Tejada Bergmann's husband, Maj. Tommy Tejada, was an ELINT operator on the flight. She had no idea of his real work until very recently. During the 1950s she had written many letters trying to find out more about the death of her husband but the USAF told her little. She said:

> And it was called a routine training flight. And I didn't know for a long long time that he was actually at an electronic machine which was doing surveillance work, spying, if you will, it's a harsh word, but he was a spy, spying over Russia, apparently.[2]
>
> But until, just within this last year, then I began to really feel maybe some of the men did survive, and that maybe my husband lived for two or three years, always saying, 'I wish I could get in touch with my family.' Maybe he survived for several years and then – and then died, alone, away from his family and his countrymen.

The Commission has found further evidence pointing to the possibility of Soviet rescue of the American flyers from the RB-50. Gen. Volkogonov, the Russian head of the Commission, said:

> Officially, all the information is such that they all perished. At the same time we have accounts that there were vessels from the Border Guards there, that there were vessels from the Navy there. Unfortunately, we haven't been able to uncover their logbooks. That is also a puzzle. There is always a logbook on every vessel. But for this period, we still do not have the logbooks. This arouses a certain suspicion.[3]

The Commission faces the diehard secretiveness of the Soviet old guard – the military and the KGB. Col. Gavril Korotkov, a political interrogator who was based in Vladivostok in 1953, suspects he knows why the Commission can't find the logbooks:

> I think they have not been successful because the people implicated are still living. They are still alive and they do not want it to be made public knowledge. They do

not want either their methods of working, nor the system to be given exposure now.[4]

At the time he heard many reports that the KGB had captured some of the crew :

> We knew they immediately, via border troops, were taken to the KGB. The KGB had their own men everywhere and they took them into their hands. The thing is that they were not considered POWs. The problem was that they were rated as spies. For this reason they could not allow us any access to these people. As for the fact that they had been taken aboard alive and held there was no doubt. The talk was such as, 'We've got so many Americans.'

Some progress has been made by the Joint Commission. The Russians have admitted that they shot down another missing RB-50 in 1952. The USAF never knew why the aircraft had disappeared. They have now retrieved the body of an American crewman whose body was washed up and buried on Yuri Island. It was reburied in the United States with a proper military funeral.

Another mystery that the commission has solved is that of an EC-130 Hercules lost on 2 September 1958. It had crossed the border into Soviet Armenia, taking a short cut, and was caught by MiGs. The slow and cumbersome aircraft was easy prey and was shot down near the village of Sassnaken. Of the seventeen crew on board the C-130, six bodies were later returned to the American government. Despite the intervention of Eisenhower eleven men had never been accounted for.

For over thirty years the files on the shot-down spyplanes were buried deep in the archives in Washington DC.[5] In 1992 Joint Commission investigators rediscovered their existence. In the case of the C-130 they included affidavits, investigations, autopsy reports. In the archives are hundreds of files and even personal effects from downed aircraft including the C-130.

The Commission found reports from Armenian and Turkish sources claiming that parachutes had been sighted, that survivors had been held by the KGB.

In the village of Sassnaken where the C-130 crashed, there is no shortage of material evidence from that day thirty-five years ago. Pieces of the planes are used for fencing and the like all over the village. However, not one eyewitness recalled seeing parachutes. Last September

(1995) the Commission called in a specialist mortuary team to dig up the crash site. The dig has produced more human bones and even a dogtag. The evidence now points to one conclusion: all seventeen crewmates died on the Armenian hillside.

It seems highly likely that the Soviets ran a secret operation to take aircrew captured in the Korean War back to the Soviet Union. Until 1990 the USSR denied any involvement in the war. According to the evidence gathered from Soviet sources, Stalin launched a major Soviet intelligence operation in Korea to obtain Western military secrets. The *Timewatch* programme revealed for the first time that two captured F-86s and helicopters were taken back in conditions of great secrecy to Moscow. Disguised Soviet intelligence officers interrogated captured pilots. As we have seen they ran a secret interrogation operation. The programme 'Russia's Secret War' revealed that the head of the Soviet air force in the war, Gen. Georgy Lobov, admitted before his death in 1993:

> I know that in the summer of 1952 at least thirty to forty American PoWs were placed in a separate and closely guarded carriage, attached to a goods train and sent to the USSR. They must have been a treasure trove. I imagine that it was specifically from these people that our intelligence people's remarkable knowledge of our adversary came.

Although fewer British families have been trying to establish what happened to their relatives during the Cold War and Korean War, they have not had much help from the British Ministry of Defence. James Baldwin received little help from the MoD so he wrote to President Clinton. The Joint Commission is now trying to find out what happened to his father, Wg Cdr Johnny Baldwin: 'The Americans are certainly much more earnest about finding out what happened forty years ago. The British have so far – I am not saying it is malicious or vindictive – shown a lack of effort and co-operation.'[6]

His father's story as a pilot is considered to be one of the most 'romantic' of World War 2. He joined up in September 1939 at the age of twenty-one as an airman. He served as ground crew in France and then on bomb disposal duties during the Blitz. In 1941 he volunteered as a pilot and was posted to No 609 Squadron in November 1942. He shot down his first enemy aircraft after only four hours flying Typhoons.

Over the next two years he rapidly increased his rank, number of decorations and 'kills'. He lead the group of eight Typhoons that attacked a convoy in France, wounding Field Marshal Rommel. By the end of the war he had sixteen enemy aircraft to his credit.

Baldwin stayed in the RAF and was one of the first four RAF pilots sent on exchange with a USAF fighter squadron fighting in the Korean War. They were flying the new state-of-the-art F-86 Sabre jet fighter, the only Western aircraft capable of matching the communist MiG-15 jets.

Shortly after arriving, Baldwin went out on a four-aircraft reconnaissance mission over communist-held territory. He was flying number two to 1-Lt Robert L. Larsh Junior, now in retirement in the USA. Larsh says that Baldwin disappeared while they were executing a turn in dense cloud at 12,000ft. Despite a search and rescue operation there was no sign of what had happened to him.

Baldwin's pregnant wife was unofficially asked to go to London on a number of occasions as the RAF thought her husband might be alive. But these visits came to nothing. Eventually in 1954, the year after the war ended, she was told that her husband had died in the crashed aircraft.

However, documents in the Public Record Office show that British intelligence received reports that Baldwin was held as a PoW. A letter from Wg Cdr C. Marshall of the Air Ministry to Mr J.M. Addis of the Foreign Office, dated 30 December 1953, discussed the possibility that Baldwin and a Canadian Sqn Ldr MacKenzie were being held. It says that while there was little direct evidence:

> I do not know the place in North Korea where Baldwin and MacKenzie are thought to be held except that it is a tungsten mine. Our unit in Korea, however, does possess this information and is trying to confirm the locality.

A later letter from the British Embassy in Washington to Addis says: 'In the course of the discussion with the State Department . . . they told me that there was some evidence that there are some United Nations Command men detained in the Soviet Union.'

Although at first the Chinese denied holding Baldwin and MacKenzie the Canadian government caused such a fuss that eventually Andrew MacKenzie was released on 4 December 1954. In his debriefing MacKenzie said other pilots were being held by the Chinese. On the British copy an Air Ministry note says, 'There appears to be an RAF officer in Chinese hands. We did not know this.'

An internal Foreign Office memo dated 29 May 1954 says:

> There are a considerable number of PoWs from the Korean fighting, mostly S. Korean and American, but including a few from the Commonwealth, who are believed to be still in the hands of the Chinese and the North Koreans.

In 1955, nearly two years after the fighting had ended, a further four US F-86 pilots were released by China. One, Lt Roland Parks, says that he does not believe he would had been released if it had not been for the pressure applied by the Canadian government over MacKenzie. British diplomatic efforts seem to run into the ground by 1955.

At the end of the Korean war some 1,036 British PoWs were repatriated and another 31 were thought to have died in captivity. About 121 remained missing, including nine RAF pilots. PRO documents also show that relatives of some of those lost believed that their loved ones had been captured.

Michael Baldwin's brother James says:

> I never knew my father – only what I have been told by his colleagues and read in his war record. He died when I was four months old and I want to get to the bottom of this. Forty years on I think it is about time.

It is unlikely that a USAF or RAF pilot will now be found, alive and long-bearded, held in some remote Soviet prison camp. However, the relatives of the missing men may finally find out the fate of their loved ones. And with the end of the Cold War the full story of the courage of the fliers who risked and sometimes lost their lives around the borders of the Eastern Bloc can now be told.

Appendix 2
SHOOTDOWN CHRONOLOGY

Date	Type	Operator	Role	Location
09/08/46	C-47	USAF	Transport	Yugoslavia
19/08/46	C-47	USAF	Transport	Yugoslavia
08/04/50	PB4Y2	USN	Patrol	Baltic Sea
06/11/51	P2V	USN	Patrol	Sea of Japan
18/11/51	C-47	USAF	Transport	Hungary
13/06/52	RB-29	USAF	Recon	Sea of Japan north of Hokkaido
07/10/52	RB-29	USAF	Recon	Kurile Islands north of Hokkaido
12/31/52	B-29	USAF	Leaflet drop	Manchuria
18/01/53	P2V	USN	Patrol	Formosa Straits
10/03/53	F-84	USAF	Intercept	Germany
29/07/53	RB-50	USAF	Recon	Sea of Japan
17/08/53	T-6	USAF	Patrol	Korean DMZ
04/09/54	P2V	USN	Recon	Sea of Japan north of Hokkaido
07/11/54	RB-29	USAF	Recon	Sea of Japan near Hokkaido
19/01/55	Unknown	USA	Training	Korean DMZ
17/04/55	RB-47	USAF	Recon	Northern Pacific near Kamchatka
22/06/55	P2V	USN	Recon	Bering Straits
17/08/55	LT-6	USAF	Training	Korean DMZ
22/08/56	P4M	USN	Patrol	North of Formosa near Wenchow
10/09/56	RB-50	USAF	Recon	Sea of Japan
23/12/57	T-33	USAF	Logistics	Albania
06/03/58	F-86	USAF	Training	North Korea
27/06/58	C-118	USAF	Transport	Soviet Armenia
02/09/58	C-130	USAF	Transport	Soviet Armenia

Date	Type	Operator	Role	Location
07/02/60	U-2	CIA	Recon	Soviet Union
25/05/60	C-47	USAF	Transport	East Germany
01/07/60	RB-47	USAF	Recon	Barents Sea off Soviet Union
27/10/62	U-2	USAF	Recon	Cuba
17/05/63	Helicopter	USA	Patrol	Korean DMZ
06/08/63	Lt aircraft	USA	Unknown	North Korea
24/01/64	T-39	USAF	Transport	East Germany
10/03/64	RB-66	USAF	Recon	East Germany
14/12/65	RB-57	USAF	Recon	Black Sea
23/01/68	Ship	USN	Recon	Off North Korean east coast
30/06/68	DC-8	USAF	Transport	Kurile Islands
15/04/59	EC-121	USN	Recon	North Korea
17/08/69	OH-23	USA	Unknown	Korean DMZ
21/10/70	U-8	USA	Recon	Soviet Armenia
14/07/77	CH-47	USA	Transport	North Korea

Other Nationality

Date	Type	Operator	Role	Location
05/06/52	DC-3	Swedish	Recon	Baltic
16/06/52	Catalina	Swedish	Rescue	Baltic
12/03/53	Lincoln	RAF	Training	Germany
23/07/54	Unknown	British	Airliner	China
27/07/55	DC-3	Israel	Airliner	Bulgaria
09/09/62	U-2	Taiwan	Recon	China
01/11/63	U-2	Taiwan	Recon	China
07/07/64	U-2	Taiwan	Recon	China
10/01/65	U-2	Taiwan	Recon	China
09/09/67	U-2	Taiwan	Recon	China
??/03/69	U-2	Taiwan	Recon	China
20/04/78	707	S. Korea	Airliner	Barents Sea
01/09/83	747	S. Korea	Airliner	Pacific

NOTES

Introduction
1   Interview with Author, Riverside, 1993

Chapter 1
1   Lane, Charles and Shanker, Thorn; 'Bosnia: What the CIA Didn't Tell Us', *The New York Review*, 9 May 1996.
2   Vulliamy, Ed; 'US Feud sealed Bosnia's fate', *The Guardian*, 20 May 1996.
3   Farquahar, John Thomas, Capt. USAF; *A Need to Know: The Role of Air Force Reconnaissance in War Planning, 1945-1953*; dissertation, Ohio State University, 1991.
4   Made a separate service and renamed the RAF in early 1918.
5   'Photographic Reconnaissance in World War II', *The Proceedings of the Royal Air Force Historical Society*, issue No 10, from seminar held 10 June 1991 at Royal Air Force Museum.
6   ACM Sir Neil Wheeler was a career RAF officer who joined the reconnaissance section early in the war. He is now retired.
7   *The Proceedings of the Royal Air Force Historical Society*, issue No 10, *op cit*.
8   The Lysander went on to a distinguished career as a special duties aircraft, landing and picking up agents from improvised airstrips in occupied territory, a task to which it was ideally suited.
9   Babbington-Smith, Constance; *Evidence in Camera*; Chatto & Windus, London 1958.
10   *The Proceedings of the Royal Air Force Historical Society*, issue No 10, *op cit*.
11   The best account of the electronic battleground of World War 2 is: Price, Alfred; *Instruments of Darkness*, London 1977 (new ed.).
12   Price, Alfred; *The History of US Electronic Warfare, Vol II, The Renaissance Years, 1946-64*; The Association of Old Crows, 1989.

Chapter 2
1   Fred Wack retired as a lieutenant-colonel and moved to Mariposa, California near the entrance to Yosemite National Park. He died in January 1996.
2   Wack, Fred John; *The Secret Explorers, Saga of the 46th/72nd Reconnaissance Squadrons*; privately published 1990.
3   Interview with the Author, Mariposa, 1993.
4   Prefabricated metal buildings, hot in summer and cold in winter. Based on the British Nissen huts.
5   The Boeing B-29 Superfortress's engines used carburettors which resulted in numerous engine fires and was partly responsible for its poor reputation for engine reliability. Gradually, fuel injection was introduced.
6   Several B-29s had been forced to land on Soviet soil after attacks on Japan. The Soviets held on to the aircraft and on Stalin's instructions reverse-engineered the aircraft in their entirety. The crews were repatriated.

7   Symington, W. Stuart; *Memorandum for General Spaatz*, 5 April 1948.

8   NARA, MRB, RG 341 entry 214, file 3-3000-99.

9   Richelson, Jeffrey T.; *American Espionage and the Soviet Target*; Quill, US, 1987.

10   Price, Alfred; *The History of US Electronic Warfare, Vol II, The Renaissance Years, 1946-64*; The Association of Old Crows, 1989; page 34.

11   Interview with Author, Kansas City, 1993.

12   Price, Alfred; *op cit* page 35.

13   Price, Alfred; *op cit* page 36.

14   Price, Alfred; *op cit* page 38.

15   Price, Alfred; *op cit* page 40.

16   Price, Alfred; *op cit* page 41.

17   Price, Alfred; *op cit* pages 42-3.

Chapter 3

1   LeMay, Curtis E. with Kantor, Mackinlay; *Mission with LeMay*; Doubleday & Co Inc, New York, 1965, page 373.

2   *Op. cit.*

3   Alpervitz, Gar.; *The Decision to use the Atomic Bomb*; HarperCollins, London, 1995.

4   Interview with the author, Mariposa, 1993.

5   Interview with the author, Riverside, 1993.

6   In line with the Truman policy, drawn up by George Keenan, of containment of the communists.

7   'If we should have to fight again', *Life* Magazine, 5 July 1948, pages 34-44. See discussion in: McGwire, Michael; *Military Objectives in Soviet Foreign Policy*; Brookings Institute, Washington DC, 1988.

8   Farquahar, John Thomas, Capt. USAF; *A Need to Know: The Role of Air Force Reconnaissance in War Planning, 1945-1953* ; dissertation, Ohio State University, 1991.

9   *Ibid.*

10   *NSC-68* was drafted by Paul Nitze.

11   US Congress, House Committee on Armed Services; *The National Defense Program – unification and strategy*; 81st Congress, 1st Session, 1949, page 183. By 1956 Ostie was arguing for the Polaris.

12   Interview with the author, Riverside, 1993.

13   I would like to thank Don Welzenbach for bringing this lecture to my attention. Dick Leghorn's lecture at Boston University's Optical Research Laboratory, 13 December 1946.

14   LeMay wrote to Gen. Vanderberg on the 12 December 1949:
'Assuming that as a democracy we are not prepared to wage preventative war, this course of action poses two most different requirements: (1) An intelligence system which can locate the vulnerable elements of the Soviet striking force and forewarn us when attack by that force is imminent, and (2) Agreement at top governmental level that when such information is received the Strategic Air Command will be directed to attack.'
Reprinted in Peter J. Roman, 'Curtis LeMay and the Origins of NATO Atomic Targeting,' *The Journal of Strategic Studies*, Vol 16, No 1, March 1993, p. 49. Although the first requirement would be adopted as national policy, the second was not.'

15   For a detailed account of the legal issues of airspace including the 1944 Chicago Convention see: Maechling Jr, Charles; 'Intrusions, Overflights & Shootdowns', *Air Power History*, Vol 36, No 2, Summer 1989.

16   Letter from Lt Farley A. Latta, Assistant Adjutant General, AAC to Director of Intelligence, USAF, Subject: Cover story for forced landing in the Far Eastern USSR, 24 August 1949, RG 341, Entry 214 File 208999, MMB, NA.

17   Major-General Bryce Poe II was a RF-80 Shooting Star pilot in the late 1940s and early 1950s based at Misawa AFB in Japan. He says that he and other pilots flew solo penetration flights over Soviet islands like Sakhalin and also the city of Vladivostock on the mainland. He says these mission continued into the Korean War. Interview with Author in Washington, 1996. Bruce Poe is now a leading figure in the Air Force Historical Foundation.

18   VP-26 was based at Port Lyantey in Morocco when on overseas duties. It performed *Elint* missions against Soviet naval targets in the Baltic and Adriatic. Declassified US files recently released in Washington DC do appear to confirm the US version that the plane was off the coast. See the Klaus Files in the Military Record Branch of the National Archives.

19   RAND was a think-tank set up to support the USAF. A.L. George is now a professor at Stanford University.

20   A.L. George; *Overflights 1935-1953*; RAND, 1955. Plus classified section 1951-55. Declassified 1993.

21   The Soviets apparently tried to salvage the aircraft from the seabed.

22   Walter Lippman, 'The Baltic Affair', *Washington Post*, 24 April 1950.

23   Farquahar, John Thomas, Capt USAF; *A Cold War in Flames: The Impact of Aerial Reconnaissance on U.S.-Soviet Relations, 1948-1960*; thesis, Graduate School of Creighton University, Omaha 1986.

24   Interview with the author, Davenport, 1993.

Chapter 4

1   *Timewatch*, 'Russia's Secret War'; BBC2 TV and A&E Channel, produced by the Author, first transmitted 21 January 1996.

2   Interview with the author, London, 1993.

3   Interview with the author, Oxfordshire, 1994.

4   *Ibid*.

5   Interview with BBC team for 'Russia's Secret War' *Op Cit*, Moscow, 1994.

6   Interview with BBC team for 'Russia's Secret War' *Op Cit*, Moscow, 1994.

7   Farquahar, John Thomas, Capt. USAF; *A Cold War in Flames: The Impact of Aerial Reconnaissance on U.S.-Soviet Relations, 1948-1960*; thesis, Graduate School of Creighton University, Omaha 1986.

8   Far East Air Force; *History of Electronic Countermeasures During the Korean Conflict*; Annex 11.

9   Price, Alfred; *The History of US Electronic Warfare, Vol II, The Renaissance Years, 1946-64*; The Association of Old Crows, 1989.

10   An example of this rare aircraft can be found at the SAC Museum, Omaha, Nebraska.

11   These cameras would be timed to be exposed for the entire sweep of the radarscope thus providing an image of the ground features below.

12   Ink-Slinger Press, Austin, Texas, 1995.

13   Rhodes, Richard; *Dark Sun, The Making of the Hydrogen Bomb*; Simon & Schuster, New York, 1995.

14   Interview with Lovell's daughter, Nancy Lovell Dean, by author, Washington DC, 1994.

15   Interview with BBC team for 'Russia's Secret War' *Op Cit*, Moscow, 1994.

16   Interview with the Author, Oxfordshire, 1994.

17   Bower, Tom; *The Paperclip Conspiracy: The battle for the spoils and secrets of Nazi Germany*; Michael Joseph, London, 1987; page 4.

18   Interview with BBC team for 'Russia's Secret War' *Op Cit*, Moscow, 1994.

19   Declassified documents obtained from the Soviet military archive at Podolsk.

20   Released to US side of Joint Commision on MIAs. Available in the National Archives, Washington DC.

21   Interview with BBC team for 'Russia's Secret War' *Op Cit*, Moscow, 1994.

22   Podolsk military archive.

23   Interview with the author, Los Angeles, 1995.

24   Podolsk military archive.

25   Interview with BBC team for 'Russia's Secret War' *Op Cit*, Moscow, 1994.

26   Interview with BBC team for 'Russia's Secret War' *Op Cit*, Moscow, 1994.

27   Farquahar, *Op Cit*.

28   LeMay papers, Library of Congress.

29   Interview with the author, Florida, 1994.

Chapter 5

1   Farquahar, John Thomas, Capt. USAF; *A Cold War in Flames: The Impact of Aerial Reconnaissance on U.S.-Soviet Relations, 1948-1960*; thesis, Graduate School of Creighton University, Omaha 1986.

2   Entry in LeMay's diary for 23 January 1951; LeMay Papers, Library of Congress.

3   Farquahar, John Thomas, Capt. USAF; *A Need to Know: The Role of Air Force Reconnaissance in War Planning, 1945-1953*; dissertation, Ohio State University, 1991.

4   These aircraft were believed at the time to be nuclear-capable. In fact they were not and it was mainly a ruse to deceive the USSR.

5   PR Conference RAF Benson 1950, PRO, Kew.

6   Letter to the author, 1993.

7   Interview with the author, Aberporth, 1993.

8   Interview with the author, Riverside, 1993.

9   Interview with the author, Wisbech, 1993.

10   Interview with the author, Riverside, 1993.

11   Colville, John; *The Fringes of Power: 10 Downing Street Diaries 1939–1955*; W.W. Norton, NY, 1985.

12   Only a few weeks later an Air France aircraft on a scheduled flight from Frankfurt to Berlin in the Berlin Corridor was attacked by MiGs. It made a miraculous landing with only a few casualties.

13   Interview with BBC team for 'Spies in the Sky', Moscow, 1993.

14   Interview with BBC team for 'Spies in the Sky', Moscow, 1993.

Chapter 6

1   Telephone interview with the author, Washington DC, 1993.

2   Bower, Tom; *The Paperclip Conspiracy: The battle for the spoils and secrets of Nazi Germany*; Michael Joseph, London, 1987.

3   Interview with the author, Davenport, 1993.

4   Oral History for Columbia University, 1964, pages 112-14.

5   The Alsop brothers, Joe and Stewart, were key figures in American Cold War journalism from the 1940s to 1960s. They had many high level contacts.

6   Goddard, George W.; *Overview, a Lifelong Adventure in Aerial Photography*; Doubleday, New York, 1969.

7   Jackson, Robert; *Canberra, The Operational Record*; Airlife, Shrewsbury, 1988.

8   The RAF's photographic reconnaissance force had moved from Benson to Wyton in 1951.

9   WE139 is now at the RAF Museum at Hendon.

10   Interview with the author, London, 1993.

11   Telephone interview with the author, 1993.

12   Interview with the author, Cambs, 1993.

13   Telephone interview with the author, 1993.

14   Letter to the author, 1993.

15   Interview with the author, Salisbury, 1993.

16   Letter to the author, 1994.

17   Interview with BBC team for 'Spies in the Sky', Moscow, 1993.

18   Interview with BBC team for 'Spies in the Sky', Moscow, 1993.

19   Interview with BBC team for 'Spies in the Sky', Moscow, 1993.

Chapter 7

1   Interview with the author, Kansas City, 1993.

2   Interview with the author, Kansas City, 1993.

3   Cargill Hall is employed by the Office of Air Force History of the USAF. He is being given access to documents of this period still denied to other historians.

4   Hillman, Donald E. with Hall, R. Cargill; 'Overflight: Strategic Reconnaissance of the USSR', Air Power History; Spring 1996.

5   The K-30 was the USAF's 100in focal length lens camera mainly used for oblique, 'over the border' photography. One had been supplied to the RAF for Operation 'Robin'.

6   Personal communication to the author, 1996.

7   Letter from Carl Espe, Director of Naval Intelligence, to Maj.-Gen. J.A. Samford, Director of Intelligence, USAF, 25 May 1954, RG 341, entry 214, file 4-1114-1290, MRB, NARA.

8   Oral history of Gen. Horace M. Wade, 1978, Office of Air Force History.

9   Interview with the author, Florida, 1993.

10   In a letter to the the author, March 1996, Bob Hubbard wrote 'you have touched on the tip of an iceberg'.

11   Interview with the author, Kansas City, 1993.

12   FRUS. Foreign Relations, 1955-1957, Volume XXIV, Soviet Union, pages 105-7. Memorandum of a Conference with the President, White House, Washington, 11.00 28 May 1956.

13   The text of the Soviet note of 14 May was transmitted to the Embassy in Moscow in telegram 12 73, 15 May. (Department of State, Central files, 761.5411/5-1456)

14   The draft has not been found, but on 29 May the Department of State presented to the Soviet Embassy a note explaining that navigational difficulties in the Arctic region may have caused unintentional violations of Soviet airspace, which, if in fact they had occurred, the department regretted.

Chapter 8

1   As the historian Robert Hopkins points out, during the early years of SAC LeMay was left to run the command pretty much on his own, a very different situation from the military today. LeMay was not required to tell the JCS or president about most of his major decisions. He did not discuss the SAC war plan, how the USA would go to nuclear war, with any senior officer for some years.

2   Interview with the author, Washington DC, 1993. Goodpaster did not join Ike's staff until later in the year so missed the 8 May RB-47 flight. However, his recollections of Ike's attitude gel with the detailed record.

3   Robert S. Hopkins III; 'An Expanded Understanding of Eisenhower, American Policy and Overflights'; Society of Historians of American Foreign Relations, Annual Conference, Annapolis, Maryland, June 1995.

4   Somewhere in the US archives there must be a full discussion of policy for 'special reconnaissance flights' but so far it has not been released.

5   Interview with the author, Davenport, 1993.

6   There was of course a covert policy of intervention ranging from CIA covert operations, manipulation of the governments of many nations through to a forceful State Department policy to keep allied nations non-communist.

7   Made to the NSC in July 1953. Memorandum by Robert Cutler, 16 July 1953, US Department of State FRUS, 1952-53, Washington, 1984.

8   Immerman, Richard H.; 'Confessions of an Eisenhower Revisionist: An Agonizing Reappraisal', *Diplomatic History*, Vol 14, No 3, Summer 1990.

9   The Brookings Institution in Washington DC is a highly regarded independent think tank that analyses foreign and military policy.

10   MccGwire, Michael; *Military Objectives in Soviet Foreign Policy*; Brookings Institute, Washington DC, 1988.

11   Biddle, Tami Davis; 'Handling the Soviet Threat: "Project Control" and Debate on American Strategy in the Early Cold War Years', *The Journal of Strategic Studies*, Vol 12, No 3, September 1989.

12   Stevens, Austin; 'General Removed over War speech', *The New York Times*, 2 September 1950.

13   Anderson thought this part of the interview was off-the-record. Mostly politicians and the military kept their advocacy of preventive war off the record.

14   Biddle, *Op Cit*.

15   LeMay, Curtis E. with Kantor, Mackinlay; *Mission with LeMay*; Doubleday & Co Inc, New York, 1965; pages 481-2.

16   Alsop, Joseph W. with Platt, Adam; *I've Seen the Best of It*; W.W. Norton, NY, 1992.

17   Power, Gen. Thomas S. with Arnhym, Albert A.; *Design for Survival*; Coward-McCann, Inc, New York, 1964.

18   Twining, Gen. Nathan F.; *Neither Liberty nor Safety : A hard look at U.S. Military Policy and Strategy*; Holt, Rinehart and Winston, New York., 1966.

19   According to former White House aide Daniel Ellsberg, that could have been as little as a division-size confrontation with the Soviets, say around Berlin. Interview with the Author, Washington DC, 1996.

20   Biddle, *Op Cit*. Also, Dean, Lt-Col. David J.; 'Project Control – Creative Strategic Thinking at Air University', *Air University Review*, Vol 35, No 5, July-August 1984. The massive documentation of Project Control is kept at Air Force Historical Research Center, Maxwell AFB.

21   Biddle, *Op Cit.*

22   *Ibid.*

23   Telephone interview with the author, USA, 1993.

24   Slessor rejected preventive war. See: Slessor, Sir John; *The Great Deterrent*; US, 1957.

25   After Project Control LeMay had his eye on Sleeper for high office. To gain operational experience Sleeper took command of a Convair B-36 Wing at Carswell AFB. However, one of Sleeper's B-36s crashed on landing. The investigation showed a number of errors at the base. LeMay had strict rules about responsibility, the buck stopped with Sleeper and his career was retarded. He left the air force in 1978 and became a professor.

26   LeMay, *Op Cit.*

27   Letter from Gen. Kuter to Gen. LeMay in the LeMay Papers, Library of Congress.

28   Burrows, William E.; *Deep Black, The Startling Truth Behind America's Top-Secret Spy Satellites*; Berkeley Books, New York, 1988.

29   Edward Land and James Killian oral histories. See: Beschloss, Michael R.; *Mayday: Eisenhower, Krushchev and the U-2 Affair*; Faber & Faber, London, 1986; page 82.

Chapter 9

1   Sergei Krushchev, interview with R. Cargill Hall and Richard Leghorn 1995. Cited in Hall, R. Cargill; *Strategic Overflight Reconnaissance in the Cold War: From Concept to Policy, 1945–1955.*

2   Interview with BBC *Timewatch* team, Moscow, 1993.

3   Goddard, George W.; *Overview, a Lifelong Adventure in Aerial Photography*; Doubleday, New York, 1969.

4   Kaplan, Fred; *The Wizards of Armageddon*; Simon & Schuster, New York, 1983; page 156.

5   *Ibid.*

6   LeMay, Curtis E.; US Senate, Study of Airpower, Hearings Before the Subcommittee on the Air Force of the Committee on Armed Services, Part 2, 84th Cong., 2d Sess., 1956, page 222; Twining, Nathan F.; *Ibid*, part 20, page 1,499.

7   Prados, John; *The Soviet Estimate: U.S. Intelligence Analysis and Russian Military Strength*; Doubleday/Dial, New York, 1982; page 44.

8   Recently declassified National Intelligence Estimates show that the highest levels of the administration and armed forces would have up to six months' warning of any Soviet preparation for military attack.

9   Kaplan, *Op Cit.*

10   Blair, Bruce G.; *The Logic of Accidental Nuclear War*; Brookings Institution, 1987.

11   Rhodes, Richard; *Dark Sun, The Making of the Hydrogen Bomb*; Simon & Schuster, New York, 1995; page 568.

Chapter 10

1   The 55th had started life in 1940 at Hamilton Field, California. In August 1943 it was sent to England as the 55th Fighter Group and undertook fighter escort work first with P-38s and later with P-51s. The group claimed 400 aircraft destroyed in the air and almost 300 on the ground. The 55th had 16 aces with a total of 90 victories. It was inactivated on 20 August 1946.

2   Bruce Bailey is another former 'crow' who flew over 400 missions between 1958 and 1974. He now lives in Tucson, Arizona.

3   Bailey, Bruce; 'We See All', A History of the 55th Strategic Reconnaissance Wing 1947-67; 55th ELINT Association historian, 1982.
4   Interview with the author, Kansas City, 1993.
5   Interview with the author, Tucson, 1993.
6   Tames, Rolf; The United States and the Cold War in the High North; Dartmouth, UK, 1991.
7   Interview with the author, USA, 1993.

Chapter 11
1   Thomas, Andy; 'British Signals Intelligence after the Second World War', Intelligence and National Security Vol 3, No 4, 1986; pp 105-6.
2   Interview with the Author, Wisbech, 1993.
3   Operational Record Book, AIR PRO, Kew, UK.
4   Ibid.
5   The same officer and former 'Dambuster' who had originally been assigned to the Sculthorpe missions.
6   Now a retired air vice marshal.
7   Wyn Shipman is now a retired USAF lieutenant-colonel living in Tucson, Arizona where I met him in 1993.

Chapter 12
1   Rositzke, Harry; The CIA's Secret Operations: Espionage, Counterespionage and Covert Action; Reader's Digest Press, New York, 1977; pages 17-21.
2   Tames, Rolf; The United States and the Cold War in the High North; Dartmouth, UK, 1991.
3   Philby's betrayal of the landings of hundreds of Albanian partisans, trained by MI6, is well documented elsewhere.
4   Faligot, Roger and Krop, Pascal; La Piscine: The French Secret Service since 1944; Basil Blackwell, New York, 1989; page 75.
5   Prados, John; Presidents' Secret Wars: CIA and Pentagon Covert Operations from World War II through Iranscam; Quill, New York, 1988; page 33.
6   Leary, William M.; Perilous Missions : Civil Air Transport and CIA Covert Operations in Asia; University of Alabama Press, 1984; Chapter 9.
7   Ibid, page 136.
8   Ibid, page 140.
9   Karalekas, Anne; History of the CIA; part of US Senate, Select Committee to Study Governmental Operations with respect to Intelligence Activities, Supplementary Detailed Staff Reports on Foreign and Military Intelligence, Senate Report 94 – 755, 94th Cong., 2nd sess., 1976.
10   Leary, Op Cit, page 143.

Chapter 13
1   Welzenbach, Donald E.; 'Din Land: Patriot', Polaroid, Optics & Photonics News, 1994.
2   Ibid.
3   In 1979, the former press secretary at the White House, Jeraldter Horst, and the former pilot of the presidential aircraft, Ralph Albertazzie, revealed in their book The Flying White House that a brand new presidential Boeing VC-137A, purchased in 1959,

had been equipped by a CIA team with a series of large cameras under conditions of greatest secrecy at Andrews AFB. This note appears to suggest that ruse had been in use for some time.

4   FRUS. Foreign Relations, 1955-1957, Volume XXIV, Soviet Union, pages 105-7. Memorandum of a Conference with the President, White House, Washington, 11.00 28 May 1956.

5   Interview with BBC *Timewatch* team, Moscow, 1993.

6   The Russians thought the British Canberra was the only reconnaissance aircraft capable of overflying the Soviet Union in peacetime out of range of the air defences.

7   Pocock, Chris; 'From Peshawar to Bodo – Mission Impossible?' Cold War Forum, Norwegian Aviation Centre, Bodo, Norway, 7–8 October 1995.

8   Interview with BBC *Timewatch* team, Moscow, 1993.

9   Interview with the author, Davenport, 1993.

10   Prados, John; *The Soviet Estimate: U.S. Intelligence Analysis and Russian Military Strength*; Doubleday/Dial, New York, 1982; page 60.

11   Ambrose, S.E.; *Eisenhower*; 2 vols, 1983-84.

12   Prados, *op cit*, page 40.

13   Beschloss, Michael R.; *Mayday: Eisenhower, Krushchev and the U-2 Affair*; Faber & Faber, London, 1986.

Chapter 14

1   Interview with the author, Hove, 1993. Robinson died in the autumn of 1995.

2   Interview with the author, Davenport, 1993.

3   Jackson, Robert; *Canberra, The Operational Record*; Airlife, Shrewsbury, 1988.

4   *The New York Times*, 12 September 1995.

5   Pocock, Chris; *Dragon Lady: The History of the U-2 Spyplane*; Airlife, Shrewsbury, 1989.

6   FRUS. Foreign Relations, 1958-1960, Vol X. Memorandum of Conference with President Eisenhower, Washington 7 April 1959.

7   Soviet defensive missiles are known generically as SAMs for surface-to-air missile or by their NATO reporting names and codes; eg SA-2 'Guideline', SS-6 'Sapwood'.

8   Wg Cdr Robinson retired from the RAF in 1972. He retains a fondness for the U-2 and has been up to see 'Article 359' that is preserved at Duxford. The aircraft continues to have a surprisingly long life and association with Britain. USAF U-2s have been based at Alconbury since 1982.

Chapter 15

1   Beschloss, Michael R.; *Mayday: Eisenhower, Krushchev and the U-2 Affair*; Faber & Faber; London, 1986.

2   LeMay, Curtis E. with Kantor, Mackinlay; *Mission with LeMay*; Doubleday & Co Inc, New York, 1965.

3   Hopkins, Robert S. III; *An Expanded Understanding of Eisenhower, American Policy and Overflights*; paper to Society of American Foreign Relations Annual Conference, Annapolis, June 1995.

4   'Russia Charges US Jets violated Siberian Territory', 17 December 1956.

5   RB-69s were converted Lockheed P2V-7s; *see* Miller, Jay; *Skunk Works: The Official History*, Aerofax Inc., updated version, Austin, Texas, 1995. An example of one of these aircraft remains in the museum at Warner Robins, Georgia.

6   Memorandum for the Record, 24 April 1958, in FRUS, 1958-1960, Vol X, page 163.

7   Kipp and Bohn; *LeMay Oral History*, 24.

8   See account in: Tames, Rolf; *The United States and the Cold War in the High North*; Dartmouth, 1991.

9   Memorandum of Discussion at the 445th Meeting of the National Security Council, 24 May 1960, 526.

10   Interview with BBC *Timewatch* team, Moscow, 1993.

11   This was the case of F-86 pilot Lt Roland Parks who misjudged his location, parachuted and was captured by the Soviets. Interviewed by author, Washington DC, 1994.

12   Yedremov, A. Ye.; *Yevropa i Yadernoye Oruzhive* (Europe and Nuclear Weapons); Moscow, 1972; page 16 reprinted in Tyushkevich, S.A. *et al. The Soviet Armed Forces: A Historical View of their Organisational Development*; Moscow 1978, translated and republished by the USAF.

13 This story is based on interviews with the author, with John McKone, Deltaville, 1993 and Bruce Olmstead, Annapolis, 1993.

14 The best account of the July 1960 shootdown can be found in the book *Little Tin Dog*, which is based on McKone and Olmstead's own stories.

15 Interview with BBC *Timewatch* team, Moscow, 1993.

16 Sam Klaus was also the official that caused Operation 'Paperclip' a great deal of difficulty. It was obviously a matter of great personal distaste to him that ex-Nazi scientists were hired for the US missile and other programmes. By standing by the letter of US law, he refused to grant visas. It forced those in charge of 'Paperclip' to bring them in as PoWs, their position normalised later by more compliant officials. For the best account see Tom Bower's *Operation Paperclip*.

17 No 51 Squadron was to suffer the RAF's most expensive aircraft accident to that date. In the early part of 1961 one of the Comets was under total refurbishment in the hangar at Warton. An electric inspection lamp was left on near a leaking pump and the aircraft caught fire. The aircraft was burnt out. Although much of the important ELINT-gathering equipment had been removed for the refit, even so the mistake cost £1 million. The Comet was the most expensive aircraft on the RAF list at the time.

18 Some published accounts have baldly stated that it was an ELINT Lincoln from No 192 Squadron.

19 Tames, Rolf; *The United States and the Cold War in the High North*; Dartmouth, 1991.

20 Älmeberg, Roger; *Flygaren som Forrsvann* (The Flyers who disappeared); Sweden, 1983.

21 Ayling, Elizabeth; 'Soviet General admits: "I shot down 'spy' plane".', *The European*; 19-21 April, 1991.

22 Mosey, Chris; 'Spy-plane mystery deepens', *The Observer*; 28 August 1983, page 10.

23 Establishment of a Joint Reconnaissance Center, Chairman of the Joint Chiefs of Staff Memorandum 451-60, 20 October 1960, National Security Archives (NSArch) microfilm #00855.

24 The EC-130 incident attracted enormous international publicity. The American Government was convinced that some of the crew had been captured and used a number of strategies to try to persuade the USSR to release them. The President even took the unprecedented step of releasing a tape of the Soviet pilots' conversations, which had been recorded by the NSA.

Chapter 16

1   Baldwin, Hanson; 'The vulnerable Soviet; Moscow Reveals Defense Weakness in Publicising US Plane Incursion', *The New York Times*; 11 May 1960.

2   Khrushchev, Nikita; *Khrushchev Remembers: The Last Testament*; Little Brown and Co, Boston, 1970; page 210. Whether this is a reference to the U-2 flight of 4 July or to another flight is not known.

3   Professor Sergei Khrushchev is now at Brown University in the United States. Quote comes from *Spy in the Sky*, a WGBH Nova programme broadcast in the US in March 1996.

4   The U-2 pilot, Gary Powers, was given a show trial but was eventually released in 1961 by Khrushchev as a goodwill gesture to the incoming President John F. Kennedy.

5   Blanton, Tom (ed.); *The White House e-mail, A National Security Archive Reader*; New Press, New York, 1995; page 169.

6   Interview with BBC *Timewatch* team, Moscow, 1993.

7   Tames, Rolf; *The United States and the Cold War in the High North*; Dartmouth, 1991.

8   The files of Sam Klaus, the State Department. A legal officer whose files contain a minutely detailed analysis of the history of the disputes over the islands between Russia and Japan. See the Klaus Files, Military Records Branch, National Archives, Washington DC.

9   van der Aart, Dick; *Aerial Espionage, Secret Intelligence Flights by East and West*; Airlife, Shrewsbury, 1985.

10 Baldwin, *Op Cit.*

11 van der Aart, *Op Cit.*

12 Personal communication to the author, 1996.

Chapter 17

1   Interview with the author, Davenport, 1993.

2   Kaplan, Fred; *The Wizards of Armageddon*; Simon & Schuster, 1983; page 161.

3   Khrushchev, Nikita; *Khrushchev Remembers: The Last Testament*; Little Brown and Co, Boston, 1970.

4   Interview with the author, Washington DC, 1993.

5   The British dependency on American missile technology was to leave them naked when, two years later, the US Defense Secretary Robert McNamara cancelled the Skybolt missile project on which the British had based their next generation of defence strategy.

6   Prados, John; *The Soviet Estimate: U.S. Intelligence Analysis and Russian Military Strength*; Doubleday/Dial, New York, 1982; page 112.

7   Prados, *Op Cit*, pages 115-6.

8   The SS-6 'Sapwood' never became a proper working nuclear delivery system. The Corona photographs showed four working missiles.

9   Burrows, William; *Deep Black: The Startling Truth behind America's Top Secret Spy Satellites*; Berkeley Books, NY, 1986.

Chapter 18

1   Post-Cold War research shows that much of the Cuban missile crisis was based on both sides misunderstanding the opposition's intentions. From 1987 a series of seminars took place involving many of the key players from both sides. For a detailed account read:

Chang, Laurence and Peter Kornbluh (eds); *The Cuban Missile Crisis 1962*, A National Security Archive Documents Reader, The New Press, New York, 1992. Also: Blight, James G., Allyn, Bruce J. and Welch, David A.; *Cuba: On the Brink. Castro, The Missile Crisis and the Soviet Collapse*; Pantheon Books, New York, 1993.

2 Part of the reason for his visit was to discuss the deployment of MRBMs and IRBMs on Cuba.

3 These would later turn out to be missile technicians and military.

4 Brugioni, Dino A.; *Eyeball to Eyeball, the Inside Story of the Cuban Missile Crisis*; Random House, New York, 1991.

5 This was named after Boston University where it had been designed. It was another example of the collaboration of Jim Baker and Gen. George Goddard.

6 Kohn, Richard H. and Harahan, Joseph P.; *Strategic Air Warfare, An Interview with Generals Curtis E. LeMay, Leon W. Johnson, David A. Burchinal, and Jack J. Catton*; Office of Air Force History, USAF, Washington DC, 1988; page 116.

7 Sagan, Scott D.; *The Limits of Safety: Organisations, Accidents, and Nuclear Weapons*; Princeton University Press, New Jersey, 1993.

8 *Ibid.*

9 *Ibid.*

10 Rhodes, Richard; *Dark Sun, The Making of the Hydrogen Bomb*; Simon & Schuster, New York, 1995.

11 Journalist Fletcher Knebel interviewed Gen. LeMay who went off the record to accuse President Kennedy. Knebel obituary, *New York Times*, 28 February 1993.

12 Blight, James G. and Welch, David A.; *On the Brink*; Hill and Wang, 1988.

13 Rhodes, *Op Cit.*

14 LeMay, Curtis E. with Kantor, Mackinlay; *Mission with LeMay*; Doubleday & Co Inc, New York, 1965.

Chapter 19

1 FRUS, Foreign Relations 1958–1960, Volume X, item 70, pages 260–262.

2 The Soviet note of 27 November 1958, set a deadline of six months, or 27 May 1959 for acceptance by the Western powers of its proposal for the conversion of West Berlin into a 'free city'.

3 Historian Greg Herken asked LeMay in the late 1980s.

4 Interview with Dan Ellsberg, Washington DC, March 1996.

5 Rhodes, Richard; *Dark Sun, The Making of the Hydrogen Bomb*; Simon & Schuster, New York, 1995.

6 Interview with the author, Washington DC, 1996.

7 Khrushchev, Nikita; *Khrushchev Remembers: The Last Testament*; Little Brown and Co, Boston, 1970.

8 Text of statement by Democratic Council, *The New York Times*, 23 May 1960; page 9.

9 Hyland, William and Shyrock, Richard; *The Fall of Khrushchev*; Funk & Wagnalls, New York, 1968.

10 Sagan, Scott D.; *The Limits of Safety: Organisations, Accidents, and Nuclear Weapons*; Princeton University Press, New Jersey, 1993.

11 Cousins, Norman; 'What We Do When We Are Wrong?', *Saturday Review*, 21 May 1960; page 30.

12 *Defence and Armament*, No 24, November 1983; page 9.

Appendix 1

1   Interview with BBC *Timewatch* team, Vladivostok, 1993.
2   Interview with the author, Pomona, 1993.
3   Interview with BBC *Timewatch* team, Moscow, 1993.
4   Interview with BBC *Timewatch* team, Moscow, 1993.
5   The Klaus Files, Military Records Branch, National Archives Washington DC.
6   Lashmar, Paul; 'Family seeks truth of pilot lost in Korea: Sons fear RAF hero was sent to Gulag', *Daily Telegraph*, 21 January 1996.

BIBLIOGRAPHY

Alpervitz, Gar; *The Decision to use the Atomic Bomb*; HarperCollins, London, 1995.

Alsop, Joseph, with Platt, Adam; *I've Seen the Best of It*; W.W. Norton, NY, 1992.

Ambrose, Stephen E.; *Eisenhower. Vol I & II*; George Allen & Unwin, London, 1984.

— with Immerman, Richard; *Ike's Spies: Eisenhower and the Espionage Establishment*; Garden City, New York, 1981.

— ; *Rise to Globalism: American Foreign Policy since 1938*, 5th edn; Penguin Books, 1988.

Anderton, David A.; *The History of the U.S. Air Force;* Hamlyn–Aerospace, London, 1982.

— ; *Strategic Air Command*; Ian Allan Ltd, London, 1975.

Babbington-Smith, Constance; *Evidence in Camera*; Chatto & Windus, London, 1958.

Bailey, Bruce: *'We See All', A History of the 55th Strategic Reconnaissance Wing 1947-67*; 55th ELINT Association historian, USA, 1982.

Bamford, James; *The Puzzle Palace: America's National Security Agency and its special relationship with Britain's GCHQ*; Sidgwick & Jackson, England, 1982.

Beschloss, Michael R.; *Mayday: Eisenhower, Krushchev and the U-2 Affair.*; Faber & Faber, London, 1986.

Betts, Richard K.; *Nuclear Blackmail and the Nuclear Balance*; Brookings Institution, USA, 1987.

Blair, Bruce G.; *The Logic of Accidental Nuclear War*; Brookings Institution, USA, 1987.

Blanton, Tom (ed.); *The White House e-mail, A National Security Archive Reader*; New Press, New York, 1995.

Blight, James G. and Welch, David A.; *On the Brink*; Hill and Wang, USA, 1988.

Blight, James G., Allyn, Bruce J. and Welch, David A.; *Cuba: On the*

Brink. Castro, The Missile Crisis and the Soviet Collapse; Pantheon Books, New York, 1993.

Bower, Tom; *The Paperclip Conspiracy: The battle for the spoils and secrets of Nazi Germany*; Michael Joseph, London, 1987.

Brendon, Piers; *Ike His Life & Times*; Harper and Row, UK, 1986.

Brookes, Andrew J.; *Photo Reconnaissance*; Ian Allan, London, 1975.

Brugioni, Dino A.; *Eyeball to Eyeball, the Inside Story of the Cuban Missile Crisis*; Random House, New York, 1991.

Burrows, William E.; *Deep Black, The Startling Truth Behind America's Top-Secret Spy Satellites;* Berkeley Books, New York, 1986.

Caidin, Martin; *A Torch to the Enemy: The Fire Raid on Tokyo*; Ballantine Books, New York, 1960.

Campbell, Duncan; *The Unsinkable Aircraft Carrier, American Military Power in Britain*; Michael Joseph, London, 1984.

Carter, Ashton B., Steinbruner, John D. and Zraket, Charles A. (eds); *Managing Nuclear Operations*; The Brookings Institution, Washington DC.

Chang, Laurence and Kornbluh, Peter (eds); *The Cuban Missile Crisis 1962, A National Security Archive Documents Reader*; The New Press, New York, 1992.

Coffey, Thomas M.; *Iron Eagle: The Turbulent Life of General Curtis LeMay*; Crown Publishers Inc, New York, 1986.

Colby, William; *Honourable Men: My Life in the CIA*; Hutchinson, London, 1978.

Cole, Paul; *POW/MIA Issues: Vol 1, The Korean War*; RAND, National Defence Research Institute, USA, 1994.

Colville, John; *The Fringes of Power: 10 Downing Street Diaries 1939–55;* W.W. Norton, NY, 1985.

Craven, Wesley Frank and Cate, James Lea (eds); *The Army Air Force in World War II, Vol 5, The Pacific: Matterhorn to Nagasaki June 1944 to August 1945*; Office of Air Force History, Washington DC, 1983.

Faligot, Roger and Krop, Pascal; *La Piscine: The French Secret Service since 1944*; Basil Blackwell, New York, 1989.

Farrar-Hockley, Gen. Sir Anthony; *The British Part in the Korean War, Vols 1 & 2, Official History*; HMSO, London, 1990 and 1995.

Freedman, Lawrence; *The Evolution of Nuclear Strategy*; St Martin's Press, New York, 1989.

Frisbee, John L.; *Makers of the United States Air Force*; USAF Warrior studies, The Office of Air Force History, Washington DC, 1987.

Futrell, Robert F.; *The United States Air Force in Korea*; The Office of Air Force History, USAF, Revised edn., Washington DC, 1983.

Goddard, George W.; *Overview, a Lifelong Adventure in Aerial Photography*; Doubleday, New York, 1969.

Hersh, Seymour M.; *The Target is Destroyed, What really happened to Flight 007 & what America knew about it*; Vintage Book, New York, 1987.

Jackson, Robert; *Canberra, The Operational Record*; Airlife, Shrewsbury, 1988.

Jolidon, Laurence; *Last Seen Alive: The Search for Missing POWs from the Korean War*; Ink-Slinger Press, Austin Texas, 1995.

Jones, R.V.; *Most Secret War: British Scientific Intelligence 1939-45*; Coronet, UK, 1978.

Kahn, Herman; *On Thermonuclear War*; Princeton University Press, New Jersey, 1960.

Kaplan, Fred; *The Wizards of Armageddon*; Simon & Schuster, New York, 1983.

Karalekas, Anne; *History of the CIA*; part of US Senate, Select Committee to Study Governmental Operations with respect to Intelligence Activities, Supplementary Detailed Staff Reports on Foreign and Military Intelligence, Senate Report 94 – 755, 94th Cong., 2nd sess., 1976.

Kerr, E. Bartlett; *Flames Over Tokyo: The U.S. Army Air Force's Incendiary Campaign Against Japan 1944-45*; Donald I. Fine, U.S. 1991.

Khrushchev, Nikita; *Khrushchev Remembers: The Last Testament*; Little Brown and Co, Boston, 1970.

Killian, James R., Jr; *Sputnik, Scientists and Eisenhower, A memoir of the First Special Assistant to the President for Science and Technology*; MIT Press, Cambridge, MA, 1977.

Kohn, Richard H. and Harahan, Joseph P.; *Strategic Air Warfare, An Interview with Generals Curtis E. LeMay, Leon W. Johnson, David A. Burchinal, and Jack J. Catton*; The Office of Air Force History, USAF, Washington DC, 1988.

Leary, William M.; *Perilous Missions; Civil Air Transport and CIA Covert Operations in Asia*; University of Alabama Press, USA, 1984.

LeMay, Curtis E. with Smith, Maj.-Gen. Dale O.; *America is in Danger*; Funk & Wagnall, New York, 1968.

LeMay, Curtis E. with Kantor, Mackinlay; *Mission with LeMay*; Doubleday & Co Inc, New York, 1965.

MccGwire, Michael; *Military Objectives in Soviet Foreign Policy*; The Brookings Institute, Washington DC, 1988.

Mead, Peter; *The Eye in the Air*; HMSO Books, London, 1983.

Miller, Roger G. (ed.); *Seeing Off the Bear: Anglo-American Air Power Cooperation During the Cold War*; Air Force History and Museums Program, USAF, Washington DC, 1995.

Moss, Norman; *The Men Who Play God*.

Nesbit, Roy Conyers; *An Illustrated History of the RAF*; Colour Library Books, Godalming, 1990.

O'Heffernan, Patrick, Lovins, Amory B. and Lovins, L. Hunter; *The First Nuclear World War: A Strategy for preventing Nuclear Wars and the spread of Nuclear Weapons*; Hutchinson, London.

Pocock, Chris; *Dragon Lady: The History of the U-2 Spyplane*, Airlife, Shrewsbury, 1989.

Polmar, Norman (ed.); *Strategic Air Command: People, Aircraft and Missiles*; The Nautical and Aviation Publishing Company of America Inc, Annapolis, 1979.

Power, Gen. Thomas S., with Arnhym, Albert A.; *Design for Survival*; Coward-McCann Inc, New York, 1964.

Powers, Francis Gary, with Gentry, Curt; *Operation Overflight: The U-2 Spy Pilot tells his story for the first time*; Holt, Rinehart and Winston, US, 1970.

Prados, John; *Presidents' Secret Wars: CIA AND Pentagon Covert Operations from World War II through Iranscam*; Quill, New York, 1988.

—; *The Soviet Estimate: U.S. Intelligence Analysis and Russian Military Strength*; Garden City. NY: Doubleday/Dial, 1982.

Price, Alfred; *Instruments of Darkness*; Jane's, London, 1977 (new ed.).

— ; *The History of US Electronic Warfare, Vol. II, The Renaissance Years, 1946-64*; The Association of Old Crows, 1989.

Pringle, Peter, and Arkin, William; *SIOP*; Sphere Books, London, 1973.

Prouty, L. Fletcher; *The Secret Team: The CIA and its Allies in control of the United States and the World*; Prentice-Hall Inc, New York, 1973.

Rhodes, Richard; *Dark Sun, The Making of the Hydrogen Bomb*; Simon & Schuster, New York, 1995.

Richelson, Jeffrey T.; *A Century of Spies*; Oxford University Press, US, 1995.

— ; *American Espionage and the Soviet Target*; Quill, US, 1987.

—; *America's Secret Eyes in Space: The U.S. Keyhole Spy Satellite Program*; Harper and Row, US, 1990.

Rositzke, Harry; *The CIA's Secret Operations: Espionage, Counterespionage and Covert Action*; Reader's Digest Press, New York, 1977.

Rostow, W.W.; *Open Skies: Eisenhower's Proposal of July 21, 1955*; University of Texas Press, US, 1982.

Sagan, Scott D.; *The Limits of Safety: Organisations, Accidents, and Nuclear Weapons*; Princeton University Press, New Jersey, 1993.

Schelling, Thomas C. and Halperin, Morton H.; *Strategy and Arms Control*; The Twentieth Century Fund, New York, 1961.

Sherry, Michael S.; *The Rise of American Air Power: The Creation of Armageddon*; Yale University Press, New Haven, Conn., 1987.

Slessor, Sir John; *The Great Deterrent*; US, 1957.

Smith, General Dale O.; *The Eagle's Talon*; Spartan, US, 1966.

Stockwell. Richard E.; *Soviet Air Power*; Pageant Press, Inc, New York, 1956.

Sweetman, Bill and Gunston, Bill; *Soviet Air Power*; Leisure Books, UK, 1978.

Tames, Rolf; *The United States and the Cold War in the High North*; Dartmouth, UK, 1991.

Taylor, John W.R., and Mondey, David; *Spies in the Sky*; Ian Allan, London, 1972.

Twining, Gen. Nathan F.; *Neither Liberty nor Safety: A hard look at U.S. Military Policy and Strategy*; Holt, Rinehart and Winston, New York, 1966.

van der Aart, Dick; *Aerial Espionage, Secret Intelligence Flights by East and West*; Airlife, England, 1985.

Wack, Fred John; *The Secret Explorers, Saga of the 46th/72nd Reconnaissance Squadrons*; privately published, 1990.

White, Ken; *World in Peril: The Origin, Mission & Scientific Findings of the 46th/72nd Reconnaissance Squadron*; privately published by Ken White Assocs, Elkhart, Indiana, 1992.

Williamson, Samuel R. and Reardon, Steven L.; *The Origins of US Nuclear Strategy, 1945–1953*; St Martin's Press, 1993.

Winterbotham, F. W.; *The Ultra Secret*; Weidenfeld and Nicolson, London, 1974.

Zimmerman, Carroll L.; *Insider at SAC, Operations Analysis under General LeMay*; Sunflower University Press, Manhattan, Kansas, 1988.

PAPERS

Älmeberg, Roger.; *Flygaren som Forsvann* (The Flyers who Disappeared); Sweden, 1983.

Austin, Hal; 'A Cold War Overflight of the USSR'; Daedalus Flyer Vol XXXV No 1, Spring 1995, US.

Biddle, Tami Davis; 'Handling the Soviet Threat: "Project Control" and Debate on American Strategy in the Early Cold War Years', *The Journal of Strategic Studies*, Vol 12, No 3 (September 1989).

Dean, Lt-Col. David J.; 'Project Control – Creative Strategic Thinking at Air University', *Air University Review*, Vol 35, No 5, July–August 1984.

East, Don, Capt. USN; 'The History of US Naval Airborne Electronic Reconnaissance'; Parts 1 & 2; The Hook, Spring and Summer 1987, US.

Farquahar, Capt. John Thomas, USAF; *A Cold War in Flames: The Impact of Aerial Reconnaissance on U.S.-Soviet Relations, 1948-1960.*; a thesis, Graduate School of Creighton University, Omaha 1986.

—; *A Need to Know: The Role of Air Force Reconnaissance in War Planning, 1945-1953*; dissertation, Ohio State University, 1991.

Ferris, John; 'Coming in from the Cold War: The Historiography of American Intelligence, 1945-1990'; *Diplomatic History 19*; Winter 1995.

George, A.L.; 'Overflights 1935-1953'. RAND, 1955. Plus classified section 1951-1955. Declassified 1993.

Hall, R. Cargill; 'The Origins of US Space Policy: Eisenhower, Open Skies, and Freedom of Space'.

—; 'Strategic Overflight Reconnaissance in the Cold War: From Concept to National Policy, 1945–1955'.

Hillman, Donald E. with Hall, R. Cargill; 'Overflight: Strategic Reconnaissance of the USSR', *Air Power History*, Spring 1996.

Hopkins III, Robert S.; 'Alaskan Observers, Cobra Ball and Cobra Eye', *World Air Power Journal*, Vol 8, 1992.

— 'An Expanded Understanding of Eisenhower, American Policy and Overflights'; Society of Historians of American Foreign Relations, Annual Conference, Annapolis, Maryland, June 1995.

— 'The Tell Two Stratojets'; *Air Enthusiast*, No 41.

Immerman, Richard H.; 'Confessions of an Eisenhower Revisionist: An Agonizing Reappraisal', *Diplomatic History*, Vol 14, No 3, Summer 1990.

Jackson, Paul; 'Cryptic Comets: The story of No 51 Squadron's ELINT aircraft', *Aviation News*, 4-17 June 1993.

Maechling Jr, Charles; 'Intrusions, Overflights & Shootdowns', *Air Power History*, Vol 36, No 2, Summer 1989.

Pocock, Chris; 'From Peshawar to Bodo - Mission Impossible?'; Cold War Forum, Norwegian Aviation Centre, Bodo, Norway, 7–8 October 1995. (Extract from forthcoming book *Towards the Unknown*, Schiffer Publishing, US.)

Proceedings of the Royal Air Force Historical Society, No 10, 'Photographic Reconnaissance in World War 2', from seminar held 10 June 1991 at RAF Museum.

Rosenberg, David Alan; 'A Smoking Radiating Ruin at the End of Two Hours', Documents on American Plans for Nuclear War with the Soviet Union, 1954-1955, *International Security*, Winter 1981/2.

—; 'The Origins of Overkill: Nuclear Weapons and American Strategy, 1945-1960', *International Security*, Vol 7, No 4, Spring 1983.

—; 'U.S. Nuclear Stockpile 1945 to 1950', *The Bulletin of Atomic Scientists*, May 1982.

Wainstein, L. (project leader); 'The Evolution of U.S. Strategic Command and Control and Warning, 1945-1972', Institute for Defense Analysis, Arlington, Virginia, June 1975. (declassified September 92)

Welzenbach, Donald E.; 'Din Land: Patriot', Polaroid, *Optics & Photonics News*, 1994.

— and Galyean, Nancy; 'Those Daring Young Men and their Ultra-High Flying Machines', *The proceedings of the Royal Air Force Historical Society*, No 7, 'The origins and development of the British Strategic Nuclear Deterrent Forces 1945-1960', from seminar held 23 October 1989 at RAF Museum.

ARCHIVES

The Klaus Files, Military Records Branch, National Archives Washington DC.

INDEX

225

11-# cotton
160 tallow